PERGAMON INTERNATIO
of Science, Technology, Engineering
The 1000-volume original paperback libr
education, industrial training and the en
Publisher: Robert Maxwell, M.C.

Social Work and Human Problems
Casework, Consultation and Other Topics

THE PERGAMON TEXTBOOK
INSPECTION COPY SERVICE

An inspection copy of any book published in the Pergamon International Library will
gladly be sent to academic staff without obligation for their consideration for course
adoption or recommendation. Copies may be retained for a period of 60 days from receipt
and returned if not suitable. When a particular title is adopted or recommended for
adoption for class use and the recommendation results in a sale of 12 or more copies, the
inspection copy may be retained with our compliments. The Publishers will be pleased to
receive suggestions for revised editions and new titles to be published in this important
International Library.

SOCIAL WORK SERIES

Editor: Jean P. Nursten

Social Work and Human Problems
Casework, Consultation and Other Topics

by

ELIZABETH E. IRVINE

PERGAMON PRESS
OXFORD • NEW YORK • TORONTO • SYDNEY • PARIS • FRANKFURT

UK	Pergamon Press Ltd., Headington Hill Hall, Oxford OX3 0BW, England
USA	Pergamon Press Inc., Maxwell House, Fairview Park, Elmsford, New York 10523, USA
CANADA	Pergamon of Canada, Suite 104, 150 Consumers Road, Willowdale, Ontario M2J 1P9, Canada
AUSTRALIA	Pergamon Press (Aust.) Pty. Ltd., P.O. Box 544, Potts Point, NSW 2011, Australia
FRANCE	Pergamon Press SARL, 24 rue des Ecoles, 75240 Paris, Cedex 05, France
FEDERAL REPUBLIC OF GERMANY	Pergamon Press GmbH, 6242 Kronberg-Taunus, Pferdstrasse 1, Federal Republic of Germany

Copyright © 1979 Elizabeth E. Irvine

All Rights Reserved. No part of this publication may be reproduced, stored in a retrieval system or transmitted in any form or by any means: electronic, electrostatic, magnetic tape, mechanical, photocopying, recording or otherwise, without permission in writing from the publishers

First edition 1979

British Library Cataloguing in Publication Data

Irvine, Elizabeth Ernestine
Social work and human problems.
- (Pergamon international library).
1. Psychiatric social work - Great Britain
- History
I. Title
362.2'0941   HV689   79-40287

ISBN 0-08-023128-4 (Hard cover)
ISBN 0-08-023127-6 (Flexi cover)

Printed in Great Britain

To
JOHN BOWLBY

Contents

Foreword

The papers which make up this volume were written at different points in a 25-year span by one of the leading social work thinkers and practitioners in this country during that formative period. It has been a period both of great social change and also of more persistent effort than ever before to understand people's subjective feelings and the effect of these on their attitudes to life and their behaviour. Such studies, which started earlier with children, delinquents and the mentally disordered, have spread steadily to include husbands and wives, parents and children, adolescents, multi-problem families, the sick, the immature and, to a lesser extent, the physically handicapped of all kinds, the old and the uprooted. Across another dimension, research and recorded observation and practice have begun to clarify similar reactions to stress, loss and deprivation in very different circumstances. Hence, for example, studies of the characteristics of bereavement in widows, which have shown some of the same essential processes at work in response to the loss of a limb, of home, employment, or a familiar neighbourhood or culture. Related to this, crisis theory, with its prescription for positive intervention, was a productive outcome of observing people's reactions to crises in their lives and the likely consequences, and is here applied to social work practice.

Other reactions of people in widely different circumstances to their life experiences have also shown certain common characteristics underlying their behaviour; for example, the individual as the bearer of roles allocated to him by his family and within his immediate culture. From this recent work in psychiatry and the social sciences has come confirmation of what the poets have always known, so now "we are forced to realise that the skin is not the only boundary around the self and that the home we live in and the people to whom we are attached are, in some sense, ours — they are parts of ourselves" (Murray Parkes, *Bereavement,* 1972, p. 191).

Most of this widening span of psychiatric and sociological

knowledge in many different directions has had dramatic consequences for social attitudes, social policy, social services and the helping professions. In the past 25 years no one has played a more productive part than Elizabeth Irvine in her ability to apply such concepts as crisis theory or the effects of early childhood experience to social work practice. Having worked with Gerald Caplan in Israel, she was for some ten years a senior staff member at the Tavistock Clinic, working closely with John Bowlby and others. In this power-house of psycho-analytic theory and practice she still kept her attention fixed on the significant ordinariness of everyday life, as her articles on casework and on "problem families" show.

At the Tavistock Clinic she was responsible for teaching and supervision of students on the Advanced Course in Social Casework, who were already experienced practitioners. Her commitment to teaching became full-time when she moved to the University of York in 1966 as the first Reader in Social Work in this country. There she developed further her conviction that it is possible for students to gain a more imaginative understanding of the varieties of human experience from creative writing, especially novels, than from some "scientific" text-books. Theory and practice are not separate entities for her, because in her professional life theory has constantly been tried out in practice and distilled from her own acute perception of people and their behaviour. Her great contribution to social work is her ability to translate psycho-analytic concepts like the transference into specifically social work rather than psycho-therapeutic practice, and to apply such understanding to the meaning that simple practical help can have for people who are deprived or under stress. In contributing to professional practice, she is equally concerned about the ethics on which such practice should be based. As she puts it, "those insights which are needed to preserve our concept of the fully human, of man and his dignity." Not least are we in her debt because her writing is mercifully free from jargon and from the turgid English which unfortunately infests much social work writing. And what better aim for social work could there be than to help people, as she puts it, "to find new satisfactions in the possible"?

Eileen Younghusband
April, 1978

Introduction

In assembling these papers, with their diversity of subjects, I have asked myself whether there is sufficient unity of theme to justify assembling them in a single book. My interests have embraced the ethics of social work intervention, the processes of casework and consultation, the special problems and needs of certain client groups and the impact on some of them of psychiatric publicity, some aspects of adolescence and some components of education for social work. This variety of topics reflects the changing circumstances of my professional life, but they have all been illuminated for me by Freudian theory, combined as time went on with a growing ability to integrate other social sciences.

As a psychiatric social worker engaged almost continuously in child guidance, I spent most of my working life at the intersection of social casework and child psychiatry. These two themes are reflected in all my writing, sometimes jointly, sometimes separately. In 1951, I also became involved in teaching social workers taking the unusual course inaugurated at the Tavistock Clinic by Noel Hunnybun and John Bowlby. Here theoretical and practical teaching were combined in the same clinical setting, as were the roles of casework teacher and supervisor. Despite the clinical setting, this was already a generic course, based on the conviction that social work with all types of client and problem required the same basic understanding of human motivation and relationships as was called for in child guidance. Until I left the Tavistock in 1965 both my teaching and my writing were thus intimately related to clinical practice.

It was, of course, a limitation that my first-hand experience was confined within the walls of a clinic, but my work offered various opportunities of applying and testing my theoretical equipment at second-hand in a variety of non-clinical situations. The clinic provided a consultancy service for the staff of certain maternity and child welfare clinics and for some nearby schools (see Chapters 7 & 8). In small inter-disciplinary teams we met groups of these other professionals and explored with them the relevance and applicability of our theoretical understanding of human relations, and the very different ways in which it could be profitably applied in their different roles and situations. In particular we, who were accustomed to deep long-term treatment, were pleased to confirm the efficacy of brief and relatively superficial intervention if appropriately made at a moment of crisis (as reported originally by Caplan and Rosenfeld, (1954)).

Since the students on the Advanced Course in Social Casework at the Tavistock mostly intended to apply what they learned there in the settings from which they came, it was important for them to test out its applicability in those settings throughout the course. It was therefore arranged for each to carry at least one case in that setting under the same supervisor as their clinical case-load. Like the consultation programme, these cases provided a constant flow of information on conditions in other services, with opportunities of testing and adapting a variety of insights and techniques to their conditions and requirements. These experiences helped me greatly in developing my interest in the non-verbal elements of communication between case-worker and client.

On moving to the University of York in 1966 I undertook the task of integrating knowledge from psycho-analysis, from other branches of psychology and from sociology. My aim was to teach "human growth and behaviour" in a way which recognised the variety of sub-cultural patterns of behaviour and relationships, and the effect of these and of social conditions and social pressures on personality development and conduct.

I also lost direct contact with clients, and felt it was essential to retain at least a second-hand contact with the field. Again, I continued to learn from the experience of students in their placements, which we discussed in casework seminars. I also became involved in a small project which provided an annual holiday for some immigrant mothers and their children, and the predicaments of some of these families contributed to the thinking contained in Chapter 11. I also gained much from continued contact with the Family Service Units, and particularly from my collaboration with Lorna Walker (Chapter 10) which gave me access to her rich material.

In teaching Human Growth and Behaviour, I was eventually able to try out an idea which had long been teasing me, that creative literature had something unique to contribute to this subject. I found that students enjoyed elucidating the psychological and sociological significance of novels by George Eliot, D.H. Lawrence and Conrad, and that these works deepened their appreciation of the experience behind the concepts. Their studies of such novels also revealed with superb clarity the extent and limitations of their knowledge and understanding, and gave clues for further teaching. Following retirement from York, a brief appointment at Smith College School of Social Work gave me an opportunity to teach entirely through the use of creative literature, and enabled me to prepare a series of lectures of which Chapter 16 was the first. (The other two are simply illustrative analyses of *The Mill on the Floss* and *The Rainbow,* Irvine, 1974.)

I am grateful to Lorna Walker for allowing me to include her material in Chapter 10, and to Elizabeth Brown for allowing me to include Chapter 17, of which she is co-author. I am also grateful to Barbara Boyle and Rosemary Deane for allowing me to use some of their case material.

Part I   Aspects of Casework

The first chapter of this section describes the gradual transformation of casework theory in this country under the influence of American casework, which had been much modified during the first two decades of this century by the impact of psycho-analysis, and which was imported into the U.K. in the late 1920s in the guise of psychiatric social work.

I was myself one of the first psychiatric social workers to be trained in this country by some of the American-trained pioneers (see Chapter 1), and practised entirely in child guidance clinics for some thirty years, except for a brief period on the staff of a psychiatric hospital. It was in the Department for Children and Parents of the Tavistock Clinic that I became involved, as a supervisor and later as senior tutor, in the Advanced Course in Social Casework mentioned in Chapter 1, and thus in the extension of psycho-analytic understanding, hitherto reserved mainly for P.S.W.s, to casework teachers and practitioners in other branches of social work. At the time of writing Chapter 2, before joining the Tavistock, I still identified myself, as the title shows, as a psychiatric social worker rather than a caseworker. I note that I was already concerned with the acceptance and management of ambivalence, so relevant to the current debates about care and control which I discuss in Chapters 2 and 5.

By 1956, when I wrote Chapter 3, I had identified myself as a caseworker, teaching knowledge and skills which could be appropriately used in a variety of settings. In my own clinical setting I had begun to feel a need to differentiate more clearly, particularly in discussion with the psycho-therapists with whom I worked, between the techniques of psycho-analysis and those of casework, which seemed to me at times to be getting blurred. It was for internal consumption that I first developed my account of the application of psycho-analytic theory in responding actively to a client's assessed

1

needs, as in many forms of casework, as an alternative to formulating insight-provoking interpretations within the framework of an otherwise passive therapeutic relationship, as in psycho-analysis.

It will be clear from the references in the first few pages of Chapter 3 that I was by no means alone in the attempt to clarify the boundaries between psycho-therapy and casework. However, the idea that "real casework" was not only a purely verbal but also necessarily an interpretive method had struck deep, and when in 1964 I was asked to speak at Barnett House, Oxford, on "What is Advanced Casework?" I took up the subject again. In this paper, now published under another title as Chapter 4, I strongly emphasised the experiential aspects of the casework process and the importance of non-verbal communication, and maintained that the appropriate use of such methods requires just as much understanding and skill as the interpretive methods which had come to be labelled "advanced".

I remained in practice long enough to see the beginnings of conjoint family therapy at the Tavistock Clinic, but had few opportunities to participate directly, while short contract casework developed after I had left the field for the university. It is not for lack of interest that I have not written about these most promising developments, but for lack of practical experience.

CHAPTER 1

Renaissance in British Casework*

Social casework in Great Britain has been passing through a considerable crisis, and seems now to be entering a period of renaissance. This branch of social work originated in the 1870s with the Charity Organization Society, which was concerned to supersede the indiscriminate and demoralising methods of relieving distress which were then prevalent by a system of constructive and discriminating private charity for the "deserving" victims of circumstance. (The beggars and professional paupers who were already demoralised were to be weeded out and consigned to the deterrent methods of the Poor Law.) There is much in the writings of the time and in more recent reminiscent writings to show what qualities of sympathy and imagination were brought to bear by some of the workers on the task of supporting or restoring the self-respect of those applicants who were considered "helpable"; and the School of Sociology, which the C.O.S. helped to establish for the training of its voluntary workers, introduced courses in social psychology into its curriculum as early as 1903. But psychology at the turn of the century was still concerned with "the formation of individual and social habit", and had little to contribute to the understanding of the irrational elements in human behaviour and motivation which have since been shown to be of vital importance, and perhaps of special relevance for the understanding of social breakdown in the individual. The C.O.S. had to make the best use it could of a psychology which was still rudimentary, and when later on the startling discoveries of psycho-analysis began to be generally heard of, they were received with great scepticism (as in many other professions) and their possible

---

*First published in *Social Work* (U.K.), 1956.

applications to social work were not perceived for a considerable time.

American casework had originally owed much to the teachings of the C.O.S., but by 1915 or so it had become independent, or was even taking the lead. A little later it proved extremely receptive to psycho-analytic teaching about unconscious motivation and the influence on personality of early experience. Much thinking was done on the relation between early experience and present stress, the nature of the relationship which develops between a social worker and her client, and the possibilities of using this relationship to free the latter for healthy growth and achievement. The caseworker learned how often the need for material help expressed or indicated some difficulty in personal adjustment, which must be dealt with if any greater stability were to be hoped for; so that her function gradually widened to include help with a number of personal difficulties, whether or not these were accompanied by practical problems. To help effectively with such difficulties required new skills of a high order, as well as new knowledge; and social agencies in the U.S.A. developed the type of casework supervision which is now so familiar, but was then a very new method for teaching these skills.

In 1927 and 1928 this new orientation was imparted to two groups of British social workers, who were assisted by the Commonwealth Fund of America to undertake a year's casework training in the U.S.A. This was carried out entirely in psychiatric agencies and they returned to this country to demonstrate the value of psychiatric social work in mental hospitals, to staff the demonstration child guidance clinic established by the Commonwealth Fund in Cananbury Square, and to undertake the training of future generations of psychiatric social workers. But the training of social workers in general did not keep step with that of psychiatric social workers, and very few of these were absorbed in the older branches of social work. Until special training for child care workers was established in 1948, psychiatric social work remained the only branch of British casework whose training included the teaching of interviewing and the management of the worker/client relationship through intensive supervision of students throughout their course.

This led to an uneasy situation, in which psychiatric social workers remained to some extent isolated in their clinics by the mutual embarrassment arising from the existence of these different levels of training. Dissatisfied as many branches of social work became with their own level of training and practice, or perhaps just because of this, they found it difficult to make as much use as might have been hoped of opportunities for consultation and discussion with psychiatric social workers, while it took the latter a number of years to acquire as a group enough professional security and understanding of the issues involved to play a part in bridging the gap. Such tensions are probably inevitable whenever an individual or small group of people is given some extra training and thus set apart from the professional group as a whole, and this makes it difficult for the two groups to reintegrate, or even to communicate freely. The few American-trained psychiatric social workers who returned directly to their own settings must have found these difficulties almost overwhelming. It is interesting, though perhaps academic, to speculate whether the development of British casework would have been smoother and quicker if the Commonwealth Fund had spread its resources more evenly, though more thinly, over the whole body of social work in this country, instead of investing them in the creation of a new type of social agency and a new specialised professional sub-group.

By the mid-1950s, however, these difficulties began to yield, and social agencies began to turn to psychiatric social workers and also to psycho-analysts for leadership in case discussions as a means of widening and deepening the insight of their workers into personality and relationships. Some of these discussion groups were greatly valued, but they were no substitute for dynamically-oriented professional training, with intensive supervision to integrate theory and practice. An interesting new pattern was established in 1954 by the Family Welfare Association (formerly C.O.S.) when, as part of the effort to improve casework standards within the agency, they appointed a psychiatric social worker as a full-time casework supervisor. A similar step was taken rather later by the Invalid Children's Aid Association.

Although the social work profession in the U.S.A. was already avidly absorbing the contribution of psycho-analysis in the 1920s, this influence was only trickling down to student level in a diluted form when the first British psychiatric social workers were trained in that country. Psycho-analysis and casework made their own contact in the United Kingdom largely independently of parallel developments in the U.S.A. Some landmarks in this process were the inclusion in the London Mental Health Course (while evacuated to Cambridge during the War) of lectures by Susan Isaacs, a distinguished psycho-analyst of the English School, followed a little later by the appointment to the staff of the Course of Betty Joseph, a psychiatric social worker who was in training as a psycho-analyst. The highest degree of integration between psycho-analysis and casework in a non-psychiatric casework agency was achieved in the Family Discussion Bureau (F.D.B.)*; established in 1948 by the Family Welfare Association in collaboration with the Tavistock Institute of Human Relations in order to explore the possibilities of intensive casework with marital problems. This agency did not require its staff to have a psychiatric social work training, but recruited workers with one of the existing qualifications in social work, relying on its own in-service training to help them develop the high level of casework required. This training consisted of individual supervision for the first two years, first by a senior caseworker and then by an analyst, together with regular group case discussions under the leadership of a psycho-analyst. However senior and experienced the workers became, they continued to have the benefit of this kind of case discussion with psycho-analytic consultation. Like the early psychiatric social workers, the staff of the Family Discussion Bureau, having left the main stream of social work to acquire a specialised skill, found it hard at first to maintain effective communication with colleagues in other agencies, but the F.D.B. eventually came to exert considerable influence on many branches of social work, the probation service in particular, through full-time training for a few Fellows each year and through a great number of short or part-time courses.

Psychiatric social workers had soon begun to play a considerable part in pre-professional education, as tutors of social science courses at various universities. The Mental Health Course at the London School of Economics which provided this specialised training had been designed to prepare social workers for work in psychiatric settings, but a certain number of probation officers and others were

---

*Now the Institute of Marital Studies.

seconded to it in the hope that they would bring new learning back to their own service. The Children Act of 1948 relieved the Poor Law and other authorities of the responsibilities they had carried for children who had to be cared for outside their own homes, and created specialised child care services under local authorities. Special training courses were established in three universities for this new professional sub-group, each of which had a psychiatric social worker as tutor.

However, the whole system of having a number of separate and watertight trainings for social workers in different settings had for some time been breaking down in America, where the common or "generic" elements in the casework process were increasingly felt to be of more importance than the special modifications required by one setting or another. In 1947, this point of view received influential expression in this country in the classic report on "The Employment and Training of Social Workers" with which Miss (now Dame) Eileen Younghusband concluded her very thorough survey of this subject for the Carnegie Foundation. She called in question the fragmentation of professional training within the profession of social work, and suggested that certain features of the training of psychiatric social workers, notably the system of professional supervision, would be equally appropriate for every branch of casework. As a means at once of unifying professional training and of raising the standard, she advocated the establishment of a School of Social Work which should enrol and qualify a small number of post-graduate students of high attainments who might be expected to rise to senior posts in social work, and ultimately to engage in teaching and research in their subject.

It was some years before the means were found to implement these recommendations, but meanwhile the climate of opinion was undergoing considerable change. Interaction between the professional social workers of Great Britain and America, which had been minimal for a quarter of a century, suddenly revived under the impact of the Fulbright programme and the activity of U.N.O., which organised from 1950 onwards a series of international casework seminars where representatives of various branches of British casework were able to meet colleagues from all countries of Europe, as well as the outstanding American social workers who did most of the teaching.

The Fulbright scholars became familiar figures, and as the novelty of American caseworkers began to wear off, a number of them were invited at different times and by different groups to conduct seminars, lead case discussions, or to give individual supervision to caseworkers. British social workers have in many cases found it more natural to turn for help to American colleagues from fields similar to their own than to British psychiatric social workers, with their clinical background.

These contacts were of very great value, both on account of the professional teaching accomplished, and in helping to create a climate of feeling in which it became easier to admit how much there was to learn, and to accept the idea of in-service supervision as well as of more intensive student-supervision. But they could not meet the need for home-grown teachers and supervisors, on an adequate supply of whom the improvement of British casework training must ultimately depend. A few British social workers from various branches of the profession were enabled by U.N.O. or by the Smith-Mundt and Rockefeller Foundations to visit the U.S.A. for periods of observation or for further training, and returned to teach in this country. This was an important contribution, but not in itself an adequate solution of the problem. In 1951, the Tavistock Clinic, one of the major channels through which the influence of psycho-analysis had been brought to bear on psychiatric social work in the U.K., decided to divert its resources for social work education from the fieldwork training of psychiatric social workers to the provision of full-time theoretical and practical training for qualified and experienced social workers who were expected to return to positions in their own fields of social work where they could pass on their psycho-dynamic learning. The course was originated and designed by Miss N.K. Hunnybun, who became its tutor for the first four years. Bursaries were provided for a number of years, first by the Field Foundation and then by the Grant Foundation, enabling five or six senior social workers a year to take leave of absence without undue financial sacrifice. Eventually the course was sufficiently established for the Home Office to second one or two probation officers to it each year, while some child care services and other agencies began to do likewise.

The establishment of this Course was timely in relation to other developments in social work training. In 1954, through the generosity of the Carnegie Trust, Miss Younghusband was able to launch, not the School of Social Work she had envisaged, but a Course in Applied Social Studies at the London School of Economics, which was to combine a common basic training for students intending to work in probation, child care, family casework or medical social work with adequate opportunities for specialisation in their chosen field of work. A distinguished British psychiatric social worker, Miss K.M. Lewis, was appointed as Tutor, and great pains were taken to incorporate in the design of the Course the ripe fruits of American experience in casework training. Both Miss Younghusband and Miss Lewis spent periods of observation and study in America before the opening of their Course; and Professor Charlotte Towle, of the School of Social Service Administration of the University of Chicago, spent a year in London as consultant to the new Course. Much of the success of such a Course depends on the knowledge and skill of the fieldwork supervisors available. The Course in Applied Social Studies recruited as supervisors mainly probation officers with psychiatric social work training and caseworkers from other fields who had completed the Tavistock Course. The fact that this newest group to receive a highly specialised training so soon became integrated into a basic training programme indicated an altered climate of opinion and morale. Miss Towle herself made a major contribution to the development of supervisory skills in this country by conducting a weekly seminar for all the supervisors associated with the Applied Social Studies Course, as well as three short Courses for caseworkers from various fields who already had some experience as supervisors, or were likely to have this responsibility shortly. No formal training in supervision had previously been available in this country, so Miss Towle's Courses, which were attended altogether by some 75 social workers, were a land-mark in British social work training.

The Course in Applied Social Studies, like the Child Care Courses and the Mental Health Course, included Freudian theory in the syllabus, with some teaching on the divergences of Freud and Jung. The validity and utility of psycho-analytic theory had by no means ceased to be controversial; rather more so in the field of psychiatry than in that of casework. Many psychiatrists were convinced of an undiscovered organic basis for mental illness, and found that physical methods of treatment often disposed of symptoms more expeditiously than psycho-therapy. However, the caseworker is dealing with people who are not as a rule psychiatrically ill, but are having difficulty in dealing with certain stressful situations, in the performance of such roles as those of parent, bread-winner or marital partner and in maintaining generally satisfying relationships of mutual cooperation. It is in relation to problems of this sort that a consistent psycho-dynamic theory of human development and interaction proves most valuable and it seemed to be slowly but surely establishing itself as the professional discipline which has the most to contribute. For many social workers, the area of controversy was shifting and dwindling; it was not so much the validity and relevance of psycho-analytic theory which were in question as the extent to which it can be assimilated and the ways in which it can be applied by the general body of social caseworkers. One important element in the situation is that it is unlikely, at least for a very considerable time to come, that any large proportion of caseworkers will have experienced a personal analysis; another is that the majority of casework settings require that great attention be paid to economy of effort, the aim being to give as much help as is needed to overcome the presenting difficulty and to restore the client to effective independent functioning, rather than to deal exhaustively with all areas of his maladjustment. The problem of applying psycho-analytic principles to their own practice has been an active concern of American social workers for several decades, and a number of solutions have been adopted and extensively tested at different times and in different centres. British psychiatric social workers acting as consultants or supervisors in family casework agencies are also working on this problem, but have turned their attention to it much more recently; and this is also true of those former students of the Tavistock Course who in their various agencies are undertaking the supervision of students among their other duties, and are individually seeking to adapt the insight gained from psycho-analytic teaching to the problems, opportunities and limitations of these settings and to the needs and capacities of those whom they teach. The early "generic" training courses made a point of learning as much as possible from American experience, which has the advantage of being richly documented as well as relatively extensive in time, and it seems unlikely that British and American training and professional practice will again become as isolated and as divergent as they were till recently. On the other hand it may be hoped that interaction will not be a one-way traffic, but that British social work will show its ability to make an independent contribution to a reciprocal exchange of ideas which will be of mutual advantage. A renaissance is a dynamic and unpredictable thing, and the next ten years will be full of interest, discovery and mutual adaptation.

CHAPTER 2

The Function and Use of Relationship Between Client and Psychiatric Social Worker*

I wish to consider in this paper methods used by psychiatric social workers in helping clients to overcome difficulties in relationships; in other words, to modify their attitudes and behaviour in the direction of greater mental health. My thinking is based on experience in child guidance clinics, but I believe that workers in the adult mental health field have a proportion of clients who are capable of this kind of change, and to whom the following considerations may apply. On the other hand, I am aware that they also have many clients with whom the objective of treatment is not to produce change, but to prevent or postpone change of a deteriorative kind. Child guidance clinics also have some clients with whom it is wiser not to aim at increased insight, but to help to a more limited extent in other ways. It may be thought presumptuous to decide which clients are capable of change, but in fact I believe such decisions to be unavoidable. They may be made, not by the psychiatric social worker alone, but by a psychiatrist, a team or a whole staff group in conference, they may be tacit or explicit, they may be right or wrong, but in fact one's approach to every client, in so far as it is discriminative, implies some assessment of how much insight this person can stand, how much change is to be hoped for. These assessments may be provisional, and may be cautiously tested out during the early stages of the work, but no action can be taken without some judgement of the situation to which it should be appropriate.

If we ask ourselves why people have such difficulties in

---

*First published in the *British Journal of Psychiatric Social Work,* Vol. II, 6, 1952.

12

relationships as to seek specialised help, the question may seem so general as to be meaningless. We have all been trained to look for the sources of maladjustment in early experience and relationships, but we also know how varied these can be. Mrs. A had a drunken father, Mrs. B a harsh step-mother, Mr. C was the only son of an embittered and exacting widow. Even these statements refer only to the outstanding factor in a whole complex pattern, of which even a full social history will give only an over-simplified account. However, I believe that amidst all this variety one can trace a factor which is highly relevant to our question: the lack in early life of the kind of relationship which could remain predominantly good while permitting the integration within it of the hostile and destructive impulses which every child must experience in relation to his love-objects. Clients' accounts of their parents tend to be either too black or too white; their early family life is described either as full of conflict and hostility, or as completely free from friction or dissatisfaction of any kind. These idealised pictures always prove on investigation to cover a great deal of hostility, which was so frightening that it had to be denied in order to preserve the loving feelings with which it could not be integrated.

Early relationships which demand the repression of all jealousy and hostility, or which are lost or broken too soon, leave the individual driven and dominated by guilt at the damage he feels he has done, anxiety at the damage he still fears to do, and fear of punishment, disapproval and rejection. The more overpowering such negative experiences have been, the more they restrict adaptability, discrimination, spontaneous diversified response to others. They cause the individual to lack faith in the possibility of good spontaneous relationships which will not be destroyed by the inevitable admixture of hostile with the loving impulses. They cause him to see people according to a few simple stereotypes, and to react to them in stereotyped defensive ways. He may expect to find them bad, hostile, punishing, accusing, and attempt to defend himself by dominating, placating, or avoiding any real contact. He may feel they are good, and therefore sure to disapprove of his own badness, so that he is always having to protest his goodness, or alternatively to confess his badness, because of the guilt aroused by friendliness of which he feels unworthy. He may try to win their regard by docility and submission, which also serve to protect them against his unrecognised aggressiveness. One of the defences most damaging to relationships is that of projection. Miss Lewis (1950) and Miss Hutchinson (1948) have both described instances in which a mother attending a child guidance clinic came to see that she had projected on to a child or a husband attributes of her own which she could not bear to see in herself, and have shown how this acceptance of the problem as her own was attended with great improvements in the relationship in question. Another factor frequently found in parent-child problems is displaced restitution, as when a mother is compelled to overfeed her child because she was unable to prevent her parents from starving to death under German occupation, or is unable to assert any authority over a child whom she identifies with a sibling of her own who died in her childhood.

If, as I think, serious difficulties in relationships are always expressions of inability to tolerate and integrate ambivalent feelings, what are the implications concerning methods of helping to overcome such difficulties? Until fairly recently I think there were two main approaches to the problem. One was to give reassurance and support, trying to increase the client's self-confidence and ability to believe in his own goodness, while at the same time trying to encourage more tolerance and understanding for others. The other approach was to examine the past and try to reveal its distorting effects on the present, thus facilitating the withdrawal of projections, the relinquishment of defences, the development of insight into the self and the capacity to identify with the former objects of projection. Either process was felt to imply the necessity of a "secure" or "good" relationship, built up as a background for the facing of the client's problems. This was the basis of my own work till recently, but the nature of the "good" relationship was rarely examined, and remained rather ill-defined, implying mainly that the client should perceive the worker as a "good" figure. If a client is able to believe in good figures, it is not too difficult to assume this role for him, and then to demonstrate that a good figure can be uncritical and benevolent despite the revelation of attitudes and feelings which the client has hitherto regarded as shocking and intolerable.

It was possible in my experience to give many clients a good deal of help in this way, but there were always some who seemed unable to accept one as friendly and helpful, and repulsed all attempts at sympathy and understanding. There is no better way of appreciating the strength of the compulsion such clients are under to recreate the present in the image of the past than to observe the determination with which they insist that one must play some role of their choosing, whether it be teacher, judge, or policeman, or how they struggle against entering into a relationship at all. I have come to realise increasingly the value of concentrating on understanding just what situation the client is trying to create, what role he is trying to force on the worker, or subtly luring her into. Since the client has difficulty in relationships, it is natural that his relationship with the worker will be disturbed, and this in some characteristic way which is an excellent guide to his problems in this field. If, for instance, a parent is overtly submissive, while trying covertly to force the worker into a dominant role, we are likely to find that problems about dominance and submission are prominent in the marital relationship and the parent-child relationship, as well as having been prominent in his own childhood. The client who resists or rejects the service, or defends himself against participation in the treatment process, does so in a characteristic way on account of characteristic anxieties. Something has to be done about this and the question is what. We are apt to try to feel our way round the defences, to seek some way of demonstrating good will which will "gain the client's confidence", and establish the psychiatric social worker as a real person distinct from the image he is trying to force on to her. But it may be more profitable to focus attention at this point not on the role one wants to play, but on the client and the situation he is trying to create. Here he is, creating a difficulty in relationship; what better opportunity of studying his problems at first hand and helping him to understand them? Instead of trying to establish a relationship which is free from the start from the usual difficulties, may it not be better to begin with all the usual difficulties and work from there, by recognising and accepting them in relation to oneself, towards a relationship which is new because these problems have been to some extent resolved in it?

I think it is useful to envisage the basic aim of our work with the client in terms of restoring his faith in the capacity of others to tolerate his aggression and hostility without hitting back savagely on the one hand, or being hurt and damaged on the other. The most direct way of achieving this end is to allow, or indeed encourage him to bring all his feelings, negative as well as positive, into the relationship with the worker, to demonstrate in one's own person the ability to accept hostility without fear, and to resist demands without anger. Often it seems not enough to do this passively. If we simply remain friendly and helpful in face of a hostile client, his guilt and anxiety will tend to mount, and I believe this is the process underlying most of those cases reported closed "for lack of parental co-operation". If on the other hand we show that we are not unaware of his hostility, that our friendliness and lack of fear is not based on ignorance of his feelings, and that we understand something of the reason for them in terms of the present situation and perhaps also of the past, then he is apt to be considerably relieved.

This method of recognising and verbalising the client's feelings about the situation and the worker in an accepting and understanding way has, I think, various advantages, of which the first is its value in overcoming resistance, as described above. Secondly, I think the admission of negative feelings into open expression in the worker-client relationship helps the client better than anything else to realise that they are less harmful than he supposed, and will reduce the guilt and anxiety attached to such feelings, and the need to project and deny them, more effectually than anything else. I think the "good" worker-client relationships, in which only positive feelings can be acknowledged, involves a danger of perpetuating a false belief in the possibility of ideal and frictionless relationships, and so constituting by contrast a reproach to the client's friends and relations. When the relationship is kept "good" in this sense there would appear to me to be a danger that the client's other relationships may be overloaded with hostilities engendered, but not expressed or recognised, in the treatment situation. On the other hand, when hostile feeling can be accepted in the worker-client relationship, I think this relationship can then serve to some extent as a lightning conductor in respect of the outside relationships.

A striking example of this occurred with a very unhappy woman who complained that nobody understood her, nobody would let her talk about her sufferings in concentration camps, and yet became increasingly anxious and unwilling when encouraged to use the interview in this way. Eventually she explained her conflict by telling of a man who had committed a crime, and was advised to ease himself of the secret by whispering it to a tree; he did so, and felt greatly relieved, but the tree died. The interesting thing was that her child had already been much less anxious and defiant for some weeks, apparently because the pressure on her was relieved by the diversion of some of the mother's hostile wishes and anxieties on to the worker. I feel it is valuable in such a case to show understanding of the feeling expressed by some phrase as "You seem to feel it wouldn't be safe for me to hear your experiences?"; otherwise the anxiety can lead to complete blocking or even withdrawal. Some workers might also take up the theme of the crime at that point, while others might prefer to wait for further clarification and more direct expression before dealing with it.

The form of comment or interpretation is very important, and difficult to illustrate in the space available. For instance, one may feel that the client's late arrival is an indication of resistance which one would like to "take up". But this phrase could cover forms of comment which might increase the resistance, as well as forms which may reduce it. If one merely says: "You are a bit late today. Perhaps you didn't want to come?" this may be felt as an accusation or reproach, and the interpretation denied, even if correct. It may be more helpful not actually to mention the lateness, but to say "I wonder if it wasn't so easy to come today?" or "I wonder if anything we talked about last week has been bothering you?" On the other hand, if the client is obviously anxious or guilty about his lateness, this may be the thing to take up. I think the criterion is to put oneself in the client's place, and to remember that the function of such an interpretation is not simply to point out something, but to make it easier for the client to admit. I think a tentative form of interpretation is also useful; it not only guards against forcing a mistaken interpretation on the client, but helps to avoid slipping into a situation in which the worker is the authority who knows best, implying instead that the client is recognised as a person who is trying to work out his problems with the help of the worker.

In discussing this self-conscious use of the worker-client relationship and the emotional situation in the interview, questions often arise as to whether psychiatric social workers can safely and properly use "the transference", or in fact whether anybody but an analyst should do so. I think there are several ambiguities involved in the use of this term. It was originally coined by Freud to connote the way in which analytic patients react to the analyst with the same intense positive and negative feelings which they originally entertained for their primary love-objects. It then became evident that, like all the other mechanisms observed in analysis and in neurosis, this was a special case of a process which also occurs in normal people and in ordinary social realtionships; namely, the distortion which people tend to impose on inter-personal situations in view of assumptions, expectations and prejudices unconsciously derived from past experience. If this is accepted, it becomes evident that such factors must also exist in a casework situation. To quote Bertha Reynolds: "becoming conscious of them does not create these emotional situations, which . . . must have existed always, and which must account for some of the failures of well-intended therapy." While recognising the importance of dealing with these derivations from the past, Miss Reynolds does not use the term "transference", in order to avoid confusion with the analytic use of relationship, since (as she says) "Psychiatric social workers are not dealing with a situation, produced as a therapeutic measure, in which the patient is brought to regress to an overt repetition, in the analytic hours, of the emotional reaction patterns of his very early childhood. They are not producing a situation in which the treatment becomes, for the time being, the overwhelmingly important thing in the patient's life."

It has perhaps created some confusion in this country that the term transference has come to be used not only in the narrow specialised sense defined above (and now distinguished by the term "transference neurosis") but also in a broader sense which denotes the total emotional response of client to worker, and includes, but is not exhausted by, these emotional residues. It is perhaps in this broader sense that a psychiatric social worker can be said to "use the transference" (if one prefers to use the term). I have been asked whether I think the relationship and the emotional situation can be used in the way I have been trying to indicate by general caseworkers, or indeed by any but analysed psychiatric social workers. I think the answer is that, while personal analysis is required for work at deeper levels (and I still mean levels far short of the deepest) I hope for a time when all caseworkers will have sufficient psychological training and insight to be able at least to recognise, accept, and explore with the client the uppermost levels of his feelings.

References

Hutchinson, D.M. (1948) Clinic and Community, *British Journal of Psychiatric Social Work.*
Lewis, K.M. (1950) The Role of the Psychiatric Social Worker, *British Journal of Psychiatric Social Work,* October.

CHAPTER 3

Transference and Reality in the Casework Relationship *

During the celebrations of the birth of Sigmund Freud, lectures were given in London exploring the contribution of his discoveries to such varied fields of human knowledge as philosophy, education, child care, social problems in industry and the understanding of art. Are we ready and able to give an account of that which our own profession of social casework has extracted from this inexhaustible mine? To some extent I think we are. It has not been easy to think clearly on this topic, largely because our vision has been obscured by the emotional significance of a number of the questions involved. For instance, was casework psycho-therapy? If so, it was often assumed, it must be an inferior form of psycho-therapy; and it was often concluded that for this reason it was preferable to think of it as something different, whether we could define the difference clearly or not. Clarity could only come as this cloud of feeling subsided, and a good deal of doubt and confusion still exists. Thus at a refresher course of the A.P.S.W. we were told by a psycho-analyst (Sutherland, 1956) that casework and psycho-therapy are for him indistinguishable; while a psychiatric social worker contributed a paper on the distinction between casework and psycho-therapy (Lloyd Davies, 1956). I have come to the conclusion that this is largely a semantic problem (once it has ceased to be an emotional problem) based on the unexamined assumption that the term psycho-therapy and the term casework each refers to a

---

*First published in the *British Journal of Psychiatric Social work,* Vol. III, No. 4, 1956.

unitary entity — or in other words that each time anyone uses one of these terms he is talking about the same thing, so that anyone else knows exactly what he means. In Dr. Sutherland's paper referred to above he cuts very cleanly through this Gordian knot: "Psycho-therapy . . . can mean almost anything in regard to its aims and methods. All kinds of people can help the psychologically disturbed in all kinds of ways. Many people even have a remarkable intuitive understanding of unconscious motives and can help through this understanding. I should like to restrict psycho-therapy, however, to any psychological treatment whose aim is to permit the individual to gain insight into the nature and origins of certain unrecognised parts of himself, when such treatment is based on theoretical principles which are formulated and which can therefore be subjected to at least some checks in regard to their validity."

I think this formulation gives us a framework in which we can see that casework, no less than psycho-therapy, is a term which in common use represents a variety of different things, and that even if we restrict the use of the term psycho-therapy as Dr. Sutherland suggests there is a considerable overlap between the two; in fact that some forms of casework are psycho-therapy in Dr. Sutherland's sense and some are not. Even among psychiatric social workers, some are much more concerned with developing insight in his sense than others; some work on the basis of a body of formulated principles, and some mainly on the basis of intuitive understanding. This latter group tend to be insufficiently represented in professional discussions, and perhaps insufficiently regarded, because they are almost by definition less able to express their methods of helping in words. If I do not explicitly include their work in the survey I am about to attempt, this is because I lack knowledge and understanding of it, not through lack of respect; and it may be that some of my formulations will in fact be found to apply to some of these ways of helping.

In taking stock of our debt to Freud, we should differentiate clearly between the two elements of his bequest to the world, both indifferently known as "psycho-analysis"; I refer to the body of psycho-dynamic theory on the one hand and to the therapeutic method on the other. As regards the theory, we can now see how much of what appeared at first so revolutionary and shocking had been contained in the mythological and artistic tradition of our own and other civilisations; Freud himself paid generous tribute to his forerunners, the great poets and dramatists of the world. What shocked us or our parents so deeply was his rediscovery and restatement, in the scientific form which alone confers respect for knowledge in our time, of insights which had been tolerable only in mythological form; his increasingly well-documented insistence that the curse of Oedipus lay heavy on us all, on the psychological reality of such poetic statements as that "we are all members of one another" and that if we ask for whom the bell tolls we shall find it tolls for us. It is true that we were also shocked by the explosion of a modern myth concerning the innocence of childhood, and by the revelation that the fairy tales which some banish from the modern nursery are in fact very graphic accounts of the inner world of the child.

In short, the knowledge of the human heart which was contained in fairy tale and saga, in Norse myth and Greek tragedy, in the Bible and in the work of Shakespeare, Ibsen and others was confirmed, elaborated, extended, systematised and brought home not only to the patient, but also to the common reader. Gradually this great body of systematised knowledge imposed itself and established its indispensable importance for the understanding of human personality, behaviour and interaction, and of the therapeutic processes by which these can be changed. Whether in its classical form or in various derived or modified forms, it became the basis for psycho-therapy in Dr. Sutherland's sense; it was gradually incorporated in the training of psychiatric social workers, and eventually, in the U.S.A., of caseworkers in general. Here, this last stage is only just beginning, with the development first of a psycho-analytically-based training for child care workers, and more recently of generic casework courses. I believe the day is coming when all caseworkers will be expected to have a sound working understanding of the nature and manifestation of unconscious processes, the influence of early experience in relationship on the development of personality and on the relationships of later life, the nature and importance of ambivalence and its relation to the various forms of anxiety, and the mechanisms of defence by which we and our clients protect ourselves against our anxiety.

Relation Between Psycho-analytic Theory and Psycho-analytic Technique

We must now consider how far the psycho-analytic technique, whose development went hand-in-hand with the theoretical discoveries, represents the only method by which such knowledge can be brought to bear on the solution of problems in personal relationships. It is probably inevitable that some of us who have experienced the benefits of personal analysis, and have realised how similar are the problems which we take to our analysts and those which our clients bring to us, have been tempted to succumb to a feeling that analysis is the method *par excellence* of dealing with such problems, and to assume uncritically that the more our work could be made to resemble analysis the better it would be — despite the vigorous protests of numerous colleagues! It is time, however, that we cease to ignore these protests and to overlook the results achieved by other methods, and endeavour to see whether psycho-analytic theory cannot provide a frame of reference broad enough to accommodate traditional casework and various forms of psycho-therapy as therapeutic methods alongside psycho-analysis itself. Freud himself envisaged that his own time-consuming technique (which has since his day developed into still more time-consuming forms) would require modification if the benefits of his discoveries were ever to be made available to any large proportion of those in need of psycho-therapeutic help. He predicted (Freud, 1924) the development of a situation in which either the State or private institutions would accept responsibility for providing free "analysis" for "the men who would otherwise give way to drink, the women who have nearly succumbed under their burden of privations, the children for whom there is no choice but running wild or neurosis". He does not in this context foresee that such therapeutic help might be given by non-medical workers, but he does explicitly envisage adaptation of technique. "I have no doubt that the validity of our psychological assumptions will impress the uneducated too, but we shall need to find the simplest and most natural expression for our theoretical doctrines. . . . Possibly we may often be able to achieve something if we combine aid for the mind with some material support. . . . It is very probable, too, that the application of our therapy to numbers will compel us to alloy the pure gold of analysis plentifully with the copper of direct suggestion. . . . But whatever form this psycho-therapy for the people may take, whatever the elements out of which it is compounded, its most effective and most important ingredients will assuredly remain those borrowed from strict psycho-analysis which serves no ulterior purpose.''

I think the crucial difference between psycho-analytic technique (especially as developed by the English school of psycho-analysis) and that of other forms of psycho-therapy, including casework, lies in the handling of transference. Some of us have been reluctant to make this differentiation; others have felt there was one, but have found it hard to formulate. Miss F.E. Waldron (1948) has posed a number of very pertinent questions.

''A further development from our realisation of our representative role may be our ability to stimulate our patient's growth beyond dependence without him transferring to us infantile emotional attitudes. We do not necessarily seek to avoid the ''transference'' situation, but if as social workers we consider we are not equipped to deal with the psychological mechanisms released by it, we must increase our awareness of how we avoid it, and what help we substitute for the parental role. By examining a process which we have evolved intuitively we can make its application more valuable, for with knowledge about it we shall gain more control over it. If we do accept our role in a ''transference'' situation there is still need to examine it, for the course of a patient's growth from dependence on his social worker is probably different from that which develops from his ''transference'' to his doctor. The psycho-therapists have examined their working relationship, have controlled it, and have taught social workers how to recognise and control the ''transference'' stage of their relationship with a patient. I think it possible that we are now in a position to show the psycho-therapist that modifications and variations of the therapeutic relationship follow from the professional participator being a social worker, for we are bound to bring to the relationship qualities inherent in our approach that are distinctively ours and different from qualities found in therapeutic relationships between psycho-therapist and patient.''

I find I agree with most of what Miss Waldron has said, provided we read "psycho-analyst" for "psycho-therapist" (and with some reserve as to the extent to which either has taught the social worker how to control the development of transference). In the years since 1948, few of us have seriously tried to answer these questions, and most of those who made the attempt have given partial answers only, describing or illustrating each particular use of the relationship in which he was interested. Thus, some of us have been in favour of interpreting the transference (as far as our limitations of insight and training permit). Miss Lloyd Davies (*op. cit.*) agrees that the client tries to force transference roles upon us, but feels it is more appropriate to deal with this simply by resisting his attempts to manipulate us into playing these roles, and by asserting our own reality as distinct from these roles. This is a most important idea to which I shall return later. Mr. Myers (1954) and Miss Laquer (1954) have published sensitive case material illustrating their own use of the relationship. Only Miss Goldberg (1953) I think, really tries to survey the variety of ways, in which psychiatric social workers do in fact use their relationship with clients.

In this situation I have become uneasy about the signs that notions of "orthodoxy" were developing; that colleagues spoke apologetically and defensively at meetings about methods of work which they clearly felt were appropriate to their clients and their settings, but unlikely to command respect from those who found more intensive methods appropriate in their own clinics. Experience in training caseworkers from a variety of fields, and continued contact with them after return to their own settings, have also led me to appreciate the value and necessity of variety. I now feel that we should stop thinking in terms of "the right way to do casework" and recognise that analysed caseworkers can sometimes work in ways which are not appropriate for the unanalysed; that even so, these ways may not be appropriate for all clients and settings; and that we have reached a stage where it is less important to demonstrate what the analysed caseworker can do in favourable circumstances than to explore what the unanalysed can do with good training (because there are so many more of them, dealing with so many more clients).

Transference and Reality in Relationships

What I want to attempt in this article is to construct a frame of reference within which we can formulate an account, consonant with Freudian theory, of the variety of ways in which we try to promote or facilitate emotional growth and development in clients, or to modify their attitudes and behaviour. How can one human being help another to change? I would like to begin by quoting Miss Pearl King* to the effect that the aim of many forms of casework and psycho-therapy is to remove some of the obstacles to the inherent tendency of human beings towards healthy development. This formulation reminds us of the existence of spontaneous creative and recuperative tendencies in human beings, without which we, as caseworkers, could do little indeed. It parallels another fact which I would like to recall, which is that every relationship combines two elements in varying proportions:

(a) Response to the reality of the other person, with ability to perceive his qualities, and to feel and react appropriately (only with the psychotic is this element likely to be absent, and often then not completely so);

(b) Transference, with its aspects of perceptual distortion, inappropriate emotion and manipulative action — its tendency to transform the present person and the present situation into the image and likeness of an earlier person and a past situation.

The more normal the subject, the more will (a) preponderate over (b) in spontaneous relationships. Nevertheless, some degree of transference is always present, and it can reach considerable intensity in a casework situation, whether client and worker recognise it or not. In fact we are coming to realise that one reason why it is important for every caseworker to be able to recognise transference phenomena is that it is necessary to recognise them in order to be able to modify and control them.

Transference is of course a manifestation of unconscious fantasy, interfering with adaptation to reality. It occurs, as I have said, more or less in all relationships, and notably in those disturbed relationships with family and friends with which the caseworker's help is so often

---

*Personal communication.

sought. Any form of psycho-therapy must therefore attempt to modify this distorting influence, so that the patient (or client) may become more discriminatingly adaptive. For this purpose psycho-analysts have come to rely increasingly on the interpretation to the patient of his transference to the therapist in both its positive and negative aspects, since it is through this transference that the therapist is in direct contact with the inner world of the patient's fantasy. It is probably true that this is the most effective way known to us of profoundly modifiying this inner world; but it is not the only way of helping the individual to deal with unconscious fantasy, and of modifying its effect on current relationships. We all know that stable parents have their own way of helping children to deal with unconscious anxieties by remaining benevolent and undamaged, and by retaining a benign control of the situation; by being in fact actively parental. I think the best of the early caseworkers must have used their relationship with their clients in just this parental way. Octavia Hill, for instance, had the warmest maternal feelings for her clients, and never went to the country without bringing back innumerable bunches of flowers for her enormous family. She offered to a very deprived and rejected group a relationship in which they could respond to her emotional warmth, learn to identify with her courage and self-confidence, and experience her genuine appreciation of their own capacity for response and self-help. Such attitudes seem to have worked remarkable changes in numbers of clients. They were not, however, easy to maintain; the early literature of social work contains much evidence of the struggle to walk this narrow way between the Scylla of over-indulgence (based on guilt towards the deprived and outcast) and the Charybdis of self-righteous contempt for the "undeserving" (based on paranoid anxieties about the danger of insatiable exploitation by these damaged people).

Role-playing in Casework

I think there are still many situations in which it is appropriate for the caseworker (including the psychiatric social worker) to play a parental role in this traditional way, rather than to attempt to foster insight by interpreting the reflection of parental images as projected on to him by the client. In this type of casework the essential process lies in the acting out of a parent-child relationship between worker and client. A psychiatric social worker, describing her work with a number of immature psychopathic personalities in a mental hospital, recently gave a good description of just this sort of work, in which she set the limits of what she could offer in terms of length and frequency of interviews, and dealt with the greedy, dependent demands of the clients for extra interviews like a firm and patient parent, showing sympathetic understanding of the wish for more attention, while holding to the limits she had set and explaining the need for these in terms of the needs of others with whom she was also concerned. Miss Goldberg *(op. cit.)* also quotes a very telling case of this kind, concerning a young alcoholic with a weak character and weak, indulgent parents, who failed to take the drug which was an essential part of his treatment. The worker found it necessary himself to play the part of a strong, controlling father, and dramatised this at a crucial moment by insisting that the patient take a tablet there and then.

It is important to recognise that the playing of even a quite authoritative role such as this can be genuine casework, provided it is dictated by the needs of the client and the situation, and not by the worker's own need to assert himself; provided also that it is a genuine expression of the worker's concern for the client, and not of rejection. If we do not recognise such a carrying of authority as casework we are going to confuse and undermine such caseworkers as probation officers and child care workers, who must often of necessity play just such a role*; it is better to admit that even the psychiatric social worker may have clients who not only need advice, but also the experience of contact with someone who is prepared to give unpalatable advice and take full responsibility for it. These will usually be the very weak and immature clients; we shall probably agree that it is a pity to give much advice to those who are capable of thinking out their own solutions and taking responsibility for their own decisions.

It seems to have been of a rather similar group of clients that

---

*This has certainly come about, E.E.I., 1978.

Ratcliffe and Jones wrote (1956): "Not only must the caseworker see the patient as a human being, but *he must also be allowed to see her as a human being*" (my italics). "She may mention some incident of her personal life; reveal her ignorance of some points, etc." This is an interesting observation, not the less so for being in striking contrast to the way in which some of us in other settings have been trying to keep our own personalities in the background. It seems to be borne out by the experience of other workers in the community mental health services and to apply also to the relationship established by Family Service Unit workers with their clients. The authors do not unfortunately give the reasons why they think this group of clients needs this kind of relationship; one can therefore only speculate, but my guess would be that they have such a florid and frightening fantasy life that they are apt to become scared of what they project on to the worker, unless he presents his own reality to them in pretty firm outline.

It is probably already clear that in the role-playing type of casework one cannot generalise about "the caseworker's role", because the role must be adjusted to the needs of each client as assessed by the worker. I have illustrated variants of an authoritative role; an article by Miss Elkan (1956) shows the worker playing a very different role, that of someone who is patient and accepting and concerned about the clients' own feelings, whatever they have done. The really fascinating thing in one case was the determined efforts of the clients to put this attitude to the test by producing sweets which were not for the children but for themselves, inducing her to sanction this by accepting a sweet, and then inviting her to inspect the ration books, knowing she would find that they had used the children's coupons. It was probably the fact that she could remain friendly and accepting after all this which enabled them to feel it worth while to keep in touch with the children.

Combination of Role-playing with Insight-promoting Technique

This role-playing casework is not psycho-therapy in Dr. Sutherland's sense; but I think there is no doubt that for many simple immature clients it is more appropriate than psycho-therapy, because they are not capable of gaining insight, and because for them deeds speak louder than words. This leads us on to reflect that even when there is much discussion of the mother-child relationship in relation to the mother's early experience, the real essence of the work may lie in something which is being tacitly acted out between worker and client. Miss M.H. Holmes (1956) recently published a study of work with a mother, in which at first glance the technique appears to have been to help the mother recall her own experience in each of the areas in which there were problems between herself and her children — fears, rebelliousness, separation, rejection, sexual curiosity, clothes, sex rivalry — thus helping in many instances to convert projection into sympathetic identification. But underneath all this, something was being acted out in the relationship: "in response to the tolerant and accepting attitude of the psychiatric social worker and the clinic staff as a whole, the parent often becomes better able to tolerate herself, and hence other people". More specifically, the mother was allowed to express a great deal of aggression against the patient, and was at the same time told how much the child needed her help (the worker's confidence that she would help in spite of the hostile feelings being clearly implied). Until this point, the mother was hostile to worker and clinic, but she then became friendly and trustful. A little later the mother expressed her conflict about smacking the child (Lynda), and the worker interpreted that she was punishing, in Lynda, rebelliousness such as she herself had felt as a child, adding that ambivalence towards one's mother is natural and universal and therefore acceptable. I think this was a crucial moment in relation to the aim "to work through her feelings of rejection, and to make her feel accepted herself". It was this experience in the relationship with the worker which made it possible "to build up her maternal, positive attitude to Lynda by allowing her to express her hostility against the child and by encouraging her to discuss her relationship to her own mother". An important element in this seems to be indentification with the warm accepting social worker.*

There is a great deal in common between what went on in this case and in some cases described by Miss Betty Joseph (1948) in an article

---

*"Modelling" in the language of learning theory, E.E.I., 1978.

whose theoretical implications were not easy to assimilate at the time. Miss Joseph describes a young mother who was having trouble with an obstinate soiling child of 22 months. She was a controlling and meticulous person, who concealed a senstitive and meticulous personality beneath "a tough defiant shell". After a very few interviews, in which the worker made contact with the mother's sensitivity and need for care, the child began to be less defiant about soiling, and to invite his mother to share his interest and pride in his motions. Miss Joseph writes: "I have the impression that it was not only the child who was allowing himself to take a proud and friendly interest in his "big jobs" with a "nose". . . . The mother's own deep interest in dirtying and anal habits, so much overlaid by her reaction-formation of over-cleanliness and tidiness, was being allowed some direct, or at any rate vicarious, expression." It is noteworthy that Miss Joseph, who is herself an analyst, gave very careful consideration to the question of whether the improvement obtained in some eight or nine interviews might be only symptom relief, and decided that there was real improvement in the mother-child relationship, and in the mother's confidence as a mother.

In another case, Miss Joseph soon had the feeling that the mother "was just like her own naughty, intolerant daughter of 2½ who could brook no frustration or waiting, and who shouted and lost her temper". Miss Joseph did not, however, try to show the mother these negative aspects of her personality, but helped her to rediscover and regain the feeling of pride and unity with her child which she had enjoyed during pregnancy. "At the same time, this mother was able to continue to behave in her emotional and immature way without risk of provoking me or losing my interest, so that she gained in her relationship with me, on, so to speak, a rarefied and verbalised level, the control and support that she could not give to her child who behaved in somewhat the same way. Within two months the situation was transformed. The mother was proud and happy with Judy, and able to tolerate and laugh about naughtiness."

Importance of Worker's Feeling Response to Client

In both these cases the mother was allowed to reveal and display to the worker interests and characteristics which she had been unable to tolerate in the child; the worker, "on a rarefied and verbalised level", acted out the part of an accepting and tolerant mother; the client then, partly by identification, became able to be similarly accepting and tolerant with herself and her child, the struggle between mother and child was dissolved, and the affection which had been blocked by this struggle was allowed to flow more freely. I am becoming increasingly convinced that this is the most important thing which happens in casework on a parent-child problem, whether we interpret or not; and I suspect that it applies, *mutatis mutandis,* to casework on any problem in relationship. For this reason the quality of the counter-transference is probably more important than the interpretation of the transference (although the understanding of the transference is very important for the control of the counter-transference). This brings me back to Ratcliffe and Jones *(op. cit.):* "The caseworker must show herself as a human being who understands the particular difficulties that the client himself is experiencing as a human being. She cannot do this unless she has a genuine and sincere concern for him as a person. Assumed geniality will be seen through." It is interesting to compare Miss Joseph's comment that in the type of work described rapid changes can occur: "if I can get a really deeply established contact with the mother, and if, in addition to intellectual understanding of the problem myself, I am able to get also an understanding of the feeling content of the situation" *(op. cit.).* This seems to imply that in this sort of work the worker's own feeling response is an essential element in helping the client. Insight, and the interpretations by which it is conveyed, may be very useful to certain clients: but just as we now believe that a particular method of feeding or training a child is less important than the attitude which the mother communicates by her way of using any method, so I believe that interpretations in general are less important than the caseworker's attitude, whether conveyed through interpretations or by other means. This is probably why different workers obtain satisfactory results with such a variety of techniques, and why any given technique can let us down if the counter-transference becomes predominantly negative.

Flexibility in Casework: Mutual Adjustment of Client and Worker

If this is so, we can afford to relax our efforts to find "the best" or "the proper" amount or kind of interpretation, and focus more of our interest on the particular way in which each client wants to use the relationship and the interviews. Some have a very clear idea of the kind of problem they want to think out, whether it be something about a child which they want to understand or something in themselves. If they are allowed to set about this self-appointed task, they may do very good and useful work, using the worker as a supportive figure in much the same way as a young child learning to walk may use an adult's finger, not to take his weight, but to give him confidence and balance. In such a case, all that the worker needs to do is to give occasional evidence of continued interest and understanding, perhaps now and then verbalising a little more clearly than the client something which was implied or hinted, or asking for clarification of some ambiguity. I think some of us have laid too much emphasis on interpretation and not enough on the value of the type of question which leads the client towards finding his own interpretation (as distinct from the "fact-finding" question which is so often used to change a subject which one is reluctant to pursue). Questions directed towards clarification have the advantage of inducing (or allowing) the client to do more of the work, and this in turn limits the client's dependence on the worker, and reduces the conflict and resistance which arise from excessive dependence.

It is true that many clients want help on impossible terms; they are apt, for instance, to limit somewhat arbitrarily the areas which they are prepared to discuss, and a time will come when we shall have to show them that the selected area cannot be understood without reference to excluded areas. If something worthwhile, but limited, can be done on the client's terms, it is often useful to do this first. For instance, a mother may be prepared to discuss her relationship with the child who is the patient, but not the marital relationship, and provided she is prepared to include her own early relationships within the discussion progress can be made; if a point is reached at which the marital relationship is clearly relevant, we must then find ways of helping her to see that this is so. I sometimes put it to a mother that she is entitled to refuse to discuss such problems, with which she has not herself asked for my help, but that I want her to understand that this limits the help I can give her with the presenting problem. Sometimes she will then agree to widen the area of discussion; in other cases we may agree to terminate a treatment which has gone as far as she can allow. I have often found that a mother who is allowed to act out her resistance in this way may ask for more treatment after an interval; having found her own need, she will then take more responsibility for co-operating and offer less resistance to the work.

Sometimes a mother's terms are less workable than this; she may, for instance, refuse to talk of her own early history, or even of her own feelings towards the child, on the grounds that the problem is all in the child, and that is the only thing she is prepared to discuss — her own feelings have nothing to do with it. We cannot usually hope to give much help with the child's problem without some exploration of what is being displaced or projected on to it; but we may be able as a first step to give some relief to the anxiety behind the mother's wilfulness by sharing with her our understanding of the anxiety underlying the child's wilfulness. In general, if interviews are being used defensively, we shall have to find some way of making contact with the underlying anxieties, in which we ourselves and our anticipated reactions are bound to be involved.

If we are sensitised to transference, we shall certainly find a great deal of it in the client-worker relationship; its proportion in the total relationship varies considerably, and a strong transference is equally compatible with excellent co-operation and with great resistiveness. Where the transference is producing resistance, one has to do something about it, whether by interpretation or otherwise. Miss Lloyd Davies *(op. cit.)* gives some excellent examples of non-interpretive handling which I would consider first-rate casework. On the other hand, I do not myself share her anxieties about interpreting the transference, provided one can see it sufficiently clearly, and provided one can see both the positive and negative aspects, and is not misled into stressing one alone. I think it is useful as far as possible to keep one's style simple and natural: "I believe you feel I am just as bad as mother", or "You pulled the wool over father's eyes, and I believe you are trying to pull it over my eyes too, aren't you?"

At this point I would like to distinguish between (a) the transference interpretation proper, of which these are very simple examples, which relates the immediate present situation to some infantile, or at least some earlier situation; and (b) the verbal recognition of feelings in the here-and-now situation which may be conscious or at least not far from consciousness, but which are denied, concealed or given only displaced and indirect expression (e.g. in terms of complaints against someone other than the therapist). This is something loosely called "taking up the transference" or even "transference interpretation", but I think the distinction is important.

The first (which we might call a "now-and-then interpretation") has become the most highly valued form of analytic interpretation. Analysed caseworkers can learn to use it skilfully, and I find that some unanalysed workers can learn to use the simpler forms, such as I have illustrated, on occasion; but I do not find it appropriate for all clients, and it cannot become a characteristic implement for a profession most of whose members are unanalysed. The second (which we might call a "here-and-now interpretation") is something which I find useful with nearly all clients, and which I think all caseworkers could learn to use, given good selection and training for the profession.

Methods of Controlling Development of Transference

I think we can now take up Miss Waldron's question *(op. cit.)* as to how we can control and limit the transference elements in the situation, if and when we want to do so. In general I believe that an interpretative technique (like other elements of analytic technique) is an invitation to a partial suspension of ego function for the duration of the session, with a view to uncovering fantasy and stimulating transference. On the other hand, the use of devices, such as the question, which enlist the active co-operation of the client is stimulating to the ego and limits the activity of fantasy. For instance, when a client is talking defensively, it might be appropriate to say:

"You feel that I am accusing you of ..." and to interpret this feeling as a projection. But it is also possible to say: "You are talking as if someone had accused you of ... and I wonder who it is? I don't think it is me." This can often elicit some such response as: "No, it's myself — that's what I feel." In other words, the client himself can recognise the projection. Some forms of interpretation can convey a reassuring reference to reality: "You find it hard to believe that I am not as critical as your mother."

Miss Joseph *(op. cit.)* deliberately saw her clients relatively infrequently; this is one way of limiting the importance one assumes for the client and the amount of fantasy one stimulates. It is clear that in the work described she welcomed and encouraged the client's independence, and let her do as much for herself as possible. (Again, one might say that she was acting out a certain kind of maternal relationship.) If a sudden dramatic improvement in the child made the mother feel as if the worker had done some magic, Miss Joseph dealt with this by appeal to the real situation, i.e. by helping the mother to see how much of the improvement was due to her own work.

This is a simple instance of a way of using the reality of the professional situation which is characteristic of the "functional" school of casework in America. It sometimes happens, for instance, that a client develops a strong ambivalent transference, and engages the worker week after week in discussing why he should continue to come. One may discern in this material very paranoid elements, together with a great deal of underlying positive feeling, and a demand for constant reassurance in the form of persuasion to continue attending. If one interprets all this, one is apt to get in very deep indeed; on the other hand, if we attempt to hold the client by stressing his need, or explaining the advantages of attending we are gratifying a neurotic need for repeated reassurance of being wanted, without reducing the need, and the situation tends to become static. The "functional" way out of this impasse is to comment on the way the client is defining the situation, e.g. as one in which he is under moral pressure to attend for purposes of the worker's which are beyond his comprehension; and to contrast this with the actual situation, in which the worker is trying to give him some help which he asked for. Has he in fact been pursuing this purpose or obstructing it? Is he still pursuing it? Has he already had the help he wanted, or has he lost hope of getting it? If the discussions have not been relevant to this purpose, has he or the worker been responsible? Does he really think this or that was so irrelevant? If he is really satisfied with the help he has had, why not stop coming? If, on the other hand, he is not satisfied, he is also free to stop coming; but it may be premature to despair of finding such help, and perhaps he has some suggestions as to the kind of discussion which might be more helpful.

Summary

To return from technical devices to essentials, I am now inclined to think that the basic element in casework consists in enabling the client to experience with the worker a kind of relationship which is new and helpful for him. I think it will always have to be one in which his ambivalence is recognised and accepted, and one which the worker is able both to understand and to resist the client's defensive attempts at manipulation. But in other respects it may vary considerably, so as to supply those experiences which may have been lacking in earlier relationships. If the transference is interpreted, I think the aim will usually be not so much to explore the inner world which is projected in the transference as to remove the veil of distortion and enable the client once more to experience the reality of the relationship; and I think Miss Lloyd Davies has shown us that there are other methods of doing this. This new experience, in which old conflicts find to some extent a new resolution, may be combined to varying extents with insight-developing techniques such as the interpretation of transference (or displacement) within the family, which is extremely valuable for clients who have the necessary intellectual and emotional equipment to achieve such insight.

This way of looking at casework recognises a basic continuity with its earlier forms, as practised by Octavia Hill and others. I think the contact with psycho-analysis should not induce us to relinquish this tradition of actively playing out the role of a parental figure such as the client needs to relate to, but should help us to manage the relationship more securely, more sensitively and skilfully so as to meet the needs of each client more precisely and more differentially. If we also aim to help the client develop insight, our casework will to that extent be classifiable as a form of psycho-therapy; this psychotherapeutic casework may be more valuable for some clients, but not, I think, for all. For this purpose we may adopt various ingredients from analytic technique, and time will show which of these are most appropriate; but they must, I think, be subordinated to the characteristic casework way of using the worker-client relationship. In the long run I think we shall find that our debt to analysis in respect of deepened insight into ourselves and our clients far outweighs our debt in respect of technical borrowings.

References

Elkan, I. (1956) Interviews with Neglectful Parents, *British Journal of Psychiatric Social Work,* Vol III, no. 3.

Freud, S. (1924) Turnings in the Ways of Psychoanalytic Therapy, *Collected Papers,* II, Hogarth Press, London.

Goldberg, E.M. (1953) Function and Use of Relationship in Psychiatric Social Work, *British Journal of Psychiatric Social Work,* no. 8.

Holmes, M.H. (1956) Mother and Child, *British Journal of Psychiatric Social Work,* Vol. III, no. 2.

Joseph, B. (1948) A Psychiatric Social Worker in a Maternity and Child Welfare Centre, *British Journal of Psychiatric Social Work,* Vol. I, no. 2.

Lloyd Davies, B. (1956) Psychotherapy and Social Casework, *The Boundaries of Casework,* APSW.

Laquer, A.M. (1954) The Caseworker's Task in Meeting the Client's Inner and Outer Needs, *British Journal of Psychiatric Social Work,* no. 10.

Myers, E.S. (1954) The Caseworker's Problems in Meeting the Client's Inner and Outer Needs, *British Journal of Psychiatric Social Work,* no. 10.

Ratcliffe, T. and Jones, E.V. (1956) Intensive Casework in a Community Setting, *Case Conference,* Vol. II, no. 10.

Sutherland, J.D. (1956) Psychotherapy and Social Casework, *The Boundaries of Casework,* APSW.

Waldron, F.E. (1948) The Psychiatric Social Worker's Professional Standing, *British Journal of Psychiatric Social Work,* Vol. I, no. 2.

CHAPTER 4

A New Look at Casework*

Casework as a method of personal help has never resolved its identity crisis. It emerged laboriously from a primary preoccupation with the material predicaments of clients and their moral character, thanks to a growing knowledge of psycho-analytic theory and technique. It then underwent a phase of identification with this very potent parent-figure, during which there was a tendency to define itself with reference to psycho-analysis or psycho-therapy of an analytic kind, and in very similar terms. Such a definition of "advanced casework techniques" is given by Arthur Hunt,[1] who adds, however, that in his experience these much valued methods do not correspond with the needs of many clients of such services as probation, who need a simpler, and sometimes a more directive, approach. Margaret Brown[2] emphasises the need for a broad range of techniques, applied with sensitive discrimination according to the needs of the client. Since I must acknowledge some share of responsibility for the tendency to equate casework skill with the narrow range of techniques described by Hunt as "advanced", it may be appropriate to record a change of heart.

To arrive at an understanding of what advanced casework is, we have to ask ourselves two questions:

(a) What is casework?

(b) In what direction should it be advancing?

Casework is one of many ways of helping people with personal and social problems. These include psycho-analysis and other forms of

---

*A revised version of "What is Advanced Casework?" Published in New Barnett Papers No. 1, *The Family in Modern Society,* Department of Social and Administrative Studies, Oxford University.

psycho-therapy and group therapy, as well as counselling and social group work. Certain things are common to all these activities. They all involve a professional relationship, an interaction between one or more professional people with one or more people seeking help; and the quality of this interaction is generally believed to be of crucial importance to the helping process. They all involve insight on the part of the worker into personality, motivation and interaction including their less rational and less conscious aspects; this insight includes awareness of one's own motivation and responses as well as those of the client. The practitioners of personal help have a number of techniques available: advice, reassurance, encouragement, explanation, questions, hints, practical help of various kinds, reminders of legal responsibility or other aspects of reality, sympathy, interpretation. I have deliberately left to the last the technique of interpretation, which is relatively new as a self-conscious device, but whose uses have been studied by analysts more intensively than those of the more traditional ways of helping have been studied by anyone, so that interpretation now tends to emerge as the figure against a ground of "simple supportive and directive work". I am also leaving aside the fascinating subject of what I might call the "near-interpretations" often used by caseworkers: the interpretive question, the interpretive comment, the interpretive reassurance. I will just give one instance of the interpretive comment. Sweet Polly Oliver in the ballad misses her soldier true-love so much that she disguises herself as a man and joins the Army in the hope of a reunion. The sergeant appeals for a volunteer soldier nurse to attend to the sick Captain — who is none other than the missing true-love. In the face of the doctor's despair, Polly nurses her lover back to life — still incognito. Finally the doctor salutes her triumph with the remark: "You have tended him as if you were his wife." This interpretive observation is highly potent, for "sweet Polly Oliver burst into tears and told the good doctor her hope and her fears". This enables him to do some effective marriage guidance.

To return to the variety of helping methods: I think it is true to say that the psycho-analysts and some, but not all, psycho-therapists, try to keep the interaction component as muted and as standardised as possible, restricting it to the verbal level and to the particular type of verbal response known as interpretation. The caseworker, on the other hand, has many more responses at her disposal, a collection of ingredients which she makes up into individual prescriptions as an adaptation to the needs of each client as she perceives them. We can see this as a continuum, a whole scale of responses, ranging from the interpretation (transference or extra-transference) which we have been learning from the analysts, to the largely non-verbal interaction in terms of practical help, gifts, loans and accompaniment to the doctor, the court or the delousing station which is appropriate to the "problem family". If we look at it this way, we by-pass all these meaningless discussions about whether casework can be combined with the exercise of authority or the giving of practical aid. Casework becomes a total interaction within which action is seen to have an aspect of non-verbal communication, and words to be one of the many forms of helpful activity. There should thus be no great difficulty in combining verbal and non-verbal aid, providing both these forms of communication are saying the same thing.

The Advanced Casework Course at the Tavistock Clinic, London, with which I am associated, was established at a time when Noel Hunnybun and her colleagues were much concerned with advancing in a certain direction; the understanding of the phenomena identified by Freud as transference and counter-transference as they occur within the setting of a casework relationship and the use, within limits which were also subject to exploration, of techniques of transference interpretation. I believe that real and important advances were made. It was a difficult but worthwhile task to determine the level at which the unanalysed social worker could be trained to understand these phenomena, and the kind of interpretive comment which such workers could usefully make. I believe that *The Caseworker's Use of Relationship,*[3] by Hunnybun and Ferard, gives evidence of considerable progress in this direction. The question of the varying needs of different *clients* for more or less interpretive help, still requires a good deal of further exploration.

Although I believe the theory and practice of social work have been greatly enriched by this effort, I consider it unfortunate that advanced casework has come to be identified with this approach, since in view of the variety of personality and culture among clients and of their manifold needs, casework should be advancing on a much broader front than this. In fact, it is undoubtedly doing so, and the kind of work described by Betty Lloyd Davies[4] and Clare Winnicott[5] represents at least as great an advance in other directions, which should clearly be included in any account of advanced casework. The most advanced casework is that which best fits the need of the client in question, and we must not allow the labelling of courses to obscure this fact.

I believe in particular that the use of transference interpretation in casework is best adapted to the needs of neurotic clients, and that although psycho-analytic theory is equally illuminating in regard to psychotics and to all the varieties of character disorder (as well as to the emotional tangles of normal people) very different techniques are required in helping these kinds of person. In this context I would like to quote D.W. Winnicott:

"I think of each social worker as a therapist, but not as the kind of therapist who makes the correct and well-timed interpretation that elucidates the transference neurosis. Do this if you like, but your more important function is therapy of the kind that is always being carried on by parents in correction of relative failures in environmental provision. What do such parents do? They exaggerate some parental function and keep it up for a length of time, in fact until the child has used it up and is ready to be released from special care."[6]

Here the emphasis is on the experiential or interactional aspect of the helping process rather than on the element of communication and insight. My own thinking began to move in this direction in 1956, when I published a paper called "Transference and Reality in the Casework Relationship".[7] Here I was beginning to formulate an account of casework process in terms of an experience in interaction, and I pointed out that stable parents provide a model which is more useful in many casework situations than that provided by psycho-analysis. I think we have made some progress in understanding our work in these terms and adapting techniques more deliberately to the needs of the individual client. I would like to quote from *The Essentials of Social Casework*.[8]

"The casework relationship is not the same for every client, but should, as far as possible, be adjusted to meet the varying need of different clients. One important function of the casework relationship is to supply in some measure those experiences necessary for satisfactory emotional development, which have been lacking in the life of the individual client. Thus an inhibited and submissive client may need to be encouraged to speak his mind to the worker, and to express his feelings of criticism and dissatisfaction as a prelude to developing the ability to stand up for himself in other situations. On the other hand, a client whose pattern of behaviour is to control and exploit people until they eventually throw him over, may need to have a relationship with someone who resists all attempts to manipulate him, while remaining friendly and sympathetic. Thus the balance between firmness and permissiveness has to be finely adjusted to the needs of the client, and should not be influenced by the worker's own need, for example, to control situations himself or to keep on the right side of everybody.''

There is no question of such work being easier or less "advanced", and it often requires just as much dynamic insight into personality and motivation.

In *Transference and Reality in the Casework Relationship* I confined my attention to the emotional interaction underlying various forms of verbal interchange. This I think we now understand more clearly, but there is still a need to apply the same kind of systematic analysis on the practical level. We need to look at the whole question of gifts and loans, not only as response to material need, but to psychological need as well. Mrs. Dockar-Drysdale, working in a boarding school for maladjusted children, and Dr. J. Lomax-Simpson, a psychiatrist working with children in care, have both evolved interesting applications of D.W. Winnicott's concepts of maternal adaptation and transitional objects. Mrs Dockar-Drysdale writes of what she calls "a localized adaptation" used in work with very disturbed children in a residential setting. Certain children are felt to need something which will give them a taste of the feelings of being understood and secure which a mother's near-perfect adaptation to her tiny baby gives him. Obviously a professional worker with responsibilities to other children cannot allow any one child to be dependent in just the same way as a baby, but some little ritual can be evolved which symbolises so much more — in one case it was the provision of a sweet of a certain special colour every day at the same time.[9] This sounds like a gimmick, but the choice of gift or service must arise directly out of a deep communion of child and adult, the symbol must be something they find together, or it will not symbolise anything, it will be just a feeble fobbing off of a hungry child. In this case his demands will not be abated, whereas if the symbol is rightly chosen, the child can bear to share his loved person with others for the rest of the day.

Dr. Lomax-Simpson[10] has worked out something similar which helps her to provide through her relationship with children and adolescents a sense of deep security, even where contact is intermittent and not very frequent. With a girl who was leaving care she provided an artificial pearl necklace rather like one of her own, with a promise that she would always have it re-threaded when necessary. Thus at the same time she gave something of hers and a built-in device for renewing contact when required. With another child it might be something quite different, whose significance derives from some allusion to a meaningful shared experience — something like always remembering to provide strawberry jam when they have tea together. Some adult clients need birthday and Christmas cards in this way, or postcards during holidays. To quote my own work with a feeble-minded woman (mother of several disturbed children), I think the only really meaningful things which have happened between us have been on the plane of action. I went with her to visit her dying husband in hospital, and to his funeral. On many visits both before and after his death, I could do nothing but listen helplessly to the continuous quarrelling in the family. I gave presents of food at Christmas, redecorated the house a bit, took her shopping once on a Saturday morning, sorted out some muddles with the National Assistance Board and the Ministry of Pensions. After some years of this she presented me with four pillow-cases; soon afterwards, I lent her money to buy furniture, trusting her to pay if off by instalments; she managed to do so, and even offered on one occasion, when she was short at the time of my visit, to send it on by post; to my surprise and joy she actually did so.

Another client was angry and despairing, and never managed to make any real use of her weekly hour, beyond letting off a blast of impotent fury. I adapted to her need as I perceived it by giving her, without being asked, a second consecutive hour each week. This had several advantages on different levels. On the one hand, the longer period enabled her to relax after venting her more violent feelings, so that we could then have a calmer and more constructive discussion, in which some insight was developed. But just as important as anything I said was the fact that I had seen her need and responded to it *without being asked,* since one of her problems was that nothing was any good if she had to ask for it. It was only later, when I judged her ready to be weaned back to a single hour, that I realised how apt this symbolic cliché was; my client wondered why she was so hungry all the time! Later, she brought me some little gifts, mostly small plants she had grown. Once, presenting a little cactus, she said: "This is one of my babies"!

Occasionally with psychotic patients I have found it was tremendously helpful to disregard our usual practice and give a little bit of factual information about myself. I realise that this is a rediscovery of something that other workers have been doing intuitively for years; but I think it needs integrating into our theoretical framework, so that we can understand and teach more clearly when this is helpful and when it is not.

We are becoming more aware and planful about our non-verbal communication as described, for instance, in *The Canford Families.*[11] But the important distinction is really not between verbal and non-verbal, it is something about the way and the purpose with which language is being used. Interpretive language is used to convey to the client something about himself, perhaps to help him communicate better with lost parts of himself, to win recognition for them. The other use of language is to communicate something about the worker's attitude, his concern, his sympathy, his empathic understanding, his hope, his acceptance. Ultimately, the aim of this too is to help the client recognise and take responsibility for disowned aspects of himself, those parts which he cannot himself accept until he has felt them accepted by someone whom he respects. These things can be communicated by words (in the right tone of voice) but also by smiles, by gestures and by behaviour, by scrupulous keeping of promises, by taking trouble or extra trouble, even by accepting a cup of tea — as one client said: "What, in this awful house?"[12]

This brings us back to the home visit and the interview with several family members. These again are nothing new, but have tended of recent years to be regarded as unavoidable necessities which make it difficult to do proper casework. However, various writers have made us take a new look at these situations and recognise them as representing both a challenge and an opportunity. Challenging they certainly are, and it is tempting to try to create an individual interview situation by withdrawing with the client into another room, or to try and exclude one or more members of the family — e.g. children. Failing success in these manoeuvres, one may be tempted to regard the situation as an individual interview in trying circumstances. We naturally fear to get "out of our depth" if we venture to interact with all the people present in a way which encourages free communication instead of trying to keep the conversation innocuous and the party clean. But these problems have been courageously tackled in various ways by various people, some of whom have attempted to describe their techniques. One of the authors of *The Canford Families* describes a visit to a family where the parents had that morning destroyed a pet belonging to one of their children, and how the worker tried "to convey that their different feelings were all legitimate and accepted". E.M. Goldberg describes a more ambitious technique: "using for one's interpretations the abundant supply of material from the past as well as from the present ... one tries to catch as much as possible of what is thrown around, showing the family members ... what they were doing and have done to each other, how they misunderstood, misinterpreted and so on".[13] This sounds more difficult (and therefore "advanced") but I am not sure whether the art of non-verbal communication is not even more so — "The use of action, symbol and inference rather than direct verbal expression."[14]

Whether or not we visit the home, whether we work with two or more members of the family or whether we find a different worker for each member, we have to take steps to improve our understanding of family functioning — of the family as a system of interacting individuals. The Family Discussion Bureau has blazed a well-documented trail[15, 16] through studies of the marital relationship in terms of conscious adaptation and maladaptation and unconscious collusion through mutual projections and identifications. We still have to extend this type of analysis to include children. This is something we are working on.

I will briefly mention some final points. There has been a tendency to regard long-term intensive casework as more "advanced" than short-contact work, which is often regarded as superficial, a necessary but unsatisfactory concession to pressing demands or adverse circumstances. These assumptions I am sure we have to revise. Skilled use of short contacts, especially in crisis situations, can be extremely effective — but to be effective it must be at least as highly skilled as so-called intensive work. We have a lot to learn about short-term focused work, the skill of helping the client just enough to restore or achieve adequate functioning in respect of the problem presented without opening up his problems in general and becoming sunk for years in the effort to resolve them. This I would regard as very advanced indeed. In work with the mentally ill we have a lot to learn about how to select the best focus for treatment (Waldron, 1961)[17] and how to identify the family member with whom it would be most profitable to invest one's major effort. We also have to learn to maintain a balanced concern for all members of the family, especially in situations where there is no team to take responsibility for different members. There is a real danger of helping our client at the expense of some other member of his family, or at least ignoring the fact that his illness is disturbing relatives or children who may not get the help they need unless we do something about it.

These are only some of the directions in which we need to advance. Perhaps I can sum up the situation by saying that we need to develop more appropriate and effective techniques for all types of clients in all kinds of agency — for the clients of the family service units, of the special problem family caseworkers in public health, of the various voluntary and religious organisations (including the protective agencies) as well as for those of the child care and probation services, local authority mental health services, the child guidance clinic and the Family Discussion Bureau.

References

1. Hunt, A. (1966) Enforcement in Probation Casework, in Younghusband (Ed.), *New Developments in Casework,* Allen & Unwin.
2. Brown, M.A.G. (1966) A review of Casework Methods, in Younghusband (Ed.), *New Developments in Casework,* Allen & Unwin.
3. Ferrard, M. and Hunnybun, N. (1961) *The Caseworkers Use of Relationships,* Tavistock Publications, London.
4. Lloyd Davies, B. (1964) Psychotherapy and Social Casework, in *Relationships in Casework,* Association of Psychiatric Social Workers, London.

5. Winnicott, C. (1964) Face to Face with Children, *Child Care and Social Work,* Codicote Press, Welwyn.
6. Winnicott, D.W. (1958) The Mentally Ill in your Caseload, *Collected Papers,* Tavistock, London.
7. Irvine, E.E. (1966) Transference and Reality in the Casework Relationship, in Younghusband (Ed.), *New Developments in Casework,* Allen & Unwin.
8. *The Essentials of Social Casework,* Association of Psychiatric Social Workers, London, 1963, p. 2.
9. Dockar-Drysdale, B.E. (1964) The Provision of Primary Experience in a Therapeutic School in *Therapy in Child Care,* Longman, Green & Co., 1968.
10. Lomax-Simpson, J.N. (1964) Needs of the Child in Care, *Case Conference,* Vol. X, No. 7.
11. *The Canford Families,* Sociological Review Monograph No. 6, University of Keele, December 1962.
12. Day, B. (1965) Supportive Casework in an Authoritative Setting, *Case Conference,* Vol. XI, No. 9.
13. Goldberg, E.M. (1960) Parents and Psychotic Sons, *British Journal of Psychiatric Social Work,* London, Vol. V, No. 4.
14. *The Canford Families, ibid.*
15. Family Discussion Bureau, *Social Casework in Marital Problems,* Tavistock Publications, London, 1955.
16. Family Discussion Bureau, *Marriages: Studies in Emotional Conflict and Growth,* Methuen, London, 1960.
17. Waldron, F.E. (1961) The Choice of Gaols in Casework Treatment, *British Journal of Psychiatric Social Work,* Vol. VI, No. 2.

CHAPTER 5

The Right to Intervene*

Social workers are frequently criticised for interfering in the lives of unoffending citizens — people who may be deviating to some extent from social norms which are represented as being matters of taste rather than of serous social import. This is a change which merits serious consideration.

Oddly enough, it is most often heard in the context of discussion of "casework" and the extension of casework training to groups of social workers who previously had no training at all. The oddness lies in the fact that caseworkers cherish an image of themselves which is strictly non-interfering, as people who much prefer to deal only with willing clients who will ideally have asked for help themselves. The principles of casework, as taught to students, lay great emphasis on respect for the client and his autonomy. How is it, then, that others see us so differently from our vision of ourselves?

I think there is no doubt that many of us have been wearing blinkers. Not all types of caseworker have been able to do this — the probation officer cannot ignore the fact that his clients may at first be far from willing, and are in fact bound by a Court order, to which they have indeed given a formal consent, but under circumstances which they often experience as duress. Some probation officers feel sorry for themselves about this, and complain that it prevents them from doing "proper casework", or that they do it only in spite of their authority and their responsibility to the Court. Others see their service as making genuine personal help available to many people who need it, but can use it only on condition that it is imposed upon them in this way (Hunt, 1964).[1] But for the purpose of our present discussion,

---

*Reprinted from *Social Work* (U.K.), Vol. XXI, no. 2, 1964.

the point is that probation officers are not alone in having to intrude.

Caseworkers are employed in three other major statutory services: Child Care, National Health and Public Health. In all of these, they will have to deal with unwilling as well as willing clients. The Child Care Officer is concerned, not only with children whose parents have requested temporary or long-term care for them on account of their own difficulties in providing a home, but also with children who have been removed from the charge of their parents by order of a Court which has found them to be in need of care and protection. The C.C.O. is not only responsible for providing substitute care, but also has great influence on decisions as to whether the child may return to his parents in virtue of a changed situation.

Turning to the National Health Service, the almoner (now the medical social worker) is often concerned with a willing client who has asked for help in relation to some practical matter or to some problem about home and family; but it is also the almoner who is called in to persuade the patient to accept unwelcome medical advice concerning operations, sanatorium treatment and so on. In the mental health field, the child guidance clinic is often genuinely non-interfering, and may inflict grave frustration and anxiety on referring agents by refusing to treat children who undoubtedly need help, on the grounds that the parents are not willing to cooperate. However, this is balanced by the adult sector, particularly in community care, where psychiatric social workers often help patients whom no-one else can help, who will not go near a psychiatrist, by persistently inflicting their company on the unwilling client till willy-nilly he begins to respond to this patient courtship and allow himself to be encouraged out of his bed, out of his room, out of his house, out of his self-imposed isolation.

The same applies to various voluntary agencies, such as the Family Service Units and the Invalid Children's Aid Association. We have to admit that social workers do interfere, whether trained or untrained, and whether we like it or not. Our initial contact will sometimes be felt to be an intrusion. But of course we shall not succeed in helping if we remain intruders, and much of the skill of the caseworker consists in penetrating these defensive barriers, earning the trust and confidence of the client, and thus transforming the intruder role into one which more resembles friendship, but which is tempered by professional responsibility and a certain detachment on the part of the worker.

Let us, however, recognise that intervention does not arise, as is often implied, primarily from the personal motivation of the social worker; it is, whether he enjoys it or not, part of the task which is laid upon him by society. In discussing the right to intervene, it is the right of society with which we must be concerned, not the personal right of the social worker, who intervenes on its behalf. We have to do with questions in social philosophy: has society the right to intervene in the lives of its members, and if so on what grounds and subject to what limitations? I would suggest, with no claim to originality, that the whole basis of democratic society rests on the need to protect individuals against each other, to limit the rights of all for the mutual protection of each. This is the basis of our legal system, which authorises the State, through its agents, to intervene in defined circumstances. Social workers are among these agents, and their intervention is often the alternative to some more drastic one. No man can be placed on probation unless he has broken the law, and the alternative would be some punishment which he would consider worse. Otherwise he would not have accepted the probation order (unless he is one of the minority who can recognise probation immediately as offering a kind of help which he requires).

To look at the other extreme, it can be argued that the patient who is in his right mind, yet will not or does not accept or follow the doctor's advice should be allowed to make his choice, however unwise, unless there is a danger of his infecting others with a serious disease. This is a seductive argument, but it would lead us to renounce the attempt to help some patients who would be only too glad to accept medical advice but for some fear which can be detected and relieved by someone who knows what to look for. It also overlooks the facts of social connectedness, that most patients have relatives and dependants who will suffer grief if they die; that many are breadwinners whose dependants will suffer poverty and deprivation if they become incapacitated, or mothers whose children may well suffer neglect if their health breaks down.

Outside the probation service, unsolicited intervention is usually made in the interests of children. Enthusiasm for civil liberties, or for the dignity of the poor, sometimes leads prominent people to insist on the rights of parents to bring up their children as they like. This seems to imply either that all parents are adequately mature, intelligent and responsible, or that whatever their characteristics their children are their property. Rightly or wrongly, society does not regard parental rights as sacrosanct. It employs health visitors to give health education and to ensure minimum standards of child care, and by so doing it has greatly reduced infant mortality. It provides a school medical service to detect all kinds of chronic illness and abnormality through periodic inspections, and authorises health visitors to visit parents and persuade them to carry out the treatment prescribed — having found by experience that a certain proportion of parents do not otherwise do so. It provides compulsory education, and finds it necessary to employ school welfare officers to exert some kind of influence on the minority of parents who do not, if left alone, send their children regularly to school. It even has to make cruelty illegal, and authorise the N.S.P.C.C. to intervene in the numerous cases of cruelty which do in fact occur. We must recognise, however, that not all social intervention is in the interests of the children; the rented home is no castle, and eviction by housing authorities in defence of the public purse often has the unintended, but predictable, side-effect of breaking up the family so that the children have to be taken into public care. But this is not an activity of social workers, in fact they often try to prevent it. Children cannot be treated as the chattels of their parents, and society has both the right and the duty to protect them against ill-treatment, neglect and cruelty, and to insist on at least some minimum standard of health and education. It could be argued, however, that this protection should be limited to the provision of education, health inspection and advice, with some legal compulsion to carry out the advice; further intervention would require legal action and would depend on a proven breach of the law. This is of course what sometimes happens in cases of neglect and cruelty, and of persistent non-attendance at school.

This would certainly preserve the autonomy of the citizen, but at a rather high cost. Neglect must obviously be pretty severe before there is enough evidence for a successful prosecution, and children suffering from all the minor degrees of neglect would be virtually unprotected.

Moreover, prosecutions and legal decisions are based on concepts of crime and punishment, whereas much parental neglect is the result of ignorance, lack of intelligence or imagination, lack of energy or efficiency, or lack of relatives who can give help and guidance to the immature and inexperienced and support in illness or unemployment. Even cruelty is often due to physical or mental illness or the vaguer forms of mental or emotional instability. There are better and more appropriate ways to help these people than punishment — there is in fact the kind of help that health visitors and social workers give.

To resume: the unsolicited intervention of social workers in the affairs of a family is usually the alternative to more drastic social action, or a means of preventing the necessity arising. It follows that an over-concern with certain rather abstract rights to privacy, autonomy, etc., would involve us in the inhumanity of withholding help which was needed but not asked for, and then punishing people for failure in tasks which they lack the ability to perform unaided. But how do we know there is a need of which they seem to be unaware? Is this claim presumptuous? There is an analogy with the problems of adolescents and their parents. Adolescents often demand independence vociferously, and many modern parents respond by refraining from interference, however strong their misgivings. Yet at the same time, the young people may be demonstrating unmistakably how dangerous, for themselves and for others, is a degree of freedom which they cannot yet manage, and how much they need parents who will not give up the struggle to guide and protect them. It is convenient in terms of political theory to assume that all adults are capable of managing their lives and those of their families within the framework of law. But assumptions which do not match the facts are of limited value, and we know that many adults actually manage their lives no better than teenagers, or even than much younger children. This is why, willy-nilly, most social workers cannot keep their hands clean form the "sin" of "interference", and learn to brave the locked door, the snub, the "slap in the face", while they patiently and skilfully offer their services to those who do not acknowledge the need. If this be "dirty work", society has laid it on the social worker, and it ill becomes society to reproach her with meddling. I am myself uneasy about the ethical position of a child guidance clinic which too readily accepts its inability to help a sick child whose parents "will not co-operate". Clearly, we are not omnipotent, but are we always ready enough to modify our technical approach and try to find some kind of help, however sub-optimal, which this particularly family can accept, at least for a start?

Intervention can of course be helpful or unhelpful, and we have a great responsibility to make sure that it helps. There was a time when the child care services were perhaps too ready to remove children from inadequate homes, thus sometimes doing more harm than good. This resulted from failure to appreciate the less tangible values of family life, from an over-estimate of what the substitute home can offer, and from a lack of the skills necessary to help parents who may be fond though inadequate to manage better, both on the material plane and on that of their personal relationships. I would underline that this was a phase when few trained workers were available, and things have steadily improved as more of these enter the field, and as training itself improves. (This hope, expressed in 1964, may now seem unduly optimistic. In 1976 the rapid expansion of social work training has predictably led to a serious degree of dilution and depression of standards on many courses, and particularly in fieldwork supervision, which has also been affected by two major reorganisations of the social services. Let us hope that progress will soon be resumed.)

Similar considerations apply to the attitude of the worker. The greater the problem or the failure in the family, the more allergic people are to the slightest hint of criticism or disapproval, however delicately veiled. This is why parents of "problem families" so often fall out with welfare officers or health visitors whose friendly advice is perfectly acceptable to those who need it less acutely. Too often these touchy, hyper-sensitive people encounter mainly those representative of society who have least training in the understanding of such sensibilities. This is why local authorities are learning from the Family Service Units, and beginning to appoint social workers for these families, and also to demand "casework" training for their welfare staff.

If the medico-social concept of prevention is to have any application in the field of "social pathology", the question is not whether to intervene, but when and how, and who should do it. Roger

Wilson[2] has provided an excellent statement of the case for unobtrusive intervention by those representatives of society who are most familiar, and whose function is not defined in relation to any kind of social failure — the rent-collector, the teacher and the family doctor. Some of his suggestions are debatable; it is not clear, for instance, whether it is best for teachers to learn to do social work, or for each school to have a social worker who would present himself as an integral part of the school, with some service to give all parents — possibly in groups. It is the general principle I wish to emphasise.

There are also important questions about the criteria for preventive intervention. Can we agree with the Ingleby Committee?[3]

"It is not enough to protect children from neglect, even if the term ... be held to include their exposure to any physical, mental or moral danger or deprivation. If children are to be prevented from becoming delinquent, and if those in trouble are to get the help they need, something more positive is required. Everything within reason must be done to ensure not only the children are not neglected but that they get the best upbringing possible." Or is this going too far? How far is enough?

All these questions remain to be answered, together with others about the choice of individual casework approaches versus those of group work or community organisation. But I do not think the general case for non-intervention holds much water.

References

1. Hunt, A. (1966) Enforcement in Probation Casework, in Younghusband, (Ed.), *New Developments in Casework,* Allen & Unwin.
2. Wilson, R. (1963) *Difficult Housing Estates,* Tavistock Pamplet No. 5, London.
3. Command 1191, *The Ingleby Report,* October 1960.

Part II Experiences in Consultation and Mental Health Education

One of the fortunate hazards of my life was the almost accidental opportunity to work with Dr. Gerald Caplan at a very seminal period of his professional development and to share the experience which led him to formulate the models of both crisis intervention and consultation, which he has so fruitfully developed ever since. The first of the following papers describes this experience and presents my own modest attempts to conceptualise it, while the second and third arose out of my work with Dr. Marion Mackenzie of the Tavistock Clinic in developing a mental health education service for the staff of maternity and child welfare clinics, for which we drew heavily on Dr. Caplan's model. Our work differed somewhat from crisis consultation in that its explicit purpose was educational; our mandate was to assist the public health staff to expand their function of preventing physical illness in young children to include the prevention of mental ill health by appropriate intervention at the first sign of risk. Yet the crisis model was invaluable, since although our meetings were regular and thus not dependent on the existence of a crisis, it was usually a crisis with which we were presented, and it was equally essential to recognise and relieve the stereotypes and anxious identifications of the presenting member and the group as a whole. Chapter 8 was an attempt to learn from the difficulties which were encountered in the course of this programme, in spite of its unusually careful preparation, and from some of the solutions which we found in response. This kind of knowledge is continually being re-discovered by trial and error, but much less attention has been paid to it than to the process of consultation itself. Forewarned is forearmed.

The demand for consultation is now so great that one fears a stampede for a new band-wagon, through which the concept of

57

consultation might become as imprecise and debased as that of the therapeutic community has become. Fortunately a considerable number of doctors and social workers have been able to attend the seminars which Dr. Caplan gave every summer in London for a number of years, so there is some hope that the concept of mental health consultation may remain distinct from simple advice.

CHAPTER 6

Two Approaches to Adjustment Problems among Children in Institutions *

It is a fairly common experience in child guidance that children who have lost or have been removed from their parents at an early age are much harder to treat than home-bred children. Much attention has now been paid to the absolute or relative inaccessibility of a proportion of children reared in institutions or in successive foster-homes — but even when children are selected who can make a promising rapport with the therapist, the response to treatment is apt to be disappointing. The Institution child tends to become the remaining member of a play group, while the other members improve and pass out; when he receives individual treatment, the therapist is usually aware of expending more effort for less result than with other children. There seem to be characteristic difficulties, not only within the child, but between himself and his environment and between his environment and the clinic. We are, of course, accustomed to the problems created for parents by the instinctual release which occurs in children undergoing treatment. But acting out hostile impulses and testing the parent-figure tend to be more violent and prolonged in the Institution child than in the home-bred child, since the parent-substitutes have to suffer for the sins and failures of the child's own parents and of all their predecessors. Few parents have to face this quality of feeling and behaviour, except with children returning from early and prolonged separation and estrangement, and not all parents can tolerate it sufficiently to ride out the treatment. The house-mother who can tolerate it is rare indeed, since she has less motivation for

---

*Originally published in the *British Journal of Psychiatric Social Work,* No. V. 1951.

doing so than the parent, and her relationship with the child means less to her. Rigid standards and unrealistic expectations are not uncommon, and the more rigid the demands made on the child the more his instinctual release has to take the form of hostile attacks on the mother-figure, while if he dare not act this out the whole treatment process is apt to be blocked.

The following story is not uncommon. A ten-year-old girl from a Cottage Home was referred to a child guidance clinic for enuresis. She had low average intelligence and certain mild hysterical personality traits. She also had a distinct gift for dramatic expression and was full of vitality, while the other children in the Home gave less trouble, but all appeared emotionally numbed or stunted. Under treatment she showed some very positive, though demanding, reactions to the house-mother, but the latter was unable to accept these as having positive value, and after a series of rebuffs the child developed her attack on her to such an extent that she had to be removed. I could easily multiply stories like this, while I can think of few successful cases to set against them. The precise symptomatic picture made little difference; the common factors which defeated treatment were a general deprivation and an uncommonly resistant environment.

It is not only that children suffering from repeated loss of love-objects and repeated rejection subject a house-mother to a severer test while under treatment than most parents undergo in similar circumstances; it is also more difficult to evoke cooperation from a house-mother than from a parent, and they sometimes lack real relationship with the children. In such cases treatment of the child may even make matters worse by awakening an appetite for emotional response which we cannot enable the house-mother to satisfy, thus leaving the child emotionally starved and more conscious and resentful than before of this starvation. Looking back on failures in this field, I find we accepted too complacently the objective obstacles to working with a house-mother other than superficially, for example her difficulty of getting time off from her group and her lack of incentive to come in her own time. This acceptance was based on a tacit theory that the house-mother is less important to the child than its own mother, less intimately involved in the child's problem. Not entering into a treatment relationship with her, it was harder to resist the temptation of identifying with the child against her, letting her threat to the child blind us to the very real threat which he offered to her. A "problem child" makes demands which interfere with the smooth performance of an exacting and arduous job, he threatens the house-mother's control of the entire group and the satisfaction and reassurance she derives from her "good" children. Above all, he arouses the guilt so often felt by those responsible for homeless children about their failure to fill a parent's role. This guilt is usually kept under by various defences, such as emphasis on hygiene and abundant diet, or on the value of discipline and control; but it is powerfully stimulated by every child who forcefully calls attention to his emotional problems, and it tends to be projected on to the child. Such projections are often made by parents, but are generally unstable, since the question: "What have I done to have such a bad child?" cannot be far from the surface of their minds. The house-mother too asks this question, but readily replies: "Not I, but the parents are to blame". Few parents really want to "put the child away", but for many house-mothers it is the obvious solution.

In this situation the direct treatment of the child reinforces the threat to the house-mother, and superficial work with her directed to securing "co-operation" looks to her like support of his demands, a confirmation that she has not given him enough. Such feelings in a mother require all the relief which treatment can give, though mothers have a basic reassurance which house-mothers lack, the knowledge that somewhere in all their ambivalence lies real love for the child. Moreover, the house-mother's guilt and need to project are not only her personal problem — they pervade the hierarchy of officials which towers above her, and which exerts on her powerful pressures, often in an atmosphere strongly suffused with dominance and submission. This pressure magnifies and sustains her individual resistance; in fact the hierarchy expresses through her a collective resistance to consciousness and change.

The mother-substitute who is an employee of a large organisation has far less control of her environment than a mother on her own home; her relation to it is in many ways more similar to that of the child, and treatment of the environment is as important a factor in enabling her to change as it is for the child. Both of them are part of a highly organised and self-protective system, and neither can respond beyond very narrow limits to any treatment which is not addressed to the organisation as a whole.

The house-mother therefore not only readily transfers to the worker the anticipation of criticism and the pattern of defence against it which have become ingrained by experience within the organisation, but she defends herself vigorously against acquiring insight. Both she and the organisation behind her tend to regard the clinic team as outsiders who are critical of their methods, and who aim to succeed by other methods where they have failed, thereby threatening the precious projection on to the child and attributing the guilt of failure to the adults. The institution staff have therefore an unconscious vested interest in procuring the failure of the clinic and the admission that the child is hopeless, which would exonerate both residential staff and organisation from all suspicion of blame. Passive resistance is often very strong; attendance may not be regular, and may be interrupted just at moments of crisis for the child, when he most needs therapeutic support; escorts change from week to week, messages go astray or are garbled, the therapist is not told of significant events in the Home or of changes in the child's behaviour, welcome or otherwise.

I was led to formulate this account of a particularly difficult field of work, and some of the reasons for its difficulty, by experience of a contrasting approach to the mental health problems of institutional children. In 1950, the Lasker Centre for Mental Hygiene and Child Guidance in Jerusalem, whose Director was Dr. Gerald Caplan, was asked to provide a mental hygiene service for Youth Aliyah, an organisation caring for over 14,000 immigrant children and young people throughout Israel. Many of these had lost their families and suffered a great variety of traumatic experiences; they were now transplanted into strange surroundings among a babel of tongues, with an unfamiliar national language and a set of norms and mores which usually contrasted strongly with everything in their previous experience. Youth Aliyah had a nucleus of trained and experienced child care workers of high quality, but a sudden and massive expansion of juvenile immigration had necessitated dilution by many hastily trained recruits, many of whom were little older than their older charges. The staff in general was vigorous, enthusiastic and idealistic, and often full of up-to-date theories, but responsibility weighed heavily upon them and their high hopes made them easily disappointed and discouraged. Placements of all kinds had to be used; many groups of young people were placed in communal settlements (kibbutzim), others in Homes and schools which were more or less institutional in type and run by religious or political groups.

For geographical reasons, Jerusalem was the only area where it would have been possible to provide a traditional child guidance service, with treatment for individual children and attempts to secure co-operation from child care staff. At first we accepted a few children for such treatment, but we soon encountered very strong resistance of the kind described above. Dramatic episodes of rebellion and punishment were not reported or discussed, and one boy was expelled from his Home on account of some trivial complaint just as he was beginning to respond to treatment.

This led us to decide to offer no more therapy for children but a counselling service to the workers, in the belief that the children would benefit from any increase in the staff's insight into emotional problems and any relief of their own feelings of tension and anxiety. Each Institution in the area referring children was assigned to one of the Centre's psychiatric social workers, who visited by appointment and saw the director and any members of his staff whom he called in to describe the problems. (A few psychologists also joined the staff as counsellors, and shared the functions described.)

At this point the Director usually hoped for the removal of the most troublesome children to special institutions, but all of these already had long waiting-lists. It was quite a surprise when we offered neither removal nor out-patient treatment, and merely suggested that the staff themselves might find the children more manageable with the help of some discussion with the counsellor. At this stage we were often asked for didactic teaching of child psychology or pedagogical method. The Lasker Centre, however, envisaged its function otherwise, since intellectual knowledge alone is not much help in establishing human relationships. It was of no importance that the workers should be able to pass a written examination; it was important that they should learn to understand actual children without labelling, that they should learn, for instance, to know whether a child was angry because he was disappointed, hurt, jealous or frightened, in the same way that a mother knows the meaning of a child's inarticulate cry. The Centre did not conceive its task as training child care staff to do a highly technical job of treatment with the children, but tried instead to develop their ability to establish warm, accepting and spontaneous relationships with children without sacrificing the ability to exert authority when required.

Another way in which the counsellor was expected to play the role of "expert" was by examining and possibly treating children during his visits. This role was avoided for several reasons. To have engaged in treatment of the children would have been to stir up all the rivalries anxieties and resentment which we have already seen in play when such children attend a clinic for treatment. Children treated in such conditions often tend to split their good and bad parental images between therapist and staff in an anti-therapeutic way; and there is an insidious tendency for the therapist to develop a strong positive counter-transference to the child, which interferes with his ability to empathise constructively with the staff. The counsellors chose as far as possible to relate only to the staff, helping them to understand better and develop more fully their quasi-parental role, and thus to derive more enjoyment from it.

In spite of the initial disappointment with the Centre's inability to remove children and its refusal to accept them for therapy, the staff often surprised us by the readiness with which they accepted the alternative offer of group discussions, and the enthusiasm which was often generated. It gradually became clear that the attempt to refer children for removal or treatment was experienced as a confession of failure, a feeling which was confirmed if the child was accepted on these terms. In contrast, the Centre's policy of leaving the staff with full responsibility for the child and supporting them in developing their role represented a vote of confidence in the staff, and did much to restore their threatened morale and professional self-respect.

It was important to distinguish the counsellor's role quite clearly from those of teacher and inspector, whose services were already available. An important aim of our service was to reduce the feelings of failure and guilt which were interfering with the staff's work, and were often projected onto scape-goat children. It was important to create a situation where the staff member need not keep his end up, where he could admit without too much difficulty his mistakes, his failures, his sense of inadequacy, the difficulty of applying the principles he had learned, or even of observing all the rules of the organisation. This was certainly facilitated by the fact that the counsellor came from outside the organisation, and had no responsibility for the staff member's work or professional advancement. Often we found a disproportionate sense of failure, since the only norms available were those for children who had received systematic education in the Western tradition; these were often quite unrealistic for children from Eastern cultures, with little formal education, and the hierarchy of the organisation tended to underestimate the difficulty of the task.

Staff members were sometimes, greatly heartened simply by the counsellor's recognition of the difficulties with which they were faced, and encouragement often restored self-confidence which had been damaged by criticism. Teachers needed support to make due allowance for the educational and cultural deprivation of the children they taught, and to adapt their teaching to the children's needs and abilities; for instance, to be content to use very simple stories and rhymes as their medium with children from Eastern cultures who were unable to respond to more sophisticated methods and approaches. Similarly, the counsellors showed keen interest in the apparently trivial situations in which some warm intuitive response had gained a child's confidence or cooperation, helping the worker, and perhaps the group, to learn from the happy accident which can otherwise so easily be forgotten.

Contact was established in the first place through discussion of the children who had been referred to the Centre. Since little history was known concerning most of the children, the counsellor tried to elicit as full a description as possible of each child's personality and behaviour from all staff members in contact with him. This was not always easy. Some Directors of institutions wished to be the only informant, some staff groups, such as teachers, felt that others, such as matrons or domestic workers, were not worth consulting, although it sometimes emerged that one of these under-valued colleagues was the only member of staff who enjoyed the child's affection or trust. An important part of the service was to encourage mutual respect and appreciation among the staff emphasising the value of each person's observations in constructing a comprehensive picture of the child, and the different ways in which various people had sometimes helped him. Staff members often became anxious on discovering how little they knew of a child for whom they were responsible, but the counsellor helped them to express and tolerate this. He was also often able to elicit observations which had been regarded as too trivial to report, or even half-forgotten, and to demonstrate their value and significance for the general picture, thus increasing staff members' confidence in themselves as potential observers. It was often possible to demonstrate how the fragmentary, or even apparently contradictory, observations of several individuals could be used to build a multi-dimensional picture of the individual child in his responses to different individuals and situations, thus encouraging communication and teamwork among the staff. The modification of unrealistic ambitions and the resultant feelings of guilt and failure, as described above, also helped to ease staff tensions, by reducing the need to project such feelings onto each other. In some cases it became accepted practice to bring up for group discussion differences of opinion which had previously been the subject of bitter and unresolved controversy.

Once this way of working was established, formal referral became unnecessary. On the counsellor's regular visits to the institution, the children originally referred could be discussed again and progress, new insights or new problems, could be reported; children with similar or different problems could also be discussed in the way which was becoming familiar, along with the staff members' feelings towards them. This constructive discussion of current problems was a situation in which both staff and counsellor had a contribution to make to the common task; the staff member his first-hand knowledge of each child (which steadily increased in volume and value as he learned to notice and observe more closely) the counsellor his knowledge of human behaviour and relationships. The cooperative effort to develop understanding of each child and his problems, the formulation of tentative ideas which could be tested in practice, the triumph of finding the key to a problem, all provided an active and satisfying learning experience, whose results were more far-reaching and durable than those of didactic teaching.

We found that different institutions and groups had characteristic anxieties and defensive systems; when the underlying anxieties could be relieved the behaviour of staff and children often changed to a surprising extent. One Home, for instance, had an elaborate (and very unsuccessful) system of rewards and punishments around the problem of enuresis, but spontaneously abandoned this after a few sessions, without direct advice or comment, as interest and insight into emotional problems developed, at the same time a whole group of recent and reactive enuretics ceased to wet the bed. Some staff groups believed that it was wrong to give differential treatment to children in a group for fear of jealousy, or to respond emotionally to them for fear of favouritism; this staff eventually began to plan individualised holiday programmes in small family-type groups for those children who had no relatives to visit during holidays. In some cases, whole groups of children who had at first appeared to be highly disturbed improved amazingly when the anxieties and tensions among the adults were relieved; it now appeared that the majority had been displaying only reactive behaviour problems, and the minority of genuinely disturbed children could now be picked out with some confidence. We realised increasingly the risk of prematurely diagnosing children in institutions without first exploring the tensions in the environment and the possibility of relieving them.

Stealing, aggression and sex were frequent foci of anxiety. Discussion was directed mainly towards relieving the sense of guilt and urgent anxiety surrounding the problem, exploring and accepting the anxieties involved. This in turn relieved the drive to find ring-leaders and scape-goats and often revealed that the incidents in question indicated underlying problems common to the whole group of children. This made it possible to consider how to diminish the tensions and frustrations in the group as a whole. Staff members who found it difficult to deal with sex play and sex curiosity or to give sex instruction tended to attribute their reluctance to lack of sufficient knowledge of biology or psychology, they often came to see that the real obstacle lay in their anxieties about the subject. If these could be allayed, they became able to let the children discuss the topic, and so relieve their own anxiety, without being forearmed with the answer to every possible question.

One advantage of this approach is that instead of separating the "problem child" from his "normal" fellows, whether by segregation or by labelling, it reasserts his fellowship with them (except in cases of really gross disturbance, which had sooner or later to be removed). Discussion was not limited to children whom the staff perceived as "abnormal"; it included other children who were considered normal but presented certain problems, as well as problems felt to be common to the whole group, while categorisation became less of a preoccupation as the meaning of behaviour became the focus. The growth of understanding, along with the relief of anxiety, benefit not only the child discussed, but the group as a whole. The "problem child" serves as a point of contact between the Centre, conceived as a mental hygiene rather than a treatment agency, and the community in which he lives. Through him the community realises its need for greater insight, and enters into relationship with the mental hygiene worker who can minister to its growth. Therapeutic and prophylactic work are therefore combined in the same process to such an extent that they become indistinguishable.

I should now like to return to a point mentioned earlier regarding the necessity of including the whole organisation in such a programme. Our meetings in each institution included different professional groups, such as house-mothers, teachers and youth leaders, with considerable difference of status and inter-group feelings of superiority and inferiority; and they included in most cases the Head of each department and the Head of the institution. But we also found we could not stop within the institution. Administrative staff of the organisation, inspectors and supervisors, were active in the same field, dealing with the same problems, acting on our reports. They could be played off against us or we against them; they were bound to be disturbed whenever they became aware of differences between our approach and theirs, or when we unearthed one of the inevitable cases of discrepancy between theory and practice in the institution. The whole question of guilt, rivalry and resistance was continually arising again at this level, and had to be repeatedly taken up and worked through. Casual informal contacts with individuals were made use of as far as possible, and more formal group meetings were arranged as required. It seems to be a condition of successful work that the two organisations should be in permanent contact at every level from top to bottom.

The essence of our method was the establishment of a relationship between the worker and the staff in institutions, both severally and collectively, within which anxieties and tensions concerning their work could be ventilated and dealt with in such a way as to dissolve the barriers to spontaneous and creative relationship between the staff and the children. Although it was found to be inadvisable to go beyond a certain depth in our contacts, a quality of relationship was established within which the attitudes and insights of the staff changed more deeply and extensively than I had ever known to occur in such a situation before. This was facilitated by a number of elements in the general approach, which I should like to sum up in conclusion. We avoided the threat to the whole adult group which is implicit in the direct treatment of children. Both group and individual contacts were used to relieve the guilt of staff members about failure, whether in training the children or in meeting their emotional needs. This in itself often did much to reduce tensions between different members or groups of members, and between the whole staff and the Director, and so produced a more relaxed and tolerant atmosphere. By extending the contact to the whole organisation we avoided setting up or exacerbating conflicts within it, and found that we could often do something to relieve those which existed. A further advantage of our method was that every bit of work done on behalf of any child had the maximum prophyictic value for the group as a whole. The criterion of success was the extent to which staff members became free to handle problems confidently, spontaneously and creatively.

An important account of this experience and the theory arising from it is contained in Caplan G. and Rosenfeld J. Techniques of Staff Consultation in an Immigrant Children's Organisation in Israel, *American Journal of Orthopsychiatry,* Jan. 1954.

CHAPTER 7

The Use of Small Group Discussions in the Teaching of Human Relations and Mental Health *

Introduction

In 1951 the Mackintosh Committee encouraged psychiatric social workers to try to compensate for their inadequate numbers by devoting some of their time to fostering the mental health insights and skills of workers in various branches of the social services where the need for such qualities arises. Many psychiatric social workers were of course already in the habit of sharing their specialised knowledge in a friendly informal way with colleagues in a variety of fields, but little had been done on a systematic basis, apart from the war-time After-care Service of the Provisional National Committee for Mental Health (Goldberg, 1957). In 1955, Dr. Gerald Caplan presented to the Association of Psychiatric Social Workers a paper on the theory and technique of mental health consultation, in which the consultant helps professional individuals or groups to resolve a problem in human relations arising in their work, which has taken on the character of an emotional problem for them. He differentiated this from mental health education, a more continuous, regular and extended process designed to foster understanding of emotional problems among such groups and the ability to relate helpfully to those who present them. In the same year Jona Rosenfeld gave a paper, in which he vividly described his experience and practice in such work. More experiment has since taken place among us, and since the techniques of these

---

*First published in the *British Journal of Psychiatric Social Work,* Vol. V, No. 1, 1959.

activities had not been included in the training of most psychiatric social workers, we have had to work them out for ourselves. Those who heard Dr. Caplan and Jona Rosenfeld were undoubtedly influenced by their papers, but these were unfortunately not available for publication, and only one psychiatric social worker in the U.K. has so far published an account of her experience (Smith, 1957). Meanwhile, a number of psycho-analysts have become interested in the in-service training of caseworkers and general practitioners in human relations and the handling of emotional problems, using small group discussions of case material provided by group members, sometimes supplemented by theoretical teaching and individual supervision. The content and technique of such work was described by Balint in 1953. The aim is formulated as being to effect in group members a "limited though considerable change of personality" through "the close study by group methods of the worker's counter-transference". This method of teaching resembles psycho-therapy more closely than the technique described by Caplan and Rosenfeld (1954), who keep discussion focused on the understanding of the patient or client presented by the worker, rather than on the worker's own involvement (which is nevertheless dealt with indirectly in ways which will be indicated below).

The Choice of Technique in Relation to Group Structure and Function

The method described below was developed by Dr. Marion Mackenzie and myself in groups established at the request of the London County Council to assist the staff of their maternity and child welfare clinics to develop their potential contribution to the prevention of mental ill-health. The groups were composed of doctors and health visitors who worked together, and the model was provided by Caplan rather than Balint. One factor in the choice of technique was the aim of the programme, which was not to teach psycho-therapy to public health staff, but simply to develop their understanding of relationships and emotional situations, and their ability to give constructive support to mothers. Another important consideration is the structure of the group. Some are composed of volunteers from a number of centres, others, for various reasons, of all the workers attached to a particular centre. This second type of group presents quite different problems, because any interpersonal tensions which exist in the work-group will find expression in the discussion group situation, and great skill is required in judging what to handle in the group and what (if anything) outside, whether with individuals or sub-groups. It is also natural that more resistance is encountered in groups whose members have not freely chosen to enter a learning situation of this kind, which necessarily involves their attitudes, feelings and values. There is little doubt that a group of volunteers is easier to run for this reason; on the other hand, one has to consider the danger that, by electing to work with volunteers only, one may foster harmful tensions between the "progressives" who join and those who cleave to tradition. In some cases it may be wiser and more responsible to avoid this danger by undertaking the more difficult task of carrying the whole group, with its tensions and resistances, and accepting the slower progress which will result from this. One psychiatric social worker, appointed as consultant to a group of less specialised caseworkers, decided to hold group discussions including all workers, while offering opportunities for regular supervision or occasional consultations to those workers who asked for them, thus leaving no one out, but at the same time offering something more to the enthusiasts.

It is important to allow for the status or hierarchial relations of group members in their own organisation; this applies whether we are dealing with two or more professions, as with doctors and health visitors, or with senior and junior members of a service or professional group. Differential status seems to contra-indicate individual interpretation of implicit attitudes, whether to leaders or clients. Sanction may be obtained for such interpretations in a "sibling" group like that for general practitioners mentioned above, but seniors cannot afford to expose themselves to such hazards in front of juniors (and often vice versa). This is especially so when, as often happens in a period of rapid professional development, the juniors tend to be more advanced and more receptive than the seniors, and the latter are more insecure and easily undermined.

The educational handling of a status problem can be illustrated by the following example:

A doctor in the group reported that, much to her surprise, a mother whom she had always regarded as particularly competent and confident had suddenly come to her in great distress and anxiety and had readily communicated a story of maternal deprivation; her mother had devoted herself to a successful business career at the expense of motherhood, but the deprivation was partly compensated by the care of the older sister who took main responsibility for her. The doctor saw her client's anxiety as almost incompatible with her previous image of her, a kind of personality change. The health visitor who was sensitive and perceptive but rather unassertive, mentioned quietly several times that the mother had seemed over-anxious to her all along, consulting her with excessive anxiety about one minor problem after another. These contributions were swept aside in favour of the doctor's contradictory picture, till one of the clinical members expressed interest that the mother had shown different facets of herself to her two advisers, adding that this was not unusual, and was one reason for the value of a team. In this case it also seemed reasonable to suggest that the mother had been relating to the doctor much as she used to behave with her own mother, to whom she had tried hard to present the competent façade she demanded, and to the health visitor as she had with her sister, who had been less demanding and more accepting of weakness. Thus it was possible to teach something about transference and to relieve the inter-personal and inter-professional rivalries at the same time.

Anxiety and Defence in the Maternity and Child Welfare Setting

The group proceeded on the understanding that the earliest signs of incipient emotional disturbance in the first year of life are difficulties concerning the basic functions of sleeping, feeding and elimination in a physically healthy child. Such problems were brought to the group when the usual advice about management had not worked, or the mother seemed unable to carry it out. At first the group looked to the leaders for better and more effective advice to pass on to the mothers, but the leaders explained that such problems could only be understood in the context of the mother's personality, her relationships with the child, her husband, her parents or other important figures in her life, and often part at least of her personal history. Such knowledge had not previously been perceived as relevant, and had often been avoided rather than sought. It was tacitly assumed that to communicate distress was to increase it, so that mothers who seemed about to cry were protected against "breaking down" by a swift though kindly termination of the interview. Advice and reassurance, which have of course a legitimate function in this setting, also tended to be used prematurely and in facile forms as devices for closing communication. Although consciously intended to protect the client, such avoidance seemed rather to defend the worker against sharing her distress.

These attitudes, evolved in the practice of health education, were not compatible with effective performance in a preventive mental health function. The public health staff gradually learned to extend their frame of reference, to pay more attention to relationships, to listen longer and with more interest to emotional communication, to follow up leads and to be more alert for clues to unspoken feelings. While all this increased their understanding of the problems they were trying to relieve, it also revealed how serious many of them were: breakdown or an acute risk of breakdown in the most basic human functions and relationships — pregnancy, childbirth, early mother-child relationships and marital relations. By relinquishing their familiar defences the workers found themselves exposed more fully to the distress of their clients, as well as knowledge of their angers and hates, and thus experienced much distress and anxiety themselves. As they lost faith in their traditional reactions they began to feel helpless to help. It took time to learn through repeated experience that sympathetic listening and the emotional release which it facilitates are often surprisingly potent in relieving anxiety and restoring self-confidence. At this stage the ability to help often outruns the awareness of being helpful.

Methods Employed in the Group

In this situation, where learning involves relinquishing defences against anxiety and painful exposure to the fuller expression of very deep human problems, there are bound to be periodic crises of disappointment and despair, with underlying resentment against the leaders, who are felt to have torn away the defences (however moderate the pace may have been) and to have given no tangible means of helping in exchange.

Why did we therefore not have recourse to the kind of interpretation which has proved so effective in therapeutic groups? We have mentioned the dangers of doing this in a group of working colleagues of varying status. Another important reason is that there is no sanction for therapeutic procedures, since the members enrolled for training, not for a therapeutic experience. It could be argued that, since the nature and content of the group discussions release anxieties which can be dealt with in no other way, the leaders cannot shirk the task of negotiating sanction for therapeutic procedures. If I believed that they could not in fact be dealt with otherwise, I should feel obliged to accept this logic.

However, Caplan and Rosenfeld (1954) have shown that members of such a group tend to seek help with cases which have aroused in themselves feelings or anxieties similar to those of the client, or which express indirectly their feelings in the group. To the extent that in speaking of the client they are also speaking of themselves the understanding, acceptance and hopefulness with which the leaders discuss the client's problems also apply to the workers themselves. An interpretive process thus goes on at second-hand, and much anxiety can be relieved without embarrassing the worker by drawing explicit attention to his own problems. Caplan and Rosenfeld also noticed that consultees (as they call the members of such a group) tend to identify with the consultants (i.e. group leaders), and use with their clients methods similar to those used by the consultants in the group. Inevitably the group leaders serve as an example, and this too is a reason for demonstrating a method which group members can appropriately use in helping their own clients to weather and surmount their anxieties, rather than a highly specialised technique for which such a group cannot provide adequate training and which is not appropriate for the work in their setting. One should add that in spite of differences in personality, ability and knowledge, all members of the group share the same situation, so many of the feelings expressed are shared by the group, rather than peculiar to the individual.

An example of the indirect expression of transference feelings in the group and the indirect response occurred on an occasion when the psychiatrist was absent, leaving the social worker as the sole leader. One of the members described a mother who had been quite upset on visiting the clinic and finding that her special health visitor was absent. Group members agreed that clients developed strong personal attachments to individual workers and then no-one else would do, however kind and able they were. The social worker agreed that this was often so. A good deal of anxiety was expressed about the dependent nature of these attachments, and whether it was compatible with a professional relationship. The social worker said that such attachments were liable to arise in any situation of professional help, and often laid the basis for increased self-confidence and self-reliance in the client. No mention was made of the feelings about the absence of the psychiatrist and dependence in the group, but the social worker's response applied to this as well as to the relations of the public health workers with their clients.

At times, of course, the group did not share the worker's counter-transference to her client. If a member was occasionally over-severe or impatient with a client, another might emphasise the difficulties of the client's situation, or possible reasons for the disturbing behaviour; another worker might be over-protective to certain clients, and this too would be questioned. Sometimes if the worker was anxious or depressed the other members might try to reassure or encourage her. At other times the whole group might share her feelings. At such times we often found it helpful to recognise the implicit feeling with a certain type of interpretive comment; one addressed to the whole group rather than to the individual, and which more or less explicitly included the leaders. For example: "I think we are all feeling pretty helpless and depressed about Mrs. X. That is how she makes people feel; she overwhelms them with her own hopelessness, but perhaps if she finds you can stand it and not give up hope completely, she will find that you have helped her after all." Whereas interpretations of the more usual form tend to increase the sense of difference and distance between leaders and group, the inclusion of the leaders in the comment tends to diminish this.

I have expressed some misgivings about describing one's own work to the group, lest through identification it becomes a model. However, I have used examples from my own professional experience to further understanding of complex situations such as marital collusion, neurotic marriage choice and sado-masochistic relationships, all of which were encountered at various times. The most useful examples for teaching proved to be those where I had eventually gained insight after a long period of groping in the dark, so that such examples had a second value; they enabled the group to identify with me as someone who had originally not known, but had been able to learn, the things which they were learning now. This was encouraging and also distance-reducing

Any such example is in some way related to the group situation. I once told a story about a depressive patient to illustrate a point about control and permissiveness; but the point that most interested the health visitors was that he had refused my advice "because I was not a doctor", but had accepted the authority of the psychiatrist!

Reality-testing and Evaluation

The difficulties and anxieties of the learning process are sometimes compounded by pressures from the client organisation. In the first of our groups we found that anxiety was being aroused by persistent enquiries from a higher level of the administrative hierarchy about its activity. In discussing this, it became clear that the group was projecting onto an administrator its own disappointment with the rate of progress and the intangible nature of its learning. This was brought into the open, while it was also suggested to the employing authority that it set up a committee to which such groups could report from time to time (see Chapter 8). The first meeting with this committee confirmed the leaders' interpretation of the situation, which the group had been unable to accept: the administrator had been expressing interest rather than dissatisfaction; and the problem had simply been how to convey the substance of the learning process — and the anxiety of not being able to do so. This produced great relief and further clarification; it was at a subsequent meeting with the committee that a member first verbalised that she had learned in the group to be more sparing with advice and reassurance. After a time, the committee expressed the hope of a rapid turnover in group membership for reasons of economy, and this provided a basis for a group evaluation session. The group felt strongly that both a fixed termination date and individual withdrawal and replacement would be premature. A member clarified for the first time the double function which the group had come to have; it not only enabled members to learn and gain increasing insight, but also to work more confidently with cases of serious emotional disturbance (e.g. puerperal breakdown) which they would not have dared to keep in the community without specialist support.

New members continued to trickle in, and in course of time the older members became aware by contrast of their own growing insight and confidence until they themselves expressed a feeling that they should now make way for others, but without losing touch completely. It was agreed to reserve one meeting a month for them, and at one of the first of these second-stage meetings it was suggested that they might like to make an evaluative report to their employing body, which was keenly interested in the promotion and expansion of such groups. This suggestion gave rise to another evaluation session, in which the members expressed not only their appreciation of what they had learned, but also a certain degree of dissatisfaction and a wish for further learning opportunities of a more formal kind; a number of promising suggestions for possible developments were then put forward.

Conclusion

It is recognised that in any training group concerned with human relations in which live cases are discussed, group members will become deeply involved, and there will be a close relationship between their feelings and attitudes towards clients and group leaders. There is a tendency, through identification with the client, to recreate the client-worker situation as between worker and leader, and so to discover by experience how the leader will behave in such a situation. Identification with the leader then modifies the reaction to the client, so that the attitude and behaviour of the leaders is a vital part of what is learned*. The leaders also have to remember that owing to the process of identification and projection between worker and client, any explanation of the client's feelings and behaviour will have an unconscious personal meaning for the worker, and often for the group as a whole; provided this is borne in mind, such comments may have both a teaching and a therapeutic value. While direct interpretation can be avoided, this kind of indirect interpretation is unavoidable, whether it occurs intentionally or not. At the same time, the leader's behaviour is consistently ego-supportive; members are treated with the respect due to their professional standing and with emphasis on their colleague status, and care is taken not to infringe their professional responsibility. The constant encouragement to continue handling their own cases rather than to refer them on is an implicit token of confidence in them. Undue dependence and regression are also avoided by consulting the group in such matters as length of membership, expansion, admission of new members and general matters of policy, and by the holding of periodic evaluation sessions.

References

1. Balint, M. (1953) *The Doctor, his Patient and the Illness,* Pitman.
2. Caplan, G. and Rosenfeld, J. Techniques of Staff Consultation in an Immigrant Children's Organisation in Israel, *American Journal of Orthopsychiatry,* 1954.
3. Goldberg, E.M. The Psychiatric Social Worker in the Community, *British Journal of Psychiatric Social Work,* Vol. IV, No. 2, 1957.
4. Smith, J. (1957) An Experiment in Consultation, *British Journal of Psychiatric Social Work,* Vol. IV, No. 2.

---

*This is the phenomenon known as "learning" theory or modelling.

CHAPTER 8

Mental Health Education in the Community: The Question of Sanction*

Mental health education and consultation have always been a secondary task of child guidance clinics, but were first studied and conceptualised by Caplan and Rosenfeld (1954). In subsequent writings (1959 a.b. 1963) Caplan has drawn a fairly sharp distinction between mental health consultation, as an occasional transaction with individual consultees, and mental health education as performed at regular intervals, and more economically with groups. Psychiatric social workers have been increasingly exposed to demands for one or both of these services in the last ten years, but do not yet receive any specific training for them, a gap inadequately filled by the short courses organised by the A.P.S.W. in recent years.

The literature on this type of activity is mainly concerned with process and method in the face-to-face individual or group situation. Little attention has been paid to the institution to which the consultees belong, the hopes and fears of other members of the institution, whether colleagues of the consultees or administrative superiors. However, the consultant in practice soon becomes aware of such repercussions, manifestations of curiosity or anxiety, rumours, misunderstandings, criticism, tensions developing. One is frequently reminded of the fairy who was not invited to the Sleeping Beauty's christening.

The literature of social consultancy is highly relevant to these problems. I quote from Sofer's *Organisation from Within:*

---

*First published in the *British Journal of Psychiatric Social Work*, Vol. VII, No. 3, 1964.

"Although one or other problem in an organisation may be singled out for study or administrative action it is rarely found that such isolation reflects sociological or psychological reality. . . . Although not all problems are equally interconnected, the organisation is a social system, i.e. a set of closely interwoven and interdependent activities functionally related to each other. Accordingly, if an attempt is made to deal with one problem without recognition of the larger problem of which it is part, it is virtually certain that the attempt will fail" (Sofer, 1961).

This is why we need to devote some systematic thought to the process of obtaining the sanction of the organisation. I use the term "sanction" in the sense of "social acceptance or sponsorship of an activity" (Pumphrey, 1959) by those members of a society or organisation in whom the appropriate authority resides.

Sofer (*op. cit.*) goes on to say that it is unwise to undertake such social consultancy without the support of leading members of the organisation who recognise a problem, regard the consultants as suitably equipped to contribute to its solution and are sufficiently influential to persuade their colleagues to cooperate. Those most closely involved must also be able to bear the discomfort which arises during certain phases of the work. It is important to clarify at an early stage who the consultant's client is, and whether this person has in fact the right to engage the consultant on his own responsibility, or requires the consent of colleagues or committees.

All these questions are equally relevant when a clinical unit enters into a relation of consultancy with any part of an organisation, whose members are likely to be unaware of the ramifications of the task which they propose. Clinically-based workers themselves have not always been sufficiently aware of these complexities, or even if aware they feel themselves in a weaker position to explore them with members of the organisation than the social consultant. It therefore happens quite often that an organisation such as a public service or local authority invites different clinical units, or even different parts of the same clinic, to undertake a variety of tasks which are demonstrably interconnected, but without perceiving the need for co-ordination or integration of these various activities. The clinical workers on their part may accept these tasks without pointing out the need for integration — sometimes even without realising till much later how many other colleagues are also in the field. This is likely to result in various degrees of incoherence or even inconsistency. Consultees may be called away from a regular on-going group to attend a shorter course of some kind; they may also be taught different and even contradictory approaches by different practitioners.

Other problems arise. The consultants are not consulted, and therefore offer no advice, on important questions of strategy, such as whether to introduce new knowledge and new approaches first to junior staff, who may well be more eager to learn, or to senior staff, who may be more ambivalent towards new knowledge, but who are likely to be seriously undermined and antagonised if this is offered to their juniors and not to them. These are subjects to which, in the present state of affairs, consultants may be expected to have given more systematic thought than administrators, but the former are often unduly shy to raise such matters, which should in my view be considered part of their professional responsibility.

Similarly a senior administrator may decide to enlist the co-operation of the consultants in some programme of change or staff development, but neglect to involve the intermediate levels of administration. Administrators vary greatly in the attention they pay to such matters, and sometimes handle them very expertly; but if they do not, and if the consultants allow this matter to go by default, trouble is likely to arise at a later stage. It is, however, clear that such matters can only be discussed with senior administrators by an equally senior counterpart in the consultant clinic — who should almost certainly be the director. The leaders of a social agency or public service are not likely to take seriously the views of lower-ranking staff in the consultant agency. Top-level participation on the consultant side will also be needed later when, as we shall see, the inevitable ambiguities of the initial contract of sanction lead to difficulties and require clarification.

Negotiating Sanction

The process of gaining sanction has parallels in the intake process in clinical work. In both cases one has to discover who wants what: who wants any kind of help (and who does not) and what kind of help do they want? The patient or his parents often suggest remedies which the clinic considers inappropriate; similarly, the institution may have attempted to prescribe for its own needs inexpertly, so that once the problem is clarified the consultant's next task may be to explain that other means to the desired end would be more appropriate. In neither setting can the implications of the cooperative task (i.e. therapy or consultation) be fully described or predicted, since they are often of a character which must be experienced to be understood. To some extent our behaviour in these early approaches provides a sort of free sample of what working with us will be like. But the whole experience is a developing one, which cannot attain its fullness until both parties know each other better. In either situation, there are many things which the client or consultee cannot face until he has developed a confidence in the helper in which time is an ingredient as well as the helper's behaviour. Grunebaum (1962), in the context of group work with parents of child patients, advocates establishing at the outset a somewhat ambiguous contract with the group, to allow of re-negotiation as experience and confidence increase.

A certain degree of ambiguity seems in any case to be unavoidable, and this is a reason for trying to establish some permanent channels of communication however tenuous with those from whom sanction emanates. It is often difficult to obtain adequate preliminary discussion at senior levels (perhaps most of all with middle management) but the lack of this is apt to lead to problems later on. It is always worth trying for more preliminary discussion than is originally offered, and provided the organisation sees the proposed service as sufficiently important it may be willing to invest a good deal of senior staff time in this way, providing also that senior members of the consultant agency participate in the discussions. Having enlisted the cooperation of the Tavistock Clinic in its efforts to equip the staff of its maternity and child welfare service for preventive mental health work, the health department of the London County Council established a working-party with the clinic, appointing to it 13 representatives. This body had twenty meetings, which provided an opportunity for cooperative definition of the problem and the task, and for designing a service which the clinic would think worth offering and the authority worth accepting. The authority's original initiative (an invitation for one or two lectures) was thus transformed into a sanctioned programme, the joint decisions being embodied in a report (Study Group, 1954) which was adopted by the authority as the basis for future action. This surprisingly great expenditure of public health time must be attributed to the authority's awareness of its own need to engage in major clarification of aims and methods in relation to its new goals.

Pilot Group as a Free Sample

We have seen that in clinical work the intake process affords something like a free sample of the clinic's service. While discussing the nature of the problem and what kind of help the clinic can offer, the clients are able to experience the professional worker's attitude and the kind of help and understanding which he can give. In the L.C.C. project described above, the "free sample" was represented by an experimental case discussion group composed of two public health members (doctor and health visitor) and two from the clinic (psychiatrist and psychiatric social worker). This group explored in practice what kind of help the public health members needed and what they could do with it, and brought its findings back to each meeting of the working-party. All members of this group found their expectations considerably modified in the light of their shared experience. The consultees found that the problems they presented could not be handled simply in terms of advice from the consultants for them to pass on to the mothers; they discovered that much more information than they expected about each family was required to enable the group to understand the problems presented. The clinicians, on the other hand, learned that child guidance practice, with "full" psychiatric history and regular long interviews with mothers, was a quite inappropriate model for public health staff. It was found to be sufficient for the public health staff to supplement their own basic records by obtaining "segmental" information about the antecedents of the mother's attitude towards the problem at issue, or even simply to enquire sympathetically about the background to the mother's current anxiety. We also found that mothers are unwilling to attend for a long series of interviews in this setting, but will attend frequently at a time of crisis till anxiety is relieved, sometimes returning after an interval if further trouble develops. We learned to appreciate the strengths of the public health setting: the ready availability in time of crisis, which renders quite simple skills unexpectedly effective, as described by Caplan (1959), and the protection of the mother's independence by not insisting on frequent regular interviews (this was mentioned by Betty Joseph in 1948, but we had to rediscover it). In fact, the pilot group had the experience of co-operatively developing something new, a kind of psychological first-aid service, an economical way of helping mothers just at the moments when help was most acceptable and most effective.

Simpler Ways of Negotiating Sanction

Rarely will a consulting organisation attach sufficient importance to the matter in hand to engage in so elaborate and time-consuming a procedure as the L.C.C. on this occasion. It is therefore necessary to consider realistically what is the most economical and effective way of obtaining sanction for consultant activity. Senior staff in the consulting organisation sometimes offer one or two meetings, after which the local officials may be introduced to the consultants, and the senior officials withdraw from systematic contact. This method presents various problems. It necessitates crystallisation of plans at top level before there has been time for proper exploration of the situation at ground level; some of the plans may thus prove to be inappropriate for some reason or even unworkable. Much remains to be worked through with local officials (middle management), and it is premature to finalise any plans until the attitudes, wishes and objections of these officials have been explored. A workable plan would be to explain to the senior officials at the first meeting that there will be much to explore locally and that this will take time, and to ask for a follow-up meeting, together with local officials, after such an interval as seems appropriate in view of the number of people and places to be visited. A period of six months or more would give time for the consultants to learn something not only about the work of those whom they are to help, but also about the structure of the field, the normal channels of communication, patterns of cooperation and failures in both these functions; about who carries which tasks and who takes which decisions. In short, it affords time to learn about both tasks and problems, and to consider possible solutions. A sanctioning meeting after all this exploration will clearly be much more fruitful than one which was held at the outset.

Sanction in the Basic Group

I am using the term "basic group" to refer to those staff members of the consulting organisation with whom the consultants are being asked to work, whether they constitute the entire staff of a school or public health clinic, for instance, or a group of self-selected individuals from such a service. Caplan (1959) has called them "the grassroots care-takers", the people who are actually teaching children, advising mothers, working directly with the public.

Some members of this basic group may have participated in the process whereby the sanction of the organisation was gained, but most of them will not have done so. (In a school, for instance, the head teacher will have been consulted, but probably not the staff.) One may try to ensure the sanction of such group members by attempts to safeguard their initiative, stipulating that every member should be a volunteer. Officials do not readily agree to this, especially if they are keen on the project and eager to see it in full operation; even when agreed it is not easy to maintain. Ostensible volunteers are often found to have joined under some degree of pressure, veiled from the official concerned by the collusive compliance with which employees in a public service accept a suggestion as an order, and "show willing". True volunteering would probably require some form of selection process in which the group leaders could explore the motivation of the applicant, but this too would be hard to establish. Experience shows it to be quite possible to work with the total staff of a clinic or school, subject to the right of staff members who find the process too disturbing to opt out. In these conditions one relies less on individual initiative and more on the processes to be discussed below, by which the consultant organisation earns the right to engage the group in a process which they may find disturbing as well as enriching.

Once the basic group has been recruited, we have to repeat at this level the process of exploring expectations and arriving at a co-operative definition of the joint task. Consultees are liable to want and expect many things which may seem to the leaders impossible, inappropriate, or less valuable than alternatives. They may want formal intellectual teaching of psychology and psychiatry; a set of rules establishing a one-to-one relationship between symptom and cause; or advice as to the management of certain types of problems which they can pass on to the mother like an unopened packet. They may want to hear about the consultants' cases rather than to discuss their own, or to watch the psychiatrist doing psycho-therapy in order to learn to do it themselves. Not all these desires are entirely inappropriate. Some leaders do find it useful to describe illustrative cases from their own work on occasion, and some didactic teaching may be required from time to time; it may sometimes be useful, or even necessary, to give definite advice on the management of a difficult case. But all these demands can be used defensively, to avoid the discomfort of thinking too closely about the consultees' own cases and facing the anxieties aroused. The leaders have to be aware of these anxieties and defences, and so to handle the group that anxieties are faced and relieved and the problems of the members dealt with in some way which is not too threatening.

We do not ourselves interpret the defensive aspects of these demands, but try to deal with them firmly but flexibly, allowing an occasional session of retreat from the exacting study of members' own cases when resistance seems to be unusually high, while seeking at the same time to identify and relieve the anxiety underlying the defences. This process has many aspects, some of which are not far removed from therapy; I have described it more fully in Chapter 7. What I want to stress here is that sanction is earned, maintained, renewed and extended through the constructive resolution of this encounter of wills. The group must experience the value of what the leaders offer before it will relinquish its unmet demands and authorise the leaders to give what they feel to be most helpful, rather than to collude with evasive tendencies. At the same time the leaders will be clarifying and sometimes modifying their understanding of the professional needs of the group, and they will in time improve their technique for meeting these needs. The process continues throughout the life of the group;

sanction has to be maintained or renewed, and also sometimes extended, as the needs and potentialities of the group develop.

All this amounts to a real experience of cooperative discovery. In the public health project described above, we could not have devised beforehand techniques appropriate for public health staff in a public health setting; we elected to focus on sharing with them our dynamic understanding of their case material, leaving them free to discover for themselves how they could use this understanding and how clients could best use their help. This holds true, *mutatis mutandis,* of similar work in schools (where it is appropriate for educational psychologists to play a leading role). On the other hand, it is important for the consultants to keep good track of their aims and their limitations — i.e. to distinguish what they are helping consultees to do from psychotherapy and interpretive casework, for which such a training method would be clearly inadequate. This is a reason for caution in demonstrating ones own work, which may have discouraging effects, or may stimulate emulation; and for not interpreting group reactions at any depth, since this is likely to encourage an inappropriate use of interpretation by group members with their clients (Caplan and Rosenfeld, *op. cit.*).

One reason why sanction needs to be negotiated by the director of the consultant body is that only he has sufficient weight and prestige to maintain control of the situation should misunderstandings emerge. This applies equally in the basic groups, and is one of a number of reasons why it is usually necessary for a psychiatrist to act as consultant for groups which include doctors. Similarly, the consultant must be a reasonably senior and experienced person. Junior staff or students will be acceptable as assistants, but are likely to be resented if given sole responsibility, and to have difficulty in resisting inappropriate demands.

Maintenance of Sanction

Both in the face-to-face group and in the institution, sanction requires periodic or occasional maintenance or renewal. In the public health project the original working party was succeeded, after an uncomfortable period without official channels of communication (see Chapter 7), by an advisory committee, similar in structure on the public health side, but broadened to represent several cooperating clinics. Meetings were not frequent, but served various purposes. They kept senior public health staff in touch with developments in the groups, and enabled group members to relieve their uncertainties as to whether the group activities were actively sanctioned by their authority. They helped to correct unrealistic expectations on the part of the authority as regards the desirable duration of groups, and to convince the administrators of the unexpectedly high incidence of severe emotional disturbance among the mothers dealt with in their clinics. They provided a forum for discussion and revision of certain practical restrictions which proved to be limiting the scope of the scheme. They produced a valuable expansion of the original public health frame of reference, which was in terms of "training" rather didactically understood. The groups reported that their meetings had another value in terms of shared responsibility and consultant support in the more acutely disturbed cases, which sometimes enabled public health staff to maintain in the community mothers whom they would otherwise have taken steps to direct towards hospital.

Conclusion

Much still remains to be thought out in this area, but a few general principles are emerging from experience of trial and error. The most important seem to be that the consultant organisation should stipulate a substantial period of exploration before allowing sanction to crystallise in any detail, and should try to engage in this process at least the middle levels of administration, with subsequent report back for further discussion at top level. Without such a process, the plans agreed will either be excessively vague and ambiguous, or if more definite they are likely to need considerable modification in relation to the various and unpredictable conditions which will be met in the field. However thoroughly this preliminary work is done, machinery for reviewing progress and renewing or extending sanction from time to time is required. On the one hand unexpected difficulties are likely to be encountered, and on the other successful consultation is likely to expand and develop in ways which, in the absence of such machinery, may be artificially arrested by rigidities in the consulting organisation. Some machinery is therefore needed both to establish sanction and to maintain and extend it, although the details will appropriately vary according to local conditions and the general relations between the consulting organisation and the consultants.

References

Caplan, G. and Rosenfeld, R.J. (1954) Techniques of Staff Consultation in an Immigrant Children's Organisation in Israel, *American Journal of Orthopsychiatry,* Jan. 1954.

Caplan, G. (1959) *Concepts of Mental Health and Consultation: their Application in Public Health Social Work,* U.S. Children's Bureau.

Caplan, G. (1959) *A Community Approach to Mental Health,* Tavistock Pubs., London.

Caplan, G. (1963) Types of Mental Health Consultation, *American Journal of Orthopsychiatry,* XXXIII, 3.

Grunebaum, H. (1962) Group Psycho-therapy of Fathers: Problems of Technique, *British Journal of Medical Psychology,* XXXV, 2, pp. 147-155.

Irvine, E.E. (1959) The Use of Small Group Discussions in the Teaching of Human Relations and Mental Health, *British Journal of Psychiatric Social Work,* V, 1.

Joseph, B. (1948) A Psychiatric Social Worker in a Maternity and Child Welfare Centre, *British Journal of Psychiatric Social Work,* No. 2.

Sofer, C. (1961) *The Organisation from Within: A Comparative Study of Social Institutions based on a Sociotherapeutic Approach,* Tavistock Pubs.

Study Group from the Public Health Dept., L.C.C. and the Tavistock Clinic (1954) Preventative Mental Health in the Maternity and Child Welfare Service, *The Medical Officer,* XCII, 303.

Part III   The Needs of Client Groups
with Special Problems

(a)   Multi-problem Families

My interest in these families was originally aroused by two books: *Problem Families: An Experiment in Social Rehabilitation*, by Tom Stephens of the Pacifist Service Units and *Problem Families: Five Enquiries*, a review of investigations carried out by health visitors in five local authority health departments, written by Dr. C.P. Blacker for the Eugenics Society. I have not included the review article which I then wrote, since the following articles embody the concept of emotional immaturity which I then introduced. This concept was used unchallenged by various authors till 1959, when Harriet Wilson argued that environmental pressures were of more importance in this connection than any personal inadequacy of the parents. When asked to write an introduction to Lorna Walker's account of a groupwork project, I was fascinated to see how strongly her material seemed to confirm the challenged hypothesis of immaturity; so I produced a short paper rather than an introduction. I am grateful to Mrs. Walker for permission to include her material alongside my comments. In the final paper (Chapter 11) I have tried to integrate the personal and social factors into a more balanced and comprehensive account of the problem.

Until quite recently the Family Service Units have regarded long-term supportive casework with the parents of these families as an essential component of the help they provide, although this often came to be supplemented by groupwork with children and later with parents, and again more recently by community work. The child guidance clinics which tried to help such families also found that a long-term commitment was essential (Howell and Parsloe, 1966; Ford, 1966). It seemed that with such severely deprived parents it was necessary to provide a corrective relationship, in which their excessive dependence was accepted, worked through and outgrown. However, Laxton (1973), and Sainsbury (1975), have questioned what had become a widespread assumption. Laxton suggests that long-term intensive casework may actually retard growth towards independence, at least in some cases, by providing too much dependent satisfaction. He suggests that in many cases short-term help with problem-solving, undertaken at a point of crisis, can produce useful results in a period of four to eight months. Sainsbury, who studied a number of clients of one F.S.U., suggests that the duration of contact might be shortened if the worker-client relationship were more clearly distinguished from friendship (though certainly friendly) and if the long-term aims of social achievement and independent problem-solving by the family were kept more explicitly in focus. Roberts (1968) of Woodberry Down Child Guidance Clinic describes some very encouraging and economical work with the "seriously disturbed family, a family with a multitude of problems, whether officially 'multi-problem' or not", which "may well turn up appropriately in a number of social work departments". Some of these families "function on a primitive level and who can only achieve maturity as a unit — in other words they share between them the psychological structure necessary for maturity." However, the clinic found that these families could often respond surprisingly well to brief family therapy (including all members) with up to six meetings spaced at intervals of several weeks. This is encouraging indeed, in view of the fact that there are many more "multi-problem families" in the community than can ever be offered long-term casework. Roberts suggests that family therapy can best be practised in the child guidance clinic, since it requires the combined skills of the multi-discipline team. If and where the child guidance team survives the present reorganisation, this may become one of its major contributions to the social services and their clients. It is not suggested that it is appropriate for all families, but it could cream off a number of them, leaving to F.S.U.-type services those for whom long-term intensive casework is still the only effective treatment known.

(b)   The Impact of Parental Psychosis on Children

At the time when I wrote the paper which is now Chapter 12 I was unable to find any published work on this subject, and wrote directly out of clinical experience. I had missed Gwen Douglas's paper of 1956. The 1960s saw a handful of articles about the advantages of admitting the baby to hospital with a mother suffering from puerperal breakdown, and possibly other children as well. Interest in the problem grew slowly in the community mental health services. A postal survey of the work of P.S.W.s in mental hospitals was carried out in 1968 (Hunter, 1969). Twenty-seven out of 47 respondents said they always tried to ascertain the effect of a parent's illness on the children, while 19 did so sometimes. The concern of psychiatrists, as reported by their P.S.W. colleagues, was rather less. Although these figures leave much to be desired, from another standpoint it is encouraging that so much concern for the children was found in the traditionally patient-centred hospital service. No comparable survey of community mental health services was carried out, and there is little indication of the present situation following the merging of mental health with other social services. However, at least one very intensive study of schizophrenic parents and their children in the home is being carried out in the United States (Anthony, 1969, a,b).

References

Anthony, E.J. (1969a) A Clinical Evaluation of Children with Psychotic Parents, *American Journal of Psychiatry,* 126, 2.
Anthony, E.J. (1969b) The Mutative Impact on family Life of Serious Mental and Physical Illness in a Parent, *Canadian Psychiatric Association Journal,* 14.
Hunter, P. (1969) A Survey of Psychiatric Social Workers in Mental Hospitals, *British Journal of Psychiatric Social Workers,* Vol. X, no. 1.
Blacker, C.P. (1954) *Problem Families: Five Enquiries,* The Eugenics Society, London.
Ford, J. (1966) What is Happening in Child Guidance? *British Journal of Psychiatric Social Work,* Vol. VIII, no. 4.
Howell, D. and Parsloe, P. (1966) Working with a Family in a Child Guidance Setting, *British Journal of Psychiatric Social Work,* Vol. VIII, no. 4.

Laxton, M. (1973) in Goldring, P., *Friend of the Family,* David & Charles, Newton Abbott.

Roberts, W.L. (1968) Working with the Family Group in a Child Guidance Clinic, *British Journal of Psychiatric Social Work,* Vol. IX, no. 4.

Sainsbury, E. (1975) *Social Work with Families,* Routledge & Kegan Paul, London.

Stephens, T. (1945) *Problem Families,* Pacifist Service Units.

Wilson, H. (1969) in Holman, R. *et al., Socially Deprived Families.*

CHAPTER 9

The Hard-to-Like Family*

I will begin this paper by quoting some of the classic descriptions of "problem families":

> The Women's Group on Public Welfare (which was set up during the last war) stated (1943) that the wartime evacuation had brought to light the continued existence of a "submerged tenth" of the population: "like a hidden sore, poor, dirty, crude in its habits, an intolerable and degrading burden to decent people forced by poverty to neighbour with it. Within this group are the "problem families", always on the edge of pauperism and crime, riddled with physical and mental defects, in and out of the courts for child neglect, a menace to the community".

Another description, widely used and repeated, is that of Wofinden (1944), written as a guide to fieldworkers wishing to identify problem families.

> "Often it is a large family, some of the children being dull or feeble-minded. From their appearance they are strangers to soap and water, toothbrush and comb. Their clothing is dirty and torn, and the footgear absent or totally inadequate. Often they are verminous and have scabies and impetigo. Their nutrition is surprisingly average, doubtless due to extra-familial feeding at school. The mother is frequently sub-standard mentally; the home, if indeed it can be described as such, has usually the most striking characteristics, nauseating odours assail one's nostrils on entering and the source is usually located in some urine-sodden, faecal-stained mattress in an upstairs room. There are no floor coverings, no decorations on the walls, except, perhaps, for the scribblings of the

*First published in *Case Conference,* Vol. XIV, no. 3, 1967.

children and bizarre patterns formed by absent plaster. Furniture is of the most primitive, cooking utensils absent, facilities for sleeping hopeless; iron bedsteads furnished with soiled mattresses and no coverings. Upstairs there is flock everywhere, which the mother assures me has come out of the mattress she has unpacked for cleansing, but the flock seems to stay there for weeks and the cleansed and re-packed mattress never appears. The bathroom is obviously the least frequented room in the house. There are sometimes faecal accumulations on the floors upstairs, and tin baths containing several days' accumulation of faeces and urine are not unknown. The children, especially the older ones, often seem to be perfectly happy and contented, despite such a shocking environment. They will give a description of how a full-sized midday meal has been cooked and eaten in the house on the day of the visit, but the absence of cooking utensils gives the lie to their assertions. One can only conclude that such children have never known restful sleep, that the amount of housework done by the mother is negligible, and that the general standard of hygiene is lower than that of the animal world.''

These purple passages of emotive prose are in marked contrast with the usual style of committees and public servants. It is evident that feelings have been deeply stirred, feelings not only of antagonism but also of disgust and loathing. We become aware, as we read them, that the families described represent an affront to the fundamental values of those concerned with health and welfare; and it is often this ill-concealed disgust which makes it impossible for many sensible and capable people to help them, as they are able to help their more fortunate or "respectable" neighbours. Luckily, the Second World War had the side-effect of breaking down the geographical segregation of these families in slums which were rarely visited by what one might call the philanthropic classes; this had enabled the philanthropic classes to relapse into the state of social unconsciousness from which such authors as Dickens and Booth had awakened them in the previous century. In particular, the young pacifist predecessors of the Family Service Units were inspired by their idealistic faith to approach these families in a very different spirit from that of the exasperated officials who so often expressed themselves in the kind of terms quoted above. This new kind of work, or should we say this warm, long-suffering friendship, not only helped a number of families who had been written off as "unhelpable", but also demonstrated the way in which they could be helped. The relative success of these methods gradually became a model for some of the more progressive statutory services. Some of these have financed a local Family Service Unit, others have appointed one or more workers to a department of education or health or to a children's department, to specialise in work with these families. Such appointments implied the recognition that the workers would need a sufficiently low caseload to enable them to make the lavish expenditure of time and attention which is essential in helping such families. Apart from demonstrating a method, these workers also created an experimental situation and proved that the new approach made it possible to recognise another factor at work in these families — the factor of emotional immaturity in one or both parents.

I will now quote from an article that I wrote some years ago (Irvine, 1954) summing up from another angle the traits generally attributed to the clients of the "Pacifist Service Units" or their successors, the Family Service Units.

"Inability for sustained or planful activity, so that appointments are not kept and arrangements not carried out. Foresight is lacking, so that money which will be needed for necessities tomorrow is squandered today on luxuries, attractive rubbish, or day-dream stimulants (such as 'the pictures'). There is no 'sense of time', no 'sense of money', no 'sense of property'; in fact, a failure to grasp three of the most important elements in our culture. There is impulsiveness and lack of control in various spheres, including those of sex and aggression. Often there is a compulsive need for oral satisfaction, whether in the form of sweets, cigarettes or drink. In some instances the usual inhibitions on anal interests have not been developed, children are not toilet-trained and faeces lie about on the floor or are stored away in tin baths or cupboards."

These characteristics seem to add up to a picture of extreme immaturity; is not most of this behaviour the sort of thing one would expect from a child of two, three or four left without adult guidance or control? The Pacifist Service Units seem to have intuitively recognised these infantile dependent needs and adapted their methods to them. With clients referred to the Units advice, exhortation, persuasion, disapproval, appeals to gratitude had all been tried and had all been proved ineffective; but the Units had the good idea of visiting very frequently, especially while they were establishing their relationship with the family, and accepted the fact that if such a family was to be helped, it must have the opportunity first to be dependent on some uncritical and accepting protective authority. Advice, exhortation and so on being all ineffective, practical help in household tasks was offered instead, and did seem in many cases to elicit cooperation; though even this had to be carefully timed, whether intuitively or in a more systematic way. In fact, it was found that "the worker had most chance of success if he played the part of a warm, permissive and supporting parent, thus supplying the basic experiences of the early stage of socialisation which, for whatever reason, these clients seem to have missed" (Irvine, *loc. cit.*). With patience and tact the client could sometimes be induced to work alongside the worker, like a child in the phase of "do it with mother"; he or she might then begin to taste the satisfaction of the child who says: "I can do it myself". I suggested at that time that it is worth considering whether the nursery school teacher would not have as much to contribute to such a process as a social worker.

I would like to take this opportunity to clear up one or two misunderstandings. Leonard, in his excellent little book *Sociology in Social Work* (1967) quotes my suggestion that "in this type of casework the essential process lies in the acting-out of a parent-child relationship between worker and client" (Irvine, 1956). He adds: "The difficulty here is that the client's expectations as to the behaviour appropriate to a parental relationship will ... depend in part upon his social class position. The social worker's and the client's expectations of the parental relationship may thus diverge ... because of the conflict between the social worker's and client's cultural definitions of the parent-child relationship."

All this is perfectly true, but I do not think it affects my point. It is no part of my argument that the client should recognise this role as parental, or that the worker should meet his expectations; I am concerned with meeting, not his expectations, but his needs. In fact, to elaborate my thesis, the whole point of this relationship is that it should *not* correspond to the client's expectations, based on early experience of parental relationships which failed to provide enough need-satisfaction to enable him to establish basic trust and all the further stages of development. Clients who have been damaged in this way expect very little of any relationship. I believe they can no longer be helped by a relationship which would have been "good enough" in the first place; they need a much better one than that; as with the child who requires residential treatment as maladjusted, they now need a parental figure who will be more understanding, less demanding, and infinitely more patient than the majority of parents are, once earliest infancy is over. It is by this kind of relationship, I believe, that Family Service Unit workers break into the vicious circle by which such clients provoke those whom they meet to respond in ways which confirm their pessimistic expectations, and prove to them that other kinds of relationship are possible. To quote myself again: "The basic element in casework consists in enabling the client to experience with the worker a kind of relationship which is new and helpful for him" (Irvine, 1956).

Philp (1963) also shows that I did not make myself clear in 1954. While admitting that the concept of emotional immaturity has a certain usefulness, he adds: "When one wished to help one of these parents, however, it seemed important to try to understand what feelings were dominant in the particular instance and how they were dealt with, how the client saw himself and other people, what he was trying to achieve and avoid by this behaviour". The "however" suggests some opposition between this view and my own, which I do not think exists; whatever the level of maturity of one's client one could not help him without understanding the motivation and dynamics of his behaviour. But one is more likely to understand the quality of his feelings if one has correctly assessed his stage of emotional development.

Philp has given certain warnings of the dangers of over-stressing immaturity, lest by mentally labelling people as immature we may fail to expect enough from them. There is a real and subtle danger of doing this, so the warning is useful; nevertheless, I think there is a crude and more common danger of expecting too much of them, of demanding that they should "be their age", and becoming impatient when they fail to do so.

If we compare some of these uncontrolled impulsive adults to children, we have to remember that one of the important things about children is that, unlike Peter Pan, they grow up. If we regard these people as having failed to grow up, as still having many of the feelings, the attitudes, and even the needs of young children, this should not (though no doubt it sometimes does) cause us to assume that they *cannot* grow up. It should not make us lose interest in helping them to do so. But it remains important to recognise "where the client is" as a starting-point, and helpful to do so in relation to the stages of early development. It also helps us to be consistent in our response at any one period of time. For instance, a worker whom I was supervising once told me of a situation in which a wife, Mrs. E, had committed some hire purchase offences, for which Mr. E was going to be charged, and was likely to be sent to prison. During the course of a visit, Mrs. E became very upset at the thought that while Mr. E was in prison her own father, who lived with them, would still be there, and still enjoying all his "home comforts". She began to complain of her father and to accuse him of all sorts of things; and when he raised his voice from an adjoining room in self-defence, she flew at him and tried to strangle him. I asked the worker: "What did you do?" and she replied: "I pulled her away and sat down on the sofa with her, and sort of cuddled her". It seemed to me that it was probably most appropriate for her to have treated Mrs. E as one would treat a small child who had lost control of herself in a quarrel. Later on, when Mr. E had to go to court, Mrs. E asked the worker to attend with her but the worker refused, promising instead to visit shortly. Now this might be very supportive and encouraging to some clients, who are sufficiently mature to endure unsupported a court hearing about a matter of which they feel guilty; but it seemed to me that if Mrs. E were as infantile as the worker's previous behaviour had implied, then she really needed someone to go to court with her and "hold her hand", either literally or metaphorically, just as one would for a pre-school child who had to encounter such a frightening situation.

One decision in which we can be guided by an assessment in terms of "emotional age" is that about how often to visit. We know that the young child's sense of time is different from ours; for him 24 hours is a long, long time — in fact, it is probably for ever! (Old people in their second childhood often regress to a similar standpoint, and feel that a week's absence is months and months.) We know how the child who does not see the object of his dependence for a "long, long time" feels rejected and punished. All this applies equally to immature adults, in proportion to their immaturity.

This is well illustrated by Reiner and Kaufman (1959). "In the early stages of our contact with the B family, Mrs. B could sometimes be seen sitting with her dogs in the park near the clinic at the time when she had an appointment with the worker. Once her son, Donald, telephoned and left word for Judy, the little girl who was in treatment, to meet her in the park; at other times Judy mentioned the arrangement. That is, Mrs. B stayed away from the clinic but made sure, through her children, that the worker would know where she was. The caseworker understood Mrs. Bs fear of rejection, and decided to go and join her in the park. We may note that in such cases the caseworker has to deal with his own fear of rejection. She also decided that a week's interval was too long for Mrs. B. After a few months of contact, she said: 'I am going to suggest something that may sound funny to you. Since you can't get here once a week, I am going to ask you to come twice.' Mrs. B replied: 'That doesn't sound funny to me. I always feel better for a few days after I've been here. I might be able to get myself here during that time'." She didn't actually keep two appointments a week, but she did attend a good deal more often.

This brings us to the question of communication. We have to remember that everything we do or do not do communicates to the client some attitude, and may also become the focus for a great deal of fantasy. In fact, we have to remember that the clients are studying us and interpreting our behaviour quite as carefully as we study them. It might perhaps have been possible to deal with Mrs. B's fear of rejection by words alone, but I think the simplest way for the worker to show that she had understood her need and to reassure her against her fear was the act of offering the extra session, which demonstrated the worker's concern and willingness to meet the need. We can also look at this as a way of giving. Many workers in the field report how necessary they find it to give to these clients, especially in the early stages of the relationship. Sometimes this giving is the literal giving of concrete objects, but the instance of Mrs. B shows that we can also give in a more abstract way — the gift of our time, our attention, can be really felt as a gift.

I will now quote from a client of my own who would certainly not have been considered a typical problem family mother, because she was good at running the home and she was good at managing money; but she was immature in many ways, and she was rather hard to like at first, though I eventually got very fond of her. One of the things she wasn't good at was getting the housekeeping money out of her husband. Mrs. D had divorced the father of her two sons, and during the time when I was working with her she married a man who had been a lodger in her house. Week after week she came to me boiling with fury against one or other of the three masculine creatures with whom she was surrounded. Sometimes it was her husband who was mean, who spent so much money on his hobbies that he had little left for her. Sometimes it was the eldest boy, who had a way of stealing whenever he was upset about anything. There was always somebody about whom she felt so angry that she was sure the only solution was to kill them, and she would sit in my room shouting at me so loudly that sometimes the secretary across the passage wondered if she ought to intervene and protect me. It occurred to me after some time that an hour a week wasn't enough for this lady, so I asked her if she would like to have two. She asked: "Did you mean two separate hours?" I replied: "Yes I did, but what did you have in mind? Did you feel you would like them both together?" She preferred this plan, because it would save her both the time and expense of travelling twice from her home to the clinic. I agreed, and for some months I did see her for two hours at a time. Certainly these sessions were much more useful, because at about the end of the first hour she had blown off her steam, and was able to relax a bit and let me get a few words in edgeways. I also realised that this was meeting her need on quite a different level, because she was a person for whom nothing was of any value if she had to ask for it. The only things she could value had to be just what she wanted at the moment and they had to be offered spontaneously, because the giver was aware of her need without being asked. The various attempts by her husband and sons to please her never really managed to comply with all these criteria. But here, for once, I had given her something which corresponded exactly to her need, and had offered it without being asked. Some time later I was getting busy and I thought that she might be ready to go back to one hour a week; I discussed this with her and she agreed. It was then that I discovered another meaning that this extra hour had held for her, of which I had not been aware until that moment. She turned up for her next session saying: "I can't think why I'm so hungry all the time"; this helped me to realise that the gift of the extra hour had been experienced as a feeding situation, so that the withdrawal had the significance of weaning. Returning for a moment to Mrs. B, the lady who sat in the park with her dogs, I think it was very important there too that the worker was able to pick up her non-verbal signals, and thus to offer what was needed without being asked. Many clients are very demanding, and more or less force the worker to make one concession after another. In fact, they are forcing him to act the part of a grudging parent, who gives to the child only reluctantly in response to whining and pestering. This kind of giving does not satisfy, and does not relieve the client's insecurity any more than it relieves a child's. It tends to arouse both guilt and hostility; the hostility because the pestering is necessary, the guilt because the gifts were not really gifts at all, but the result of extortion and blackmail.

There is a very useful saying: "Deeds speak louder than words". This I think is true in all relationships, but particularly with the very young and the very immature. They themselves tend to express their feelings in action rather than talk; indeed, much of their speech can be regarded as a kind of action rather than as communication proper. Curses and accusations are often used as blows or missiles.

In one of the few problem families I have worked with, the most unlikely accusations of infidelity were flung around. The father of this family was practically blind, and very neglected and unkempt in appearance; the mother equally unattractive. It occurred to me one day to ask them if they really believed their mutual accusations of infidelity, and it was quite clear that they didn't: "but if he says that to me I've got to say something back", so each of them in turn invented some hurtful accusation. People who often use words to deceive rather than to inform have little reason to believe the words of others, so the social worker may have to help in very concrete ways before they will trust her. We have to approach the problem of material aid in terms of what it will mean to each individual. Will it help this particular client to trust the worker better, or will it confirm his fantasies of helplessness and inevitable dependence? Will it represent a successful exploitation of the worker, making the client feel both powerful and guilty? Will it perhaps humiliate him? The Pacifist Service Units used to place tremendous emphasis on cleaning and decorating the home and supplying essential basic equipment. Later the service became much more differentiated and discriminating on the basis of more diagnostic thinking. Various authors have emphasised that problem families do have genuine and serious economic difficulties — in fact, that only a genius of thrifty personality could make both ends meet in the situation in which some of them find themselves. Eastman (1959) gives an account of work with a number of such families in which minor financial assistance was an essential component. I would suppose that help of this practical kind would be frequently required, but I am sure it cannot be effective except as an integral part of a total casework process, that it has to be given in full cognisance of what this means in relationship terms. We have often said that in giving financial aid we must take into account what it means to the client; I think we should add that it is equally important to be aware of what it means to the worker, and that these two things are closely connected. The client will know whether the worker is giving grudgingly out of weakness or generously out of kindness. For instance, we know of families who sell or pawn or give away the clothes and bedding which social workers give them; whose children play with the rag doll mother made for them, but not with the much better toys donated by the kind ladies of some charitable organisations. I think the clue is to be found in the behaviour of young children in hospitals or homes, who often interpret the separation as rejection by their parents, and quickly lose or destroy the costly toys these parents bring them when visiting. The children seem to regard these gifts as poor substitutes for the affection which (rightly or wrongly) they believe has failed them; or perhaps, more simply, they take out on the gifts the angry feelings they have towards the givers. Similarly, I think clients destroy or neglect gifts which they feel were not given with love, or gifts which are felt to have invisible strings attached to them.

Of course, the phrase "rightly or wrongly" is the crux of the matter. Some parents do reject their children; and some social workers do find it hard to like, and hard not to reject, the kind of client we are discussing. Sometimes we do give with disapproval rather than with concern and understanding, however much we try to conceal the disapproval. Some of us do give with strings attached, in terms of some implicit bargain that if we do this for them they will do something for us, make some kind of effort. Sometimes when we give, we are giving *in* out of weakness, giving more than we intended because of the client's pressure, and because of our own reluctance to say "no". In this case we usually have some feeling of resentment towards the client. It is also possible to give with a hint of self-righteousness. This I think is why, although many of the families referred to the Family Services Unit have already received quite large amounts in cash or in kind from a number of different agencies, none of these gifts have helped in any way, because they were not given in the right spirit. Whereas with some less touchy, less prickly clients one can get by with controlling such feeling in oneself, with these families this is usually not possible because, I think, they have the sensitiveness to non-verbal cues which you also find in the very young child. In order to help these families, we have not only to try and control these feelings in ourselves, we really have to succeed in doing so, at any rate in the early stages of the relationship. At later stages a slip which reveals to the client that one really is feeling annoyed or disappointed is less of a disaster, provided that one is prepared to admit that the client is right in sensing this. I would emphasise that although we have to try and deal with these feelings in ourselves in order to help these clients, it is natural to have them, just as it was for all the social services which have tried to help them without success. It is natural to feel this way towards a type of client who can be so very exasperating, and to work with them requires either a rare quality of natural insight and sympathy or an extremely good training, which helps us to build up the right kind of attitude as second nature. Those who criticise from outside the unfortunate attitudes which some social workers fall into when dealing with these families should try working with them and honestly study how they themselves respond to the broken promises, the plausible excuses and even the accusations and abuse.

References

Eastman, R.T.H. (1959) Preventive Work in Children's Departments, *Case Conference* VI, 4 and 5.

Irvine, E.E. (1954) Research into Problem Families — Theoretical. Questions arising from Dr. Blacker's Investigations, *British Journal of Psychiatric Social Work,* IX.

Irvine, E.E. (1956) Transference and Reality in the Casework Relationship, *British Journal of Psychiatric Social Work,* III, 4.

Leonard, P. (1967) *Sociology in Social Work,* Routledge & Kegan Paul.

Philp, F. (1963) *Family Failure,* Faber.

Reiner & Kaufman (1959) *Character Disorders in Parents of Delinquents,* Family Service Association of America, New York.

Wofinden, R.C. (1944) Problem Families *Eugenics Review,* 38, 127.

Women's Group on Public Welfare (1943), *Our Towns: A Close-up,* O.U.P.

(i)   Group Work with the Inarticulate
by Lorna Walker

This is an account of group work in a Family Service Unit with
mothers who were at the same time receiving traditional family
casework support.

The decision to experiment with group methods was made as a
result of a growing feeling amongst Unit workers that casework alone
did not meet the needs of the very isolated, housebound mothers on
our case-loads. It was felt that if these deprived and usually immature
women were to be able to function more adequately in the community
they would need social experience and the opportunity to test
themselves against their peers. Because of their muddled lives, low
standards of hygiene, inarticulateness and lack of control they were
unacceptable to any of the existing social groups in the community.

"Problem families" have been described as "families who arouse
strong hostility and condemnation in neighbours and authorities
alike".[1] In her book *Working with Groups*[2] Josephine Klein refers to
the socially ignorant who do not know the "proper" way to behave or
are unable to behave in conformity with the expectations of others and
will express themselves "inappropriately". She suggests that "social
ignorance can only be mended with experience or by teaching. If
therefore an individual is isolated from social life, he becomes
progressively more ignorant, behaves more inappropriately, is again
rejected, and loses touch still further because of his ignorance of social
realities. Social ignorance thus creates social hunger. This is a very real
hunger, for the individual's assurance of his worth depends on group-
membership."

However, the material which follows suggests that in the F.S.U.

Mothers' Group something more complicated than ignorance was involved. On the one hand, in the early meetings members were visibly on their best behaviour, and only later, one by one, revealed aspects of their behaviour of which they were clearly ashamed, and of which other group members were critical. Shared norms identical with those of the rest of the community were clearly involved here. On the other hand those members who had some simple domestic skill carefully concealed this till after 20 meetings had elapsed instead of parading it as might have been expected, thus appearing more incompetent than they actually were. The motivation of this is not clear, but could be seen as consistent with deep-rooted feelings of worthlessness. The "good behaviour" of the early meetings was a façade, while genuine skills could only have been presented by individuals possessing at least some ability to value themselves.

Klein explains the origins of the need for group membership as follows: "The expectation of satisfactions from group membership derives to a large extent from the primacy of the family in the individual's experience. By being born into a family, he is shaped so as to seek out others for the satisfaction of his needs in many ways. Before he is aware of himself as a self-conscious being, while he is yet entirely dependent on others for the satisfaction of his material wants, he and others already depend on one another for the satisfaction of social and emotional needs. This need for interdependence will remain with him for the rest of his life: he will need to live his life in the context of small groups of others."

Family Service Unit clients have frequently had unsatisfactory experience of family life. Approval has been minimal, rivalry and jealousy intense, and they have grown up to feel unvalued, or even lacking a sense of identity. It seemed that any agency attempting to help such people must include opportunities for group experience in addition to individual casework.

It was decided to approach women in the age group 25-35, who had the largest families and the most problems. Only the seriously psychotic were ruled out.

Five women were keen to join the group, and four more were admitted after the 7th meeting. No pressure was put on anyone to join. The group was offered as an opportunity for mothers to get away from their homes and children for one afternoon a week and to meet other women faced with similar problems. The pre-school children were to be cared for in a separate room by volunteer helpers. Tea and biscuits would be provided and the meetings were presented as opportunities for social activity, which would be unstructured to begin with, but which could be developed in any way the mothers chose. We hoped it would be an enjoyable break in the week. The leader (myself) would be one of the caseworkers whom they already knew by sight. (I was also involved in a normal casework relationship with two members, Marion and Violet, and their families.) They had all visited the Unit house on several occasions, so the only strange factors would be themselves *vis-à-vis* each other, though even here there were some previous encounters — (Meg and Jessie had met in maternity hospital, Jessie and Pam were neighbours).

This was the original group as described by individual caseworkers:

MARION — aged 29. Cohabited 9 years with Pakistani aged 50+. Has 4 children aged between 9 and 3. Round-faced, overweight, long straight black hair, usually tied in a ponytail, making her look much younger than she is. Behaves immaturely, afraid to tackle problems, soon overwhelmed and relapses into inactive depressed state. Has difficulty in controlling children.
Religion — Mrs. — Protestant/Mr. — Muslim.
On contraceptive pill.

MEG — aged 28, a Londoner. Married to West Indian, 7 children aged between 11 years and 18 months. Strong feelings of worthlessness which become overwhelming, driving her into depression. Subject to mood swings. Is small, thin, with soft fair hair which usually looks ragged and untidy. Has difficulty in controlling children.
Religion — Mrs. — Protestant/Mr. — Roman Catholic.

JUNE — aged 33. Married, 3 children aged 7 to 3 years. Tall, dark, thin, haggard-looking. Suffered slight cerebral haemorrhage after birth of last child, which has left her with little use in her right hand. Has difficulty in controlling children.
Religion — Mrs. — Protestant/Mr. — Roman Catholic.

BRENDA — aged 26. Married, 5 children aged between 6 and 2 years. Short, rather stocky, lank hair, usually dirty. Looks and behaves like a teenager. Very lively. Incompetent at financial and home management, control of children and elementary hygiene.
Religion — Both Protestant.
Sterilised.

PAM — aged 26. Married, 6 children between 7 years and 3 months. Average height, very overweight, gives impression of being cheerful and easy-going. Incompetent at managing money and children, but reasonably competent housewife. A manipulator, unable to make stable friendships.
No contraception.

JESSIE — aged 28. (Joined at 8th meeting). Married to West Indian, 6 children aged 6 years to 5 months. Dumpy, overweight, suffers from bronchitis. Subject to violent mood-swings. When depressed everything goes, when elated is very lively and humorous. Difficulty in controlling children.
Religion — Mrs. — Protestant/Mr. — Roman Catholic.
No contraception.

LINDA — aged 28. (Joined at 8th meeting). Married, 4 children aged between 9 and 4 years. Short, stocky, round-faced with bleached hair usually tied in ponytail. Immature, sees herself as incompetent, especially regarding money, but hides behind cheerful voluble manner. Suffers from indigestion and constipation. Difficulty in controlling children.
Religion — Both Protestant.
Uses cap method of contraception.

VIOLET — aged 29. (Joined at 9th meeting). Married, 3 children aged 3 to 1 year. Short, overweight, round florid face crowned with red crinkly hair. Behaves like borderline sub-normal, slow in speech, thought and movement. Housework suffers from her slowness rather

than incompetence. Low standards of hygiene. Control of children likely to be problem, already difficulties with eldest.
Religion — Mrs. — Protestant/Mr. — Roman Catholic.
No contraception.

DORIS — aged 28. (First seen at 9th meeting). Small, dark, timid. Low intelligence. Separated from husband, has 5 children aged between 8 to 1 year, by different fathers. Needs constant support to maintain even a low standard of home and child care. Did not become a regular member of the group.
Sterilised.

Deprivation and immaturity were the common characteristics of the mothers who had been selected. The burdens they had had to carry, of ill health, poverty, marital difficulties, might well have brought down women with far stronger natural resources; but these women without exception had been exposed during childhood to undermining experiences such as illness, rejection, institutional care, death of parent, or large poverty-stricken families. Their exposure to the educational system had been minimal and unpleasant, and none of them could easily write a complete sentence. Meg reads women's magazines, and they all occasionally read the local evening paper, but with little comprehension.

Establishing Elementary Social Control

The group began in October, 1965, meeting weekly except during school holidays, which meant that it was possible to have 36 meetings a year. At first the women were shy; they spent the first five meetings getting to know one another, and kept to safe subjects like housing and having babies. Reference to themselves and their children was in unreal idealistic terms; marital difficulties were spoken of in a jocular manner. Once the shyness had worn off they were keen to talk but reluctant to listen, and the resulting babble echoed their family life, everybody making constant demands which nobody was able to meet.
They were like siblings competing for the attention of mother, as represented by myself. This was particularly noticeable in Marion's case, probably because I was also "her" worker. They all had to learn

to share me, but it was harder for her. It took 20 meetings before they showed signs of attempting to listen helpfully to what others were trying to communicate, and it was not until the 35th meeting* that they at last became aware of this. I had been absent the previous week and had suggested as an experiment that they should meet without a leader. It proved a frustrating experience, and they told me the following week how "boring" it had been. I waited until they were all talking at once, then stopped them and said: "I think I know why you were bored last week. You came here bursting with anxiety and things you wanted to talk about, and none of you were prepared to listen. I think you were bored because there was no-one to listen to you." There was a moment's startled silence, then they burst out laughing and Meg turned to Marion saying, "I was listening to you, cock!" After this they made conscious efforts to improve, and the babble would suddenly be interrupted by one of them shouting. "Who's talking to who?"

Providing Primary Experience

I began to realise that my role in a group of such immature women would be that of mother providing the experience of a secure, caring relationship. Irvine (1954)[1] has suggested that the methods of the nursery school teacher might well be used in casework with very immature families.

My group members all lacked good mothering; there was rivalry for my attention, and in the early meetings I could only deal with this by looking fixedly at one member and ignoring the others. I also had to decide when that particular member had made her point and transfer my attention to another.

Like children they needed to be accepted. I have said that they began by showing themselves in unrealistic ideal terms. Gradually they began to test me out. In M.5 Meg was regretting her inability to cut down on smoking when she knew the money was needed for other things. June admitted to the same difficulty. I was uncritical, and

---

*Meetings will subsequently be referred to by the initial M, and the number of the meeting, e.g. M.35.

when Meg remarked sadly that a cheap home perm hadn't taken I became a comforter, and told her that her hair was an attractive colour and very shiny. A week or two later I combed her hair, to show her and the group that even without expert cutting hair could be made to look attractive. Meg almost purred with delight as I did this, revealing that this had been an emotional experience as well as an educational one.

Each week I made the tea and handed round the biscuits. No attempt was made by members to help, and I did not ask for help, as they obviously enjoyed the experience. Not until after M.25, when members had improved their general appearance and were revealing and developing practical skills, did they begin to share in the tea-making and washing-up.

I realise now, though I was not aware of it at the time, that I was filling in gaps in my members' childhood experience. Only by regressing and allowing me to close some of these gaps were they able to feel secure enough in the group to expose themselves, and eventually to progress towards maturity and an improved ability to care for their own children. My caring for and involvement with them were most important.

Revealing the Negative Identity

At M.5 Marion exposed herself dramatically by telling us about her latest suicide attempt the previous week. This provoked group criticism. The group challenged her right to attempt suicide. "Don't you think about what would happen to your children if you succeeded?" and questioned her feelings and motives. Both Brenda and Meg showed shocked incredulity, then Brenda recalled finding her mother with her head in the gas oven and the shock it had caused to the family, even though the mother recovered. The group became quiet and thoughtful for the first time.

Marion had felt it safe to confess and to risk unfavourable group reaction. She was able to talk in subsequent meetings about her deepest feelings connected with childhood rejection, although she had been unable to do this in a one-to-one casework relationship.

By M.8 Meg was prepared to risk exposing the "bad side" of

herself. She described herself as a woman who let her appearance go, as a housewife who hated and neglected housework, and as a mother with an uncontrollable temper who hurt her children.

She also talked about her fears of illness and childbirth. It was all said with an air of bravado, interspersed with much swearing and high-pitched laughter. The group were unsure how to react to this, and took the lead from me. I said we all had our "bad" sides, and that it could be reassuring for children to realise their mothers could get angry. Children often felt angry. Marion in particular tried to be reassuring, as if having been accepted she could now identify with me and give acceptance.

The following week, M.9, Meg arrived dressed in a bright newish skirt and with her hair washed and curled. I drew attention to her improved appearance and the others joined in with admiring comments. Meg was more relaxed and confident. When I suggested sending a get-well card to Jessie in hospital they all readily agreed, either through identification or compliance with me. (Further reference to the need to identify with a leader will be made later, but for a fuller statement on the subject of providing primary experience read Dockar-Drysdale, *Therapy in Child Care.*[3]

Part of my plan for making the members feel accepted and nurtured was to initiate a visit to the film "My Fair Lady", to be paid for by the Unit as a New Year's treat. We discussed this plan at M.9 and they were delighted, but almost incredulous that the treat was to be free. I remarked that the Committee had wondered if they would feel able to pay 2d. or 3d. for their weekly fee, and there was unanimous agreement that 3d. a week was reasonable. I felt that this readiness to give — to the Unit, to another member — was a result of the nurturing they had been receiving, and was in marked contrast to the self-centred "sibling rivalry" of the first few meetings.

As with children, encouragement and reassurance produced better results than criticism (though in due course criticism of each other would become effective). I was continually looking for members' strengths and examples of "good" child management, praising their efforts to improve their personal appearance. At the same time I encouraged them to look on the bright side as well as the black side of their lives, reminding them of their husbands' good points when they were dwelling on their faults, helping them to recall pleasant experiences to counterbalance the unpleasant.

At first I was not altogether conscious of the role I was playing. My handling of the group dynamics was on the intuitive level, and it was vital to keep a weekly record of what actually happened so that the group dynamics could be looked at and analysed later. As with individual casework, one's initial approach is tentative and one hesitates and loses opportunities. It was a learning experience for me, and I have now learned to pick up a member's half-revealed anxiety and draw out group reflection and comment.

By M.16 I was reproving Brenda very sharply for her unkind remarks about "niggers" and "wogs". She well knew that three of the members were married to coloured men, but either lacked sensitivity or was reacting to the general group disapproval of her. She took the reproof as a child would from her mother, looking shamefaced, and subsided. When Brenda was out of the room I urged the three injured parties to stand up for themselves, but it was not until M.49 that they were able to tackle Brenda on this issue, and even then only obliquely (see Brenda's case history).

Violet needed nurturing and controlling. She was slow in speech and movement, lacking in intelligence and completely self-centred. She had an irritating way of repeating herself over and over again. She craved friendship and tried to buy it, for example by producing Dinnefords for Meg's crying baby, but ruined her efforts because of her inability to listen and her interminable monologues. I have described my work with Violet in her case history. She represented a challenge for me because the group used her as a scapegoat. A group of individuals with so many handicaps, and so much feeling of inferiority, is almost bound to use its weakest member in this way. They were all self-centred, they all talked too much, they saw themselves as less intelligent and competent than most people they met. They all had difficulty in being ready on time, and in feeding their children adequately. Vi being the weakest member suffered from their projected dislike of these attributes in themselves. I had to persevere to get them to recognise that they could use their intellectual superiority to help Vi instead of cold-shouldering her. In this way they learned to recognise their own relative advantages and to have compassion for someone less well endowed.

Brenda was also scapegoated. She expressed prejudices and a hostile attitude to authority which were present in all of them. Her difficulty in separating from her children was also a common one. By adopting a firm but sympathetic attitude, and by my disapproval of intolerant attitudes, I helped members to identify with me and thus modified their hostility towards Brenda.

In the beginning group members had few expectations beyond the provision of a room in which they could relax and escape from their home and children for two hours. Indulging in fantasy about their lives was another means of escape. They did not expect to have to take any decisions or to be allowed to do so, and were quite surprised when I consulted them at M.19 (Easter, 1966) about accepting new members. Their attitude towards the Unit, and towards the leader as "mother figure", was wholly dependent. They saw the group as something provided by the Unit for them, but after the outing to "My Fair Lady" I sensed the emergence of "us".

From then onwards the group became increasingly a group in its own right. During the August 1966 school holidays (following M.30) Marion, Jessie, Pam and Meg managed to visit each other, and thus provide a few group family outings for themselves. This entailed bus journeys and getting several children ready. I felt it showed their growing self-confidence, and the wish to break away from their old pattern of isolation.

At the end of a year's meetings (M.36) Meg suggested without any prompting that they should collect for a present for June in hospital, and then decided with Marion to visit June. Meg was entrusted with the money for the present. Thus in a year we had arrived at group decision-making, some ability for organisation, trust in each other and altruistic feelings.

Developing Skills

Few members had skills in housewifery, sewing, knitting or cooking, and those who did possess such competence — Meg in knitting and dressmaking, Brenda and Pam in cooking — concealed them.

When the group first began, I had suggested sewing or knitting as possible group activities. This had met with no response except from Meg, who sometimes brought knitting but actually did very little. However, Pam brought knitting after a few weeks, and when Vi joined the group she brought knitting too. I have described Violet's progress in her case history. I suspected that her perseverance stirred up resentment among the others and contributed to their hostility. By M.19 Brenda seemed to be wanting to improve her self-image, and I will describe later how she asked for help with menus and cooking. At this meeting the group expressed concern that Doris seemed unable to continue to attend. I reminded them of their first weeks in the group, and they recalled that they had once been as shy and isolated and incompetent as Doris. This was a significant point, at which they realised the progress they had made. From this time on they showed a growing drive to acquire skills. We went at their pace. Brenda asked for recipes; I wrote some out for her. Linda wanted to diet to lose weight; I told her about vitamins, proteins and starch, and suggested menus for balanced meals containing less starch and fat than Linda normally took. She lost 8 lb in six weeks. Linda at M.23 brought a coat to shorten. I showed her how, and she did the job. The next week she boasted that her husband wouldn't believe she had done it; she had shortened a dress at home to prove it. Brenda began buying dresses at jumble sales and bringing them to the group to alter — often with Pam's help. Pam, who confessed to being lazy, could not allow herself to be outdone, and brought a home-made cake to make a tea-party to celebrate her birthday.

Along with developing confidence in these newly-acquired or newly-revealed skills came developing concern for each other. Meg eventually allowed the group to discover that she had considerable skill at simple dressmaking, which she had not previously revealed. At this point (M.25) she offered to make dresses for Pam's children out of spare material or old dresses, charging 2s. 6d. for the labour. The group were generous in their admiration, and asked her to make dresses for the children of Vi, Brenda and Marion. Brenda and Vi also exchanged dresses which did not fit, and altered the hems during M.27. Marion (M.28) sewed buttons on to a coat for one of June's children (June was handicapped by a partly paralysed right arm).

My role, once the momentum was gained, was to act as enthusiast, adviser and teacher, but always at the group's pace. If someone merely felt like relaxing or talking I did not press. I encouraged members to notice each other and to praise achievement. These developing skills improved the members' self-images, contributed to the development of mutual concern and also lessened the need for scapegoating.

General Aim of the Group

The caseworkers saw the aim of the group as helping the members to function more adequately and happily in the community. The members were reluctant to see it as anything other than an escape. Every time I introduced a new member I asked the older ones to explain what we did, and the result ran like this: Meg: "We come to have a natter and get away from the kids for an hour". I remarked that their "nattering" often took the form of discussing their anxieties, e.g. houses, money and children, and wondered if they felt better for talking about them.

Meg: "No, we just like talking."

Marion: "It's the company we like."

I said I understood how isolated they must feel at times, and wondered if they found it a help meeting people with similar problems. Meg and Marion nodded without enthusiasm.

Not until M.65 (second Winter session) was Jessie able to say "I think ours is the best group, where we all have the same kind of troubles. We understand what each other is up against. We all get depressed and ill, and the children get too much for us, and we are all hard up and it helps to talk about things to each other. It doesn't seem so bad when you can share your troubles".

In her way she was saying what Somers[4] says — "As we try to change our old ways we are familiar with the need for strong identification with one or more persons who have what we are attempting to learn, the need for peers to help us copes with the new, to reassure us in certain ways, to support us as we change". I have already commented on the ways in which members at first identified with me. Now they were also identifying with each other.

If they were to become competent and acceptable members of the community there had to be a change, and change is usually painful.

"Since change always produces some stress, current disorder, uncertainties about the future, and fantasies about losses incurred, it is necessary for individuals to have meaningful interpersonal nurture and emotional support during the process of changing, and until equilibrium is again established, if change is to be successfully achieved and maintained" (Somers)[4].

Each member needed to learn to re-evaluate herself in a more realistic way. A group can help a maladjusted member by listening, clarifying, reassuring, comparing (Klein)[2].

It was remarkable that Marion was able to talk in the group about her deepest feelings connected with childhood rejection, whereas she had previously been unable to do this in a one-to-one casework relationship. By comparing her marital situation with that of others in the group she discovered that others were facing similar difficulties. Then she realised that her husband could be compared favourably with other husbands, and could therefore be given some sympathy. Finally, she learned that running away from problems did not solve them. With group support she began to resist the urge to flight and gradually learned to revalue herself and to defend herself against husband, neighbours and officials whenever she felt they were behaving unjustly. This was especially noticeable when the main sewer was blocked just outside her flat. The group encouraged her to persist with her complaints to the Housing and Health Departments, even finally to the point of threatening to write to the local newspaper (M.39).

My role in this kind of supportive group behaviour was that of final arbiter and supporter. Individuals would look questioningly at me to see if I was in agreement. I always did try to avoid giving my opinion until everyone who wanted had had their say, because I knew that my opinion carried more weight than that of any other individual. My opinions were not always acted upon; nevertheless, I was very conscious that the group were looking to me to set standards, as representative of society in general. They were wanting to learn how to conform and earn society's approval. "It is in the small group that the individual and society confront each other at close range for better or for worse in their inter-relatedness'' Somers[4].

The climax for this group was reached in July 1967, when the group solidly supported Meg during a period of marital difficulty, complicated by her advanced pregnancy and conflict about sterilisation.

"M.61 (4th July 1967): I was not in the group for the first half-hour, and when I joined them I found a heated discussion in progress about husbands. Marion had explained about her difficulties the previous week, and Meg had burst out with her feelings about her husband, and not being cared for. This was a group reaction, and one could sense a tremendous concern for Meg. The general opinion seemed to be that Meg was allowing herself to be bullied; it was interesting to hear these women, who two years ago had undervalued themselves and lacked self-confidence, holding the floor in turn and saying how they were coping with different marital problems. They no longer talked chaotically. They listened to each in turn and were able to question and comment. They were really discussing themselves as individuals entitled to some consideration at home and what they should do about selfish and violent husbands. They were concerned particularly with Meg's distress, and searching for ways in which she could change her situation. They felt that it was not right that she should be bullied and browbeaten. The discussion was brought to a lull by Meg's dissolving into tears, and it was obvious I think to everyone that her difficulties would not be easily resolved, because her husband appeared to be a man with very little ability to feel for other people. Jessie got up and sat by Meg in a comforting gesture, but nobody tried to stop her from crying, and I felt for the first time since the group began that Meg had been able to reveal her despair.''

Meg had probably resisted change more than anyone. Initially her contributions to the group had been flippant; then she had tested-out, describing herself as a foul-mouthed, violent-tempered mother, frigid wife, slovely housewife. When she found the group did not accept this picture of her (and I took part in this, by describing her good qualities) she allowed herself to be seen as a softer, kinder, more competent person. She was presenting her skill in dressmaking by M.25 and it was she who at M.36 suggested visiting June in hospital. She talked a good deal about her phobias concerned with darkness, illness (every pain was thought to be cancer), and riding on 'buses.

The group tried, with some success, to encourage her to fight these phobias, and without group support I doubt if Meg would have faced sterilisation. However, fighting her phobias necessitated facing her real fears — that nobody loved her and that she was not worth loving. The group's solid identification with her when she broke down demonstrated that at least some people thought she was worth loving.

M.61 was a serious discussion of the marital relationship, however biased, with ego development showing in awareness of members' rights as human beings. All shared their experiences, and at least one, Brenda, was able to attempt to describe how she and her husband had resolved their difficulties. She was not very clear as to how they had overcome these, but talking it out with her husband had been part of it, as well as her improvement as a housewife. But it struck an optimistic note against the depressed and aggressive solutions being advanced by the others.

Caseworkers reported that in the cars on the way back to their homes all the members were commenting on the afternoon's discussion. I felt considerable anxiety as to possible repercussions in their domestic lives, now that these women were becoming aware of themselves as worthwhile individuals. Obviously this would make its first impact in the only area in which they had any existence at the time, i.e. their homes and marriages. I wondered how individual workers would be able to cope with this, and sure enough, during the same week, caseworkers were reporting marital crises in their families. The general conclusion in the Unit, however, was that as ego development had been consciously aimed at, then somehow the results of this must be coped with in the individual casework as well as in the group. (It was merely a coincidence that the group meeting took place on the 4th of July.)

The following week the members switched their paranoid feelings from husbands to neighbours — much safer! Later they began to find ways of gaining satisfaction and forming social relationships outside the group. Marion began part-time cleaning at a church, and gradually became involved with its social activities. A continuing growth in self-assurance was noticeable in Meg, Pam, Brenda and

Linda. As they became happier and more competent at home their need for the group became less, and their attendances dropped off. By May 1968 there were five new members, and it was virtually a new group.

June, Jessie and Violet continued to attend regularly; they still had a long way to go in terms of maturation and self-confidence. Only Jessie showed resentment at the changes, but the departure of the others gave her the opportunity to play a leading role, and thus to take a further step in maturation.

Time and Structure

Time and structure emerged as group requisites. Ruth Smalley[5] states that "the effectiveness of any social work process is furthered by conscious, knowing use of time phases and of structure and form".

The staff took the initial decision that the group should be held from 2.00 to 3.30 p.m. on the same day and time each week, with the exception of school holidays. This was making immediate demands on women whose sense of time was vague or completely lacking (according to Irvine, a trait which is directly connected with emotional immaturity)[1]. To get the numbers there at all in the early days it was necessary to provide transport.

Gradually the group meeting became a focal point for the week, and members made great efforts to be ready on time. Some, like June and Jessie, were months before they were able to attend regularly, because they had difficulty in distinguishing one day from another. Even when they overcame this difficulty there remained the problem of being ready for the transport.

Gradually the meeting itself developed a pattern. The first half-hour would be taken up with friendy chatter, enquiries about absent members, and welcoming returning members. Then more serious subjects would emerge, gradually tailing off as 3.00 p.m. approached and the kettle boiled for tea. Tea was usually the time for jokes and relaxation before taking up their children and the week's burdens again. Within this framework they could all begin to develop ego strengths and practical skills at their own pace, and in the appendix I shall show how this process worked in the case of Vi and Brenda.

There can be no time-limit on a group of this kind, and because the objective is maturation a closed group would be unsuitable. There needs to be flexibility of membership, with new members arriving and old ones leaving, to reveal the process of maturation to the members. A visitor to our group would always be able to pick out the most recent recruit. For a few weeks her unkempt and grubby personal appearance will distinguish her from the other members. She will either talk too much or not at all. Gradually she will modify her appearance and behaviour to conform to the group, or like Doris she will drop out. This does not mean that members lose their individuality; the point has already been made that increased maturation and ego strength results from membership of the group.

The individual casework relationship was continued with each mother who attended the group, though it was found that some needed less frequent home visits. We had originally hoped that group-work would economise on casework resources, but in fact group experiences often provoked fresh crises for the caseworker to tackle (as in M.61). A constant exchange of information between group worker and individual caseworkers was required, and the keeping of records was essential. Any change taking place in the mother had its repercussions on the rest of the family. A serious example of this occurred in Meg's family. For all her increased self-confidence she was unable to resolve her marital difficulties and tried to do so by projecting them on to her eldest son, aged 6. A short return to our group did not help, as members colluded with her fantasies about her "terrible" child.

Meg now needs a group with a therapeutic aim. Her case has confirmed that we were right to limit our group purpose to that of social education, and in the case of a person like Meg I believe the social hunger needs to be dealt with before a therapeutic group can hope to be effective. We have recently received a new member who had already tried a therapeutic group run by a mental health department. Although seriously neurotic, she finds our group helpful because she has much in common with our members, whereas "the women in the mental health group were better educated than me and didn't have money problems like me. They all had a better upbringing and I didn't fit in at all."

Discussion

The role of the leader in a group such as the one I have described is not an easy one, particularly if some group members are also on the leader's own caseload. Tilbury, 1968[7] draws attention to many of the pitfalls faced by social workers involved in social clubs "where the work in the individual relationship is intensive and the feelings aroused strong, it is less likely that they can be separated from the group situation. Rivalry and jealousy may arise, making the whole situation infinitely more complex". However, providing one recognises the complexity the pitfalls can be avoided, and the results are extremely rewarding.

The leader, like the nursery school teacher, must steer rather than command. The members need to feel free to take advantage, or not, of opportunities for growth, and in fact they cannot escape the influence of the changing and maturing group.

Rivalry and jealousy were the first problems and I have described how I dealt with these. It took a year to establish elementary social control.

Group development and individual maturation did not wait for social control to be established. Here were people who as children had lacked good mothering, and they cast me in the role of mother. They made demands, tested me out, used projection, showed hostility by failure to attend, tried to please, "acted out". Some of this I was aware of, but I was also involved in learning what their needs were, and I have described some of the ways in which I developed a secure, caring relationship. The reward was in seeing the members learning to trust and care for each other, and observing a disorganised collection of individuals cohering and giving mutual support and encouragement, as well as developing greater capacities for mothering their own children.

They looked to me to set standards in dress, behaviour and the acquisition of skills, but it would have been impossible to impose these. I used praise, encouragement and their rivalry as constructive elements, enabling them to raise their sights as mothers, members of the group and of the wider community. I have described in detail in the appendix the process of change in two members.

A minimum amount of structure was necessary to enable the group to begin. A comfortable room, a beginning, an ending and a cup of tea were basic. We learned that an optimum number for a group is 8, and because of frequent sickness in large families one needs a roll of 12. Provision had to be made for the under-fives, and by having a play-group we helped mothers and children to face separation anxieties; we discovered that the children later adapted to school with greater ease than their older siblings had.

The success or otherwise of this kind of group depends very largely on the support given to the leader by caseworkers involved with the individual members. Caseworkers need to see how and where the group work complements their work. This is part of the complexity referred to by Tilbury[7], and is only coped with through mutual trust and the sharing of information between group leader and caseworkers.

The Original Group Two Years Later (October 1967)

MARION. Has gained in self-confidence and social poise. Her appearance — slimmer, short hair, neat clothing, brisker movements, reflect these gains. Control of children more effective and consistent. Has taken part-time cleaning work at an office at the church. Has been drawn into membership of the church and attends women's meetings, mixing happily (after initial difference) with women from a range of social backgrounds.

MEG. Less phobic. Has become more aggressive and turns her destructive feelings outwards, particularly towards her husband and eldest son. Occasionally a destructive and disturbing influence in the group, and is often openly critical of other members. However, usually takes the initiative in suggesting new activities or outings for the group. Socially is now ahead of the group and needs one with a therapeutic aim.

JUNE. Has become more active and keeps her home cleaner and tidier. Depressions less acute, but she still undervalues herself. Has little to say at group meetings, but shows interest in the other members and greatly appreciated their concern for her when she was in hospital. Has visited members at their homes.

BRENDA. Great improvement in care of herself, children and home. Socially acceptable in the local community, and accompanies husband to darts matches. Keeping up with the neighbours in providing an incentive to wiser management of her housekeeping money.

PAM. Seems to have been little affected by the group. Her social isolation seems to be due to her personality. She is deceitful and manipulative, and unable to make lasting friendships. Was helpful in the group because she enjoyed helping others, thus demonstrating her superiority in practical skills. She admitted to being lazy. Finally left after quarrelling with Jessie, who was a neighbour.

JESSIE. Has become less self-centred. Depressions less acute. Has made very slow progress socially, and is only just beginning to realise how the group can help her. However, has become strongly attached to Meg and Marion, who have both visited her at home seeking comfort in marital crises. They have helped Jessie to reveal herself as warm-hearted and with a capacity for leadership. She is now beginning to take over Meg's role as initiator.

LINDA. Has used the group as a support following the death of her child. The acquisition of practical skills increased her self-confidence, and she made great efforts to improve her management of the housekeeping money. Persevered with her diet and has become slim and attractive. Began to go out with husband, and her attendances at the group tailed off.

VIOLET. Has become less self-centred. Now listens to what other members say and acts upon criticism. Still isolated in local community, and will need longer period with the group. Home standards have improved but her treatment of her children remains inconsistent and ineffective.

APPENDIX:

Case Histories of Two Members

(1) Brenda

Brenda was not a popular member of the group, but because of her liveliness and fund of witty anecdotes she filled the role of clown and awful child. She could be trusted to put into words sentiments which no one else dared to utter. In the early meetings she would arrive looking dirty and unkempt. She had great difficulty in separating from her two youngest children, and frequently swung between annoyance with herself and them and over-protectiveness towards them. She swore a lot, complained about her husband and generally exposed herself as "bad" mother, unsatisfactory wife and incompetent housewife. Her bawdy jokes and witty comments were an attempt to win admiration, but even in this sphere she overstepped the mark by making flippant and sarcastic remarks about coloured people (3 of our members had unions with coloured men). The group was at first unable to challenge her directly, and resorted to ignoring her and sometimes literally freezing her out by sitting with their backs turned to her.

It was not until the 19th meeting (and Brenda's 11th attendance) that she made her first attempt to present herself in a better light. Other members had been talking about meals and how much they disliked cooking. Brenda said she liked cooking, in fact her last meat and potato pie had been "gorgeous", and she asked if anyone could suggest some alternative recipes. With one exception (Linda) the group looked resentful and left it to me to make suggestions, but Brenda was serious, and the incident marked the beginning of a change in the way she presented herself to others. For six months the group, though covertly hostile, had contained her, and her clowning had gained her a precarious foothold in spite of her unpopularity. In fact it had more than once provided a much-needed antidote to a general feeling of depression. By the 23rd meeting we were succesfully persuading her to separate from her children, and she was asking for help in mending a tear in her coat. She also persuaded the group to talk about food and recipes. She was noticeably cleaner.

At the 24th meeting she was participating in an easy manner, admitted to having lost the recipe I had given her last week, and took the group's good-natured bantering in good part. The following week she brought a dress which needed a zip sewing in the back. She was hoping I would do this for her, but with very little encouragement from me she got down to doing it herself, and was taken in hand by Pam; between them they coped admirably with the zip. Afterwards she proceeded to undo the hem and shorten it. The group were quite impressed with her competence, and she said archly: "Oh, I'm not as daft as you think I am". I hastened to say that I knew she was a good deal more able than she usually showed, adding: "And that goes for all of you, if it comes to that".

The 26th meeting represented a climax in Brenda's development. It was the first meeting after Whitsuntide, and Meg, Marion and Violet were congratulating each other on their neat appearance — clean dresses and cardigans, and hair washed and curled — when the door slowly opened and a voice drawled: "Hello girls". It was Brenda wearing a new blue tailored costume, with her hair dyed dark brown. She was also clean! The contrast to her previous appearances, with patchy ginger hair and slovenly clothes, was so dramatic that everyone gasped and then burst out laughing. She was holding a box containing a chocolate sponge which she placed on the table with a flourish, saying: "It's my birthday tomorrow". There was a chorus of congratulations and Brenda, rather embarrassed, said: "I've hardly been able to keep off opening it all morning". They wanted to know all about her hair and the suit. She said her husband had done her hair; the suit had been given to her, and she had shortened the skirt hem herself. For the remainder of the afternoon Brenda enjoyed her new-found popularity. She acted as hostess at teatime, and this was the beginning of a tradition of celebrating members' birthdays with cakes for tea.

Brenda maintained her improved appearance, and I saw this as a bid for popularity, but her tactless remarks prevented any lasting change in the group's attitude. They were, however, beginning to feel secure enough to criticise each other openly, and Brenda came in for her share. If she came in a pinafore she was told off, but they were still unable to deal with her racialist attitudes except by ignoring her. They now only discussed racial discrimination when she was absent, yet with three members married or cohabiting with coloured men it was a constant source of anxiety.

Brenda continued to develop her cookery skills at home, and would report her progress to the group. Her caseworker reported that her standards of housewifery had improved all round. I had felt all along that Brenda was tactless rather than prejudiced, though her prejudiced remarks could have been an aggressive response to the way in which the group scapegoated her.

One afternoon Jessie burst into a tirade against colour prejudice and described a recent incident in her street. Brenda immediately identified with Jessie and said how shocked she was, adding that her best friend was married to a West Indian, who was a very nice fellow! It had taken 49 meetings over 18 months to reach this point, and may have been as much due to the growing self-confidence of group members, who no longer needed a scapegoat, as to Brenda's own social development.

Following this the group was kinder to Brenda, and she became less flamboyant both in dress and manner. She seemed to have less need to shock, and was able to enjoy herself and her children. During the summer of the second year, when Meg and Marion were having serious marital difficulties, it was Brenda who was able to offer advice and hope, her marriage having emerged into much calmer waters. She was now accepted by the group and participated fully. She had achieved a "respectable" look, and I noted that she would now pass in any group of working-class women. She had in fact become more acceptable in her local neighbourhood, and was going out regularly with her husband or with friends. Consequently her attendances at our group tailed off, and after the second summer break we only saw her twice.

(2) Violet

Violet joined the group at its 9th meeting. I had had reservations about her inclusion because of her low intelligence, and also because she and her family were on my caseload. However, she was desperately in need of social outlets, and it seemed possible that contact with other mothers might do more to improve her very low standards of home-making than I could through a one-to-one contact. Also I hoped it would encourage her to take a greater interest in her personal appearance; this would improve her relations with her husband, who was intensely critical of the way she had "let herself go".

At her first meeting, in January 1966, she got off to a good start; her curly red hair was admired, and she produced a bottle of Dinnefords, which quietened Meg's crying baby. However, she showed little interest in the group conversation and kept trying to buttonhole someone into listening to her monologue. The next week members made critical jokes about her need to rush into the next room when her baby cried and bring it back to nurse. She defended herself, saying she liked nursing babies. She had difficulty in getting herself and three children ready in time, and was nearly always late for the group. She would arrive with bottles and tins of food, saying she hadn't had time to give the children their dinner, and would hopefully expect the voluntary helpers to feed them. This caused resentment among the other members, but they were unable to be openly critical, and would mutter about her during her frequent sorties to look at her children. Also the state of her clothes and the children's caused critical comment.

She often brought knitting to do, and at this time was clearly a beginner — dropping stitches and making other mistakes. However, in her dogged way she saw the group afternoon as providing her with the opportunity to persevere with knitting, and needing help with dropped stitches was an excellent way of getting attention from me. I felt she was also using the knitting as a necessary defence because of her lack of social acceptability. She hid behind it, emerging from time to time to throw a remark to anybody who would catch it. This was quite irritating to the others, who did their best to ignore her. I was often the only one willing to listen and reply, but I had to show her that I was not prepared to turn from listening to someone else, so that she must wait till that person had finished.

After attending 6 meetings and a group visit to the film "My Fair Lady" she got herself a part-time job in a mill, and we didn't see her for 5 weeks. Having found the job too much for her, she returned to our Tuesday group like an "old girl" and was given a friendly reception. Being in the mill had had a good effect; she was less self-centred and showed more interest in the others. She continued to knit.

By M.27, she was wanting to enlarge her skills and joined Brenda in turning up dress hems. She had no idea of simple hemming or slip-stitching but, as with the knitting, she persevered and brought her efforts to show the group. They were grudging with praise, still needing a scapegoat, possibly resenting her persistence and resulting improvement, so they tended to ignore her; this forced her to break into conversation if she was to say anything at all, and then they showed irritation at being interrupted, but were still unable to tackle her directly. I felt it would be inappropriate to force the issue, but expressed my concern to members who complained, explaining that Violet was rather backward and that I was hoping they would try to be tolerant and help her. This had quick results — when Violet's husband was in hospital Marion offered to mind her children while she visited him.

Soon afterwards, (M.32, October 1966) Violet incurred direct criticism in the group. (Perhaps, having helped her, they felt freer to be critical.) She announced that she was pregnant and trying to abort herself with Pennyroyal. Both Marion and Meg protested strongly against abortion on moral and medical grounds. Violet, possibly hoping for sympathy, complained of the amount of washing she had, and asked if she could bring it to the Unit to do in our washer. Marion jumped on her again, pointing out that she herself had 4 children and did all her washing by hand at night; why couldn't Vi do the same? Meg supported her, and Vi retired crestfallen. During all this I tried to convey to Violet my understanding of her despair and her feelings of being overwhelmed, although I disagreed with her attempts at abortion on the grounds of risk to health or life.

She continued to attend regularly, and at M.35, when I pointed out the lack of willing listeners, she remarked quite brightly that she thought because they were so alone all the week, with nobody to listen to them, they got used to talking to themselves; in the same session the other members tried to make some helpful suggesions as to how she could cope with her washing problem. Pam described different types of launderette and their prices. The following week, when Meg suggested a collection for flowers for June, who was in hospital, Vi gave 2 shillings, quite a sacrifice.

In spite of her efforts at abortion her pregnancy continued, and she was coping even less well at home. In December she arrived looking so dirty and bedraggled that I took her off to the clothing store and found her a suitable smock and underskirt. The latter was too long, and the group insisted that she must take it off and shorten it rather than just pinning it up. Then she was encouraged to shorten her coat, while Meg took a proprietory interest in her and offered advice on fixing a washing-line in her kitchen. She made a bid for respect by telling them she had used the weekly menu list which I had given out last week, making Wednesday's dinner on Wednesday (stewed meat and vegetables), and it had been a success.

There were several instances of helpfulness towards Vi in spite of her irritating ways — (she was still self-centred and a poor listener). She announced that she intended to be sterilised after this child (her fourth) and received a good deal of support from Jessie, who had had the operation some ten months previously. She began taking more pains with her appearance, brought a cake to celebrate her birthday, and responded to Jessie by offering a bra which had become too small for her. The group became more maternal as Vi's pregnancy wore on. They put pressure on her to wear elastic stockings and pressed her to persevere with her second child's toilet-training.

In May 1967 the group had an outing. Vi's baby was only 3 weeks old but she would not be left out, and turned up on time with all four young children. Within ten minutes of setting out her third child was sick, and there were mutters of: "I bet she stuffed him with breakfast". She had brought a flask of milk for the baby, and incurred more muttered criticism for overfeeding him. She ignored all advice, and allowed her other children to overeat; inevitably they were all sick again on the homeward journey.

For the next few meetings she kept the baby with her, and bottle-fed him during the sessions. The group prevented her from overfeeding him, but got very irritated with her habit of handing him to someone else to hold. Explosion point was reached one day when we went to the park, and Vi left Marion holding the baby while she took the other three children to the cafe and stuffed them with orange juice and crisps. Meg was the spokesman, and scolded Vi ferociously for always needing to feed her children when she was out, demanding why she could not do it at the proper time like everyone else. Improvement was gradual; two weeks later she incurred the group's displeasure by not being ready when called for, and thus making two other members late. However, she had fed the children first, so I made a point of praising this, while suggesting that with a little more effort she might even be ready on time. She missed the next meeting, but after that there was no more bother about feeding the children during the session. She began taking much more trouble over her appearance, but was still not always ready on time. Her first attempt to "look smart" resulted in a "tarty" look which provoked a good deal of leg-pulling, and she added to the amusement by recalling some of the men who had "pursued" her.

Violet's socialisation is still not complete, but over the three years in which she had attended the group she has made tremendous gains in poise and confidence. She now contributes to conversations and listens with interest to what other people say. Her appearance receives group approval; she is invariably neat and clean, and has slimmed down to quite attractive proportions. Her standards of housewifery have improved. Her knitting is now of quite a high standard, and she makes all her children's sweaters and cardigans. She can also do simple sewing repairs. New members have come and the original members, except June and Jessie, have left. On two occasions recently, when visitors called at the Unit during Tuesday afternoons, Vi has talked to them about herself and the group, taking the role of responsible member. Her husband is much happier with her new image.

References

1. Irvine, E.E. (1954) Research into Problem Families, *British Journal of Psychiatric Social Work.*
2. Klein, J. (1961) *Working with Groups,* Hutchinson University Library.
3. Dockar-Drysdale, B. (1968) *Therapy in Child Care,* Papers on Residential Work, Longmans, Green & Co.
4. Somers, Dr. M.L. (1966) *The Small Group in Learning and Teaching,* University of Chicago.
5. Smalley, R.E. (1967) *Theory for Social Work Practice,* Columbia University Press.
6. Irvine, E.E. (1967) The Hard-to-Like Family, *Case Conference,* Vol. 14, No. 3.
7. Tilbury, D. (1968) Social Work and Social Clubs, *British Journal of Psychiatric Social Work,* Vol. IX, No. 4.

(ii)   Helping the Immature to Grow Up
by E.E. Irvine

This is one of the most fascinating descriptions of work connected with multi-problem families which I have read since I first became interested in the subject in 1954. It is primarily an account of a service rendered to a group of very deprived women as part of a more comprehensive programme of rehabilitative work; a programme whose results are very modest from one point of view, but yet remarkably good in terms of what can reasonably be hoped for in work with clients of this character. Mrs. Walker has given us a sensitive account of a very sensitive piece of work, and has succeeded to an unusual degree in the extremely difficult task of recounting in words the essentials of a group process. I would like in this foreword to explore the implications of the work reported in relation to some of our existing formulations about deprived and immature people, and of some concepts which have perhaps not previously been used in this context.

In the last chapter I suggested that many aspects of the behaviour of the clients of Family Service Units were characteristic of extreme immaturity, and this hypothesis was subsequently adopted by Rankin (1956), Bodman (1958), and Ratcliffe (1958). Wilson (1959) suggested that immaturity had been overstressed as a factor in relation to problems of income, housing, health and employment. Mrs. Walker's clients certainly had their share of all the more tangible problems listed by Wilson; on the other hand I would suggest that these were compounded by the personal characteristics which are represented by the concept of immaturity. The reader may find evidence that as this particular factor was dealt with in the group its members gained in ability to deal with the other unfavourable factors in their situation.

Philp and Timms (1959) consider the concept of immaturity to lack precision, and find it of limited value. In itself it is of course no more precise than that of maturation, which is, however, far from useless. The function of such a concept is to provide a frame of reference within which more or less precise statements can be made. The most elaborate attempt to discriminate personalities on the parameter of maturity is that of Reiner and Kaufman (1961) who distinguish four types of personality disorder corresponding to the four phases of pre-genital development described by Freud (1933, 1949).

Without attempting quite such a cut-and-dried categorisation, I think that in Mrs. Walker's material we can clearly see adults behaving in many ways like quite young children, and then gradually like older children, until some of them at least became able to carry their adult roles in ways which fall within the bounds of normality for their local sub-cultures. In 1954, I suggested that in relation to immature clients, a social worker might have much to learn from the nursery teacher. However, Mrs. Walker's material reminds us strongly that before the nursery school and its teacher, there are a home and a mother. During the interval since I wrote that article a number of authors (in particular D.W. Winnicott, 1958 and B. Dockar-Drysdale, 1966), have clarified for us the nature of that once-vague concept "good mothering", for lack of which the deprived child is in danger of remaining for ever deprived of the capacity for satisfying relationships and the ability to learn from experience to deal effectively with present problems and plans for the future. They have helped us to understand that the kind of therapeutic relationship which provides the matrix for the growth of insight rests itself upon a foundation of primary experience of "good enough" mothering. Where this is lacking in a child it is hard, but not impossible, to supply — provided one understands what needs to be supplied, and has the motivation and the considerable emotional resources required by the task (Dockar-Drysdale, 1966). For those who have achieved adult status without this basic experience and the maturation which depends on it, it may be even harder to provide, both because they are more deeply entrenched in distrust and discouragement, and because it is hard to find therapists who can perceive and respond to the hurt and starving child concealed within the "hard-to-reach" and "hard-to-like" adult who is often labelled "inadequate" or "psychopathic", and so dismissed. However, just as Mrs. Dockar-Drysdale has demonstrated the possibility of providing primary experience for the over-five, so Winnicott (1958) and Family Service Units have demonstrated that it is still possible for those who have reached adult years and adult status.

In reporting a complex therapeutic process, it is very difficult to evaluate the relative importance of the various elements involved. The theories of therapy concerned with insight, and the technique of verbal interpretation based on them, are formulated with great elaboration, but I suspect that even in respect of orthodox psychoanalysis this theoretical emphasis may sometimes distract the practitioner's attention from non-verbal elements in his interaction with the patient which may be of greater therapeutic import than he realises. Theories concerned with the provision of primary experience at a non-verbal level have been elaborated much more recently, and in a language with which few of us are as yet familiar. Thus, even those workers who intuitively or otherwise appreciate the need to engage in such primary interaction with their clients often tend to underrate its importance in the total therapeutic process; it is difficult to focus it as sharply as can be done with verbal interaction. However, this seems to be only partly a cognitive difficulty; there is also an anxiety factor. Mrs. Dockar-Drysdale has graphically described the tremendous appetite of the emotionally starved individual, the tremendous pressures he exerts on those who defeat his despair and arouse his hopes; the tremendous responsibility which they undertake in working with him, and the inevitable anxiety attendant on this. To sharpen the focus may well sharpen the anxiety.

Thus I have often noticed that a worker who has made physical contact with a client on some occasion does not spontaneously mention this in reporting the session, and is likely to account for it, when it emerges, as having been secondary to some other purpose; a touch on the arm to arrest a compulsive flow of speech, an arm around the shoulder of a separated combatant. In our text, Mrs. Walker describes how she combed a client's hair, ostensibly "to show her and the group that even without expert cutting hair could be made to look attractive". It was the client's response which revealed to the worker that she was also providing a deeply satisfying experience of maternal care. Perhaps we should learn to be less shy of physical expression of concern. I remember a French psycho-analyst demonstrating in a role-playing session how one could relieve the anxiety and hostility of a frantically complaining mother, whom a succession of caseworkers had failed to mollify by verbal means. He placed his hand over that of the client as it lay on the table, and said sympathetically: "It's very hard, isn't it?" None of those present could doubt the rightness of the gesture. There may be something in the suggestion that the English-speaking peoples impoverish their social life and relationships by excessive avoidance of physical contact, thus increasing social distance; it must certainly be harder to make a parental role convincing if all physical contact has to be avoided.

However, there are other ways of making that contact at an unconscious level which makes primary experience possible in adult life. Mrs. Walker brings out very clearly how by giving to her clients she enabled them in their turn to give. But even this formulation could be more sharply focussed; the particular giving to which she refers was actually feeding — symbolically the most significant and basic giving of all. To put it like this may arouse in some readers anxieties lest response at this level should encourage interminable dependence. But if we take the mother/infant relationship seriously as a model, we shall perhaps remember that it is only mothers with a certain kind of emotional pathology who try to prolong dependency beyond its usual term. The "ordinary devoted mother", the "good enough mother", responds to the developing child not only with acceptance of his dependence, but also with encouragement for all signs of increasing maturity and independence. (There was a period when the fashion in child care was to force the pace of maturation and curtail the phase of accepted dependency, but this proved to be ill-advised, and was relatively short-lived.)

It is easy to trace the progress of nurtured maturation in Mrs. Walker's group. After only a couple of months, we find a symbolic weaning. During this time, the worker has provided a weekly cup of tea with biscuits, which is not perceived as a gift but taken for granted, as the infant takes for granted its daily milk. But the offer of a visit to a film is definitely perceived as a gift, an amazing treat, which reveals surprising things about the giver in relation to the group. At this point, when gift and giver are sharply perceived, the worker suggests that the unconditional feeding should be discontinued. She invites the members to pay for their weekly tea and I think it is not too fanciful to see in this an analogy to weaning, or perhaps to the moment at which the infant is encouraged to feed itself.

The process of stimulating maturation continues with Mrs. Walker's assumption that the members are now mature enough to take a collective decision about admitting new members. At this point we can see her beginning to move into the role of nursery teacher. An interesting feature of the account is the premature attempt to introduce constructive activities at the outset. Some of the members, as we know, possessed some of the skills in question, and were presumably using them to some extent in their homes; but they were not prepared to use them in the group situation because, I think, they were not compatible with the phase of infantile dependence which was then being symbolically enacted in the group. The time was not ripe for constructive activity, for the learning and practice of skills, till the nineteenth meeting, when Brenda revealed some accomplishment and a wish to learn more. The whole group gradually manifested a readiness to learn, and the atmosphere changed to one of purposeful activity and learning, which seem to correspond to Erikson's phases of preoccupation with mastery and industry.

I have suggested one reason for the early concealment of skills, but I suspect there is more to it than that. It is interesting that most of these mothers not only had little skill in cooking, but hated to cook. Why should this be? I suggest that in the home, as well as in the group, this was an expression of their unreadiness to be mothers, their identification with the dependent child who has to be fed. This seems particularly clear in respect of Vi, who was continually stuffing her children with food which others had prepared. The facts that she persistently left other people to hold her baby and that she repeatedly made her children sick by over-feeding suggest that this was not an expression of genuine maternal feeling, but rather of projective identification with an insatiable child. One suspects also that, reared in homes where very young children, as soon as they betray any capacity for independence, are liable to be exploited as "mother's helps'', these women defensively concealed their accomplishments for fear that to reveal them would automatically debar them from further nurturing. They had to be secure in the dependable support of the worker before they could venture to taste the joys of accomplishment and giving — and eventually accept a responsible mother role. Philp, in an unpublished communication, has suggested that it is misleading to regard these clients as immature, since they are physiologically mature and sociologically invested with adult roles. This is of course true. The same women to whom I have attributed such childish experiences and attitudes are all the mothers of families; one has seven children, none less than three. One reveals at the fifth session (i.e. in the phase when the group was manifesting the greatest dependency) ''her latest attempt at suicide'', and the others are quick to remind her of her responsibility to her children. Later, we find Violet attempting abortion and the other members disapproving. Later still, she plans to be sterilised, and is supported by a member who has already undergone this operation. The group gets involved in Vi's pregnancy, encouraging her to wear her elastic stockings and to get her children toilet-trained before she has a new lot of nappies to wash. These women are undoubtedly rich in some kinds of adult experience; they are also capable of responsible thought and action (as well as of much irresponsibility).

Perhaps it may help us here to refer to Berne's reformulation of the Freudian id, super-ego or ego in terms of an internal Child and an internal Parent, both of whom interfere with the appropriate adaptation to present situations of the Adult (Berne, 1964). In any group the members act at different moments at each level, and if one plays the Child role the others often adopt the strict Parent role. The worker, in our particular group, can be seen first in the role of nurturing Parent, later in that of Adult, in each case setting an example which encourages group members to adopt similar roles. We can see very clearly how the members adopt the strict Parent role in relation to Vi and her abortion plans, and how the worker by precept and example encourages them to exchange this for the Adult role. Every mother and every nursery teacher helps little girls to develop through identification the potential wife and mother (among other things) in themselves. This worker does the same, as she cares for the members and encourages them to care for each other, as well as to sew and to cook; the only difference is that her "children" are already wives and mothers. It is sometimes feared that to recognize the immaturity of certain clients and to relate to them on this basis implies some lack of respect. We could reply that the good mother or nursery teacher respects even the young child as an individual. Be this as it may, we can clearly see Mrs. Walker respecting and supporting these women as individuals and as mothers, at the same time as she is teaching them the elementary nursery lessons of taking turns and thinking of others, of not all speaking at once.

I would now like to consider a most challenging question which arises from the account of this group. Why did the members seem compelled to present such distorted and unfavourable pictures of themselves before they were able to admit their good points and assets? We have seen them as presenting themselves as weak and helpless, but this is not the whole story. In the fifth meeting Meg and June present themselves as both weak and selfish; in the same meeting Marion speaks of suicide. Mrs. Walker regards this as a confession of "badness"; the group saw it like this, and probably Marion did too, though it must also have been an expression of desperation or despair. Some weeks later the worker combs Meg's hair (which may well have been experienced not only as acceptance and reassurance, but also as a reward for truthful self-exposure) and very soon Meg goes further than before, accusing herself of idleness, neglect and cruelty. The week following this confession she allows herself to dress better and to appear relatively well-groomed.

It seems, to use a concept from Erikson (1968), that these women have been strongly possessed of a negative identity, which has to be revealed and exorcised by acceptance before they can find their more positive identity. In the initial phase of "best behaviour", they present "ideal, unrealistic pictures of themselves", motivated presumably by guilt or shame and fear of rejection if they "come clean". But this deception probably increases their guilt towards a worker who is perceived with increasing clarity as kind and understanding. Guilt increases as fear decreases, till first one and then another confess their faults. Each confession accepted by the worker makes the next one easier. Accepted confession is followed by relief of both fear and guilt, till eventually it becomes possible to admit and take credit for real assets, and to integrate them into a more realistic self-image, including both good and bad qualities.

In this context, I would like to draw attention to the passage where Mrs. Walker sums up her ego-strengthening (or Adult-strengthening) activity. "I was continually looking for members' strengths and examples of "good" child management, praising their efforts to improve their personal appearance. At the same time, I encouraged them to look on the bright side as well as the black side of their lives; reminding them of their husbands' good points when they were dwelling on their faults, helping them to recall pleasant experiences to counterbalance the unpleasant." In other words, she was gently but persistently bringing them back from fantasy to reality, both as regards depressive and paranoid fantasy (exaggeration of the faults and denial of the virtues respectively of the self and of others.)

It will be apparent that this is not an essay in "applied social studies". It is an application of certain psycho-analytic concepts to a group process. My interpretations are susceptible of discussion, but not of proof; they represent a way of looking at certain phenomena which seems to me fruitful, and I offer them in the hope that others may find them fruitful and illuminating too. I have also used imagery, such as that of possession and exorcism, where this seems to me to reflect most clearly what was afoot in the minds of those concerned. In a way this kind of study resembles literary criticism more than social science. As F.R. Leavis has put it, one can only say to the reader: "Isn't this so?"

References

1. Berne, E. (1964) *Games People Play.*
2. Bodman, F. (1958) Personal Factors in the Problem Family, *Case Conference,* 4, 99-104.
3. Dockar-Drysdale, B. (1966) The Provision of Primary Experience in a Therapeutic School, *Therapy in Child Care,* 1969.
4. Erikson, E.H. (1968) *Identity, Youth and Crisis.*
5. Freud, S. (1933) *New Introductory Lectures on Psycho-Analysis.*
6. Freud, S. (1949) *An Outline of Psycho-Analysis.*

7. Irvine, E.E. (1954) Research Into Problem Families, *British Journal of Psychiatric Social Work, No. 9.*
8. Philp, A.F. and Timms, N. (1959) *The Problem of the Problem Family,* Family Service Units, London.
9. Rankin, T.G. (1956) Problem Families, *Case Conference,* 13, 94-99.
10. Ratcliffe, T.A. (1958) *Personality Factors in the Problem Family,* ISTD London.
11. Reiner, B.S. and Kaufman, I. (1961) *Character Disorders in Parents of Delinquents*
12. Wilson, H. (1959) Problem Families and the Concept of Immaturity, *Case Conference,* VI, 5.
13. Winnicott, D.W. (1958) *Collected Papers.*

CHAPTER 11

The "Problem Family" and Society

"Problem family" is one of those categories which has become a label. Labelling has become a formidable accusation, yet without categorisation no social analysis would be possible. Labelling appears to denote assignment to a stigmatised category — e.g. "mentally ill" or "problem family". Here we are on the horns of an ugly dilemma. If we do not identify categories of problem or need and those who suffer from them, we cannot provide any selective service, or even discuss what kind of service is appropriate. So we must have a term to denote such categories; but if the members of the category are generally disliked or feared, connotations of dislike or fear become attached to the term which denotes it. Stigmatisation and rejection of deviance seem to be deeply rooted in society; more violent and harsh in some than in others, but never absent. Those who wish to help or treat stigmatised groups often try to ward off the stigma on their behalf by changing the terms which have acquired or constellated such connotations: "lunacy" becomes "insanity", "insanity" becomes "mental illness"; "asylum" becomes "mental hospital" or "psychiatric hospital" (but remains "loony-bin" in the vernacular).

All this is relevant to the term "problem family". A recent conference called by the Family Service Units was entitled "The Deprived Family and the Social Services". I suspect that the term "problem family" was avoided because it is so often used abusively by those who dislike such families. I have demonstrated elsewhere (Irvine, 1967) that these families do in fact arouse violent antagonism in many people, and that this is an important part of their problem: I shall say more about this later. The change to the term "deprived family" exemplifies the same strategy as the change from "insanity" to "mental illness"; the stigmatised group is assimilated to a much wider group, which is the object of sympathy rather than stigma. But at least the adjective "mental" indicates a reference to a sub-group, whereas if "problem families" are simply merged with the much wider category of the socially deprived we are left with no basis for positive discrimination on their behalf, no way of identifying those who need a special quality and quantity of service.

The Family Service Units were in fact set up to help a certain type of client, who required a great deal more time and attention than most social services were equipped to give, and a different kind of service (including more home visits) than most child guidance clinics could offer. This inability to use existing services was one feature of this group of client. They were also distinguished from the general mass of suffering humanity by "failure ... to meet the community's minimum expectation of social behaviour, parental responsibility and domestic management" (Philp, 1963) or, to put it rather more strongly, as I did, by "child neglect and squalor" (Irvine, 1954).

Thus "the problem of the problem family" was a double-edged one: more than their fair share of suffering in many cases, and of problems (as reflected in the variant term "multi-problem families"), but also a special problem for society. This was only partly because of marked deviation from social norms (working-class, not only middle-class, norms) and partly because society could not ignore such deviation, inasmuch as it appeared to involve various degrees of serious risk for the development (or in some cases the survival) of their children. It was also partly because of the special difficulty these families presented, both in respect of social help and of social control.

So the original concept of problem family, as formulated both by public health authorities and by the Family Service Units, was essentially concerned with failure in social functioning, particularly in the crucial role of parent. Some of the public health people were frankly exasperated and hostile towards the parents, as shown by the quotations in "The Hard-to-like Family" (above). About this I shall have more to say later in this chapter. The great strength of the Family Service Units was that they could approach the families without this hostility, indeed with genuine friendliness and concern for parents as well as children, but without shutting their eyes to the problems of social functioning — or indeed to problems of social handicap. The balance of emphasis on personal and societal factors has shifted from time to time as social conditions and our public knowledge of them have changed. In the 1950s there was a period of optimism, when it was possible to believe that slums, unemployment, malnutrition, ill-health were yielding or had already yielded, to the growth of general prosperity, full employment and "the Welfare State" (see Philp, 1963). During this period there was perhaps an over-emphasis on personal problems. But later in the sixties the Child Poverty Action Group, of which Philp was a founder member, blew sky-high these complacent assumptions, and proclaimed very loudly that all was far from well. It was then that the ideology of social deprivation took over, and the pendulum swung to the other extreme, since it was now suggested that "problem families" were simply the worst equipped, or the worst injured victims of the general calamity of social deprivation; that this current deprivation was their only problem, and that all the studies of personal factors reflected an ideology of personal responsibility which was apparently without foundation.

Certainly it is possible to regard the condition of the problem family as an extreme form of failure to cope with difficulty and stress. The C.P.A.G. has clearly demonstrated that large numbers of families in our society are exposed to very severe stress, confronted for instance with budgeting problems which "only resourceful and very self-disciplined people would be able to solve" (Wilson, 1970). Failure to solve the budgeting problem is likely to lead to malnutrition, poor health and impairment of earning capacity in the parents and learning capacity in the children — whether or not the illness of a wage earner first set up the vicious circle. Similarly, as Wilson argues (*ibid.*), while mental illness may be a cause of failure to cope with adverse circumstances, it may also be a response to the stresses of unemployment, poverty and bad housing, thus helping to perpetuate and aggravate the circumstances which provoked it. Individuals vary in their ability to cope with stressful situations; some surmount them, others suffer some degree of failure or damage, others give up the unequal struggle. At any given level of stress, it is the weakest who go to the wall. Of the half million families with dependent children estimated by the Ministry of Social Security in 1966 to be living on incomes below what is now called supplementary benefit level, probably only a fraction could have been described as problem families. Nevertheless, the vast majority were exposed to various degrees of damage to health and child development, and a certain proportion of families exposed to such stress would be likely to succumb sooner or later to discouragement and bitterness, and swell the ranks of problem families.

However, if problem families are simply the severest casualties of social deprivation, then social action which protects families against such stress might be expected to eliminate the problem — prevention rather than cure, a consummation devoutly to be wished. But the premise is dubious. Woodhouse's research, reported by Philp (*ibid.*), found that some 25% of sample families had income at or below the "minimum need" level recognised by the then National Assistance Board, 21% had incomes over 50% above this level, and another 10% over 100% above, although some of these incomes fluctuated. Thirty-seven per cent had major debts — i.e. debts amounting to at least three times their available weekly resources — but 38% had negligible or insignificant amounts of debt. Naturally, debt was heavily associated with fluctuating income, and the proportion of those free from debt rose with income. In all, financial hardship can be seen to be a common factor in the situation of a problem family, but by no means a universal one. Indebtedness was partly due to poor and irregular incomes, but not in all cases; other factors were the difficulty of remembering that what is consumed on credit must be paid for later, and the perennial hope that the day of reckoning may never come.

For these reasons, one cannot accept that *current* poverty and hardship fully account for the condition of most "problem families", many of whom are overwhelmed by problems which most of their neighbours find manageable, if difficult. Hence the need to study their personal vulnerability, as described earlier in this book; the inability to control impulse, to plan for tomorrow, let alone till the end of the week; all that I have summed up as immaturity (or in Freudian terms, ego weakness). Certainly these characteristics often result from early deprivation, whether this is mainly material or emotional or both. (Some "respectable" families can be emotionally very depriving.)

In this global sense the social deprivation hypothesis is much more acceptable. It has been suggested that many hyper-active, impulse-ridden children are suffering from minimal brain damage — that is from very mild degrees of the kind of intra-uterine damage which results, when more severe, in epilepsy, spasticity, etc. (This kind of damage shows observable neurological signs for a brief period after birth, but these vanish as neurological compensation occurs; Pasemanick and Knobloch, 1961; Prechtl, 1963.) This hypothesis is difficult to prove in the absence of observable neurological symptoms, but it seems not unlikely. There is also evidence that the incidence of the major conditions mentioned above is correlated with various concomitants of poverty — malnutrition, ill-health and poor housing, and general stress as they operate on the expectant mother (*ibid.*). It therefore seems likely that these conditions will also produce a high proportion of children who, even if not brain-damaged, have some degree of physiological handicap resulting from a sub-standard intra-uterine environment, and will therefore be less well equipped to cope with stress. But these vulnerable children are now exposed to the same stresses which may have affected their pre-natal environment; they have both impaired ability to cope, and more than average stress to cope with. There is likely to be less reliability of maternal preoccupation and devotion for the first year or two of life, abruptly withdrawn on the early arrival of the next baby. This abrupt transition is often dramatised by the sudden removal of the displaced baby into the care of strangers in a strange place. Group care means increased exposure to infection; and I suspect that the stress for a young child of sudden removal from mother and home reduces resistance to infection. In any case, I have often been struck, when pursuing the histories of children from such families, by the frequency with which admission to short-term care, during the mother's confinement, was followed by the contraction of an infectious illness and admission to hospital for a longer period, with all the extra stresses and strangeness of that experience. Quite apart from these double transplantings, malnutrition and insanitary housing also increase the risk of hospitalisation in the early years, with all its hazards for the mother-child relationship and the child's capacity for affection, trust and trustworthiness. Others, as well as I, have described the salient characteristics of immaturity, all so unacceptable to society. Graham and Rutter (1971) and Rutter (1972) have pointed out that the risk of disturbed development associated with early separation of mother and child depends very largely on the presence of another factor — disturbed relationships in the home. We know that emotional disturbance can be found at all levels of society, but there seems little doubt that extreme poverty shortens tempers and exacerbates rivalries — I have in extreme cases known members of problem families hide food from each other, as well as quarrelling endlessly about who ate more than his share.

I have sketched in only a few of the ways in which poverty may have contributed to the emotional deprivation and immaturity of many of the parents of problem families, which not only incapacitate them for coping with social stress, but also increase the risk of unemployment, or irregular employment, poverty, bad housing, etc.; and which often make them unable to manage in conditions which more mature people find manageable enough. A common result of premature separation of more than a few weeks' duration is an increasing shallowness of affective ties, with progressive loss of discrimination between persons, who are welcomed increasingly solely for the physical and material gratifications they provide, while there is a general shift of interest from people to goodies, and the attitude to other people becomes predominantly one of exploitation. All these traits are frequently found in the parents of problem families.

There has been very little discussion of the role of anxiety in the "problem family" syndrome, and this seems to me to be a crucial factor in the deadlocks and cross-purposes which arise between such families and the various agents of society. It seems likely that one of the things which cause problem families to manage worse than equally poor neighbours is a dysfunctional way of reacting to anxiety. As Nicholas Bond very relevantly pointed out (Bond, 1970) a moderate degree of anxiety operates as a stimulus for improved role performance, or social functioning, and the necessary problem-solving activities; whereas past a certain threshold, anxiety produces apathy and paralysis. He argued from this that those concerned with inducing clients to improve various aspects of their performance should be alert to recognise those whose performance disintegrates still further under any increase of anxiety, since the kind of pressure which helps some families to mobilise their resources is dysfunctional with these others, and defeats its own ends. I suspect that this is an important reason for the "intractable ineducability" of which problem families have been accused; for the negative response to well-meant intervention, and the mounting hostility to social workers and other agents of society. I suspect that two things go together in these people, which are closely connected; a poor and rather primitive repertoire of problem-solving devices, and an inability to manage anxiety, which rapidly reaches an intensity which either induces paralysis or frantic spending on inessentials, drinking and gambling. This is simply a special case of the widespread use of consumption as a mechanism of defence. (Any cigarette-smoker knows that his consumption goes up at times of stress.) I have recently been in touch with Mrs. X, an unsupported mother of seven, living on the supplementary benefit scale. There are chronic rent arrears, and a fine of £15 to pay in respect of an unpaid television licence which is, not surprisingly, also in arrears. She has been threatened with eviction on the first count and prison on the second. At each warning, the anxiety engendered is smothered by the reflection that she got off this time, and it may never happen — and by rushing out to spend any loose cash on some piece of personal finery. (Here we have comfort-spending at the exhibitionist rather than the oral level.) Extravagant spending, or wild gambling, can also be an expression of anger with the marital partner or others, or may represent an act of revenge on them.

I am still persuaded that the special vulnerability of these families, in a situation of undoubted difficulty or stress, is largely due to the immaturity of their parents, whether primary or secondary (regressive). Nevertheless, we should recognise that their interaction with society is pathological on both sides. Firstly, there is exploitation. Mrs. X was induced by a representative of the firm from which she rents her television set to have the meter adjusted to a higher rate, to finance the hire-purchase of a three-piece suite. Door-to-door salesmen are quick to cash in on the customer's mood. One of them was lucky enough to call on a former client of mine when she was in a fury of resentment against some official visitor who had criticised her mucky home. It was the work of ten minutes to persuade her that by contracting to buy a colourful blanket on easy terms she would somehow be scoring off this unkind critic.

This phrase sums up two of the things to which such people are most vulnerable — unkindness and criticism. Even quite friendly and gentle criticism, such as would be quite acceptable in most families, is perceived and experienced as unkind and hostile. But in fact such families arouse strong and widespread attitudes of criticism, disapproval and hostility; in relations, neighbours, society and its agents — teachers, rent-collectors, magistrates, officials in general. Consider the Court which imposed a fine of £15 on a woman living on supplementary benefit. This is punitiveness run riot, and has inevitably led to failure to pay, and thus to the threat of prison. Why not tell her to spin straw into gold? Why expose the community to the risk of taking 7 children into costly care to redress the failure to pay a few pounds for a licence? It might have been really constructive to have put this woman on probation, thus providing contact with a social worker who could give close personal supervision and support in the management of the tiny budget — and an atmosphere of care and concern which might reduce Mrs. X's anxiety to a level where more self-control and foresight were possible. But not all probation services are well enough staffed to provide as much help as such people require. Perhaps a voluntary auxiliary could help — as fortunately, since being rehoused, Mrs. X is proud of her home and keeps it clean and tidy, and since she also responds readily to a friendly approach. But to suggest such remedies, there would have to be less hostility.

For these reasons, I do not classify this as a full-blown problem family, which is so much harder to like. However, I have heard it referred to as such, and it was very much at risk at the time of rehousing. The new home was basically a great improvement on the old, but had been left in a filthy condition by the previous tenants. Mrs. X, an immigrant with no very encouraging experience of public authorities, lacked the know-how to get rubbish removed and repairs carried out, but fortunately had some contacts with a university social service project. A friend from the university obtained the services of the housing and sanitary departments, and parties of students spent several days cleaning and redecorating. Without all this help it is unlikely that Mrs. X, with her seven young children, would ever have got the Augean stable clean, and her new home might well have presented the typical picture of "domestic squalor" which arouses so much hostility and provokes reactions in the community which drive the family further and further into the Slough of Despond.

In "The Hard-to-Like Family" I devoted some attention to this social hostility which problem families arouse, emphasising both its intensity and its normality. "The families described represent an affront to the fundamental values of those concerned with health and welfare . . . this ill-concealed disgust. . . . It is natural to feel this way towards a type of client who can be so very exasperating. . . . Those who criticise from outside the unfortunate attitudes which some social workers fall into when dealing with these families should try working with them and honestly study how they themselves respond to the broken promises, the plausible excuses and even the accusations and abuse." On the other hand, we have to recognise that the impact of such attitudes can only make matters worse. Harsh, punitive, threatening or unfriendly behaviour from the agents of society defeats its own ends, and collusively exacerbates the problem it was intended to resolve.

Perhaps we should think some more about why such irrational attitudes are so strong and so widespread, and why so many people react to these families not only with hostility and disgust, but in much more primitively aggressive ways than they usually manifest. I am reminded of certain London families which evacuated their young children to some distance during the last world war, and more or less lost touch with them. Some of these evacuated children, whose return "home" was for them the second or third uprooting in their young lives, reacted by regressing into incontinence, which sometimes provoked parents into such uncontrolled cruelty that the child had to be removed to safety. But such cruelty was often "out of character", although indignant authorities were often reluctant to recognise this complication. They were not cruel parents, except to the child in question; to younger children, who had not suffered the experience of separation and reunion and who were developing normally, they were affectionate and loving parents. Society was in a quandary; some of its agents wanted to punish the cruel parents by imprisonment, while others argued that to do this would be to deprive their other children of good parents for whom there was no substitute. It seemed to me that these parents were normal people, capable of normal parental affection towards the "normal expectable child" who matured at the usual pace. What they could not stand was a great boy of five who had reverted to soiling like a one-year-old and who, being "old enough to know better", must be doing it out of pure diabolic spite. Their outrage at this primitive behaviour released in them the deeply buried capacity for primitive rage and violence which had been repressed at the time of their own toilet-training, when they renounced forever their own freedom to soil and mess.

This seems to me an apt analogy for the violent feeling response and punitive fantasies of so many nice, kind normal people towards "problem families". Some of us can stand anything but filth, others anything but child neglect or cruelty; others may be more antagonised by lying and prevarication than anything else. And in any case, all these things and many more may be combined in one family or individual. For one reason or another our blood boils, or they "make us sick", and we react to these families, who are so vulnerable and who need more sensitive help than most, in crudely hostile or manipulative ways which simply intensify their despair and their hatred and mistrust of Them. Such families are scape-goated in the fullest and deepest sense of the term.

In "The Hard-to-Like Family" I suggested that this was a reason for assigning special social workers to such families — workers who were special mainly in their ability to accept what is unacceptable to so many, even among trained social workers — and to give them very small caseloads. I mentioned that certain local authorities had copied the Family Service Unit model in this respect, but this trend has been very limited; naturally, again, because the service described is relatively costly in terms of money and professional resources, and the results are modest rather than dramatic. Scarce resources have to be distributed between "problem families" on the one hand and elderly and handicapped people on the other and, partly because they are so hard to like, problem families are unlikely to be accorded priority. It is only when we remember the cost of taking Mrs. X's seven children into care that it might seem an economy to spend a good deal of social work time on keeping her out of prison! But this kind of issue is not often faced, and some rather pathetic compromises are tried. Each homeless family is allotted to a social worker — but the social workers have caseloads so heavy as to allow half an hour or less per month for each family. In these circumstances, the more vulnerable homeless families hang around inertly in their temporary accommodation, while the staff become increasingly hostile to them, and thus reinforce their negative self-image as hopeless, helpless and bad. They are reproached with not changing their ways — but with a worse situation than before, and with half an hour's help a month, why should we expect them to change for the better? Both social workers and families are expected to make bricks without straw.

Much has been said, by me and others, about the qualities required by a social worker in order to remain understanding and helpful in working with such families. Less has been said about the social pressures which they must be able to endure, but there is little doubt that the hostility aroused by their clients rubs off onto the social workers, who are often concerned with trying to rehabilitate a family with which other groups in the community have already lost patience and hope. These other groups (housing departments, some social agencies) may already have decided that the family should be evicted, charged with child neglect, or otherwise assaulted and broken up, and may in fact be very angry that the social worker, or the agency for which he works, has staved off this rough justice (or injustice) by undertaking an attempt to rehabilitate. This resentment and frustration are liable to be taken out on the social worker in terms of refusal to cooperate, amounting sometimes to sabotage, demands for instant results, etc. The worker needs both personal toughness and institutional support in his agency to withstand these pressures and continue to work patiently with the family without getting rattled. He also needs skill in overcoming, or at least reducing, the hostility and prejudice I have described. This in turn demands more than a simple faith in communication, as sometimes suggested in the literature, but also an understanding of the motivation of the prejudiced, and the value-system to which the problem family is such a threat. As with clients, if we are to have any hope of changing attitudes, we must be able to empathise with those who hold them.

One begins to feel that this is asking too much of a single human being. Very likely there has to be a certain division of labour, since those workers who are most accepting of the problem family are likely to have difficulty in relating effectively and constructively to the authorities who make life harder for them than it need be. So there may be a need for other workers, or at least some one in the agency who can do this, and whose main job may be to protect the families and their workers against outraged members of society, and to obtain as much cooperation as possible from the relevant organs of the community.

References

Bond, Nicholas (1970) The relationship between Anxiety and Performance in Clients, *Social Work Today*, I, 8.

Graham, P. & Rutter M. (1971) Organic Brain Dysfunction and Child Psychiatric Disorder, *Brit. Med. Journ.*, III, 695.

Irvine, E.E. (1954) Research into Problem Families, *Brit. Journal of Psych. Social Work*, No. 9.

Irvine, E.E. (1967) The Hard-to-like Family, *Case Conference*, XIV 3 (Chapter 9, this volume).

Miller, D.H. (1964) *Growth to Freedom.*

Pasamanick, B. and Knobloch, H. (1961) Epidemiologic Studies on the Complications of Pregnancy and the Birth Process. In Caplan, Ed., *Prevention of Mental Disorders in Children,* Tavistock Pubs.

Philp, A.F. (1963) *Family Failure.*

Rutter, M. (1972) *Maternal Deprivation Reassessed.*

Wilson, H. (1970) In Holman R. *et al., Socially Deprived Families.*

Women's Group on Public Welfare (1943) *Our Towns,* O.U.P.

CHAPTER 12

Psychosis in Parents: Mental Illness as a Problem for the Family*

I propose to present some case materials to illustrate common reactions to mental illness in the family. This is not intended to contribute anything new to our knowledge of the subject, but to emphasise the need of the relatives for help in their own right, a topic about which very little seems to have been written in our country.

In 1954, psychiatric social workers in 15 mental hospitals in various parts of the country collaborated in a small survey of how they actually spent their time. It had till then been generally assumed that the psychiatric social worker in such hospitals was mainly concerned with service to the relatives, or at least with working with them; but to our surprise it emerged that the proportion of total working time actually spent with in-patients varied from 36% to 85%, and that spent with out-patients from 21% to 80%. Nor were the higher figures atypical. Workers in nine of the fifteen hospitals and seven of the out-patient clinics spent over 50% of their time with patients. As the commentary to these figures said: "Intriguing questions arise about the function of the psychiatric social worker in adult work. Is her direct therapeutic role with the patient assuming more importance? Is she less concerned with the family and the social background of the patient?"

In the face of these figures, one reflects that it is perhaps natural for those working in a mental hospital to have a predominantly patient-centred approach. Perhaps one should rather look to Community Care for a comprehensive community mental health programme in which preventive work with relatives would bulk as large as the pre-

---

*Based on a paper presented to a general meeting of the A.P.S.W. in November, 1960.

care and after-care of patients? On consulting Power[1], I found the following statement: "The community care setting . . . calls for a change in emphasis. Traditionally, the main focus of the work has been with the patients' relatives . . . but *most of the community worker's time is spent with the patients themselves*" (my italics). the author mentions the difficulties and resentments of the families of incurable psychotics, and the fact that other agencies may be involved with such families, but he did not at that time appear to envisage that the community care worker might take responsibility for helping these relatives. (This may well have been due to the tremendous imbalance of supply and demand at the time.) He also states that "although the first need is to treat the sick person, this cannot often be accomplished in isolation" because the patient's illness may satisfy the needs of the relatives, and he mentions a case where successful work with the patient produced a need for casework with the mother, to enable her to accept her son's reviving initiative and independence.

This concept of work with the relatives in the interest of the patient is rather more fully presented by Goldberg in an article[2] on the forerunner of community care, the Social After-Care Service of the Provisional National Council for Mental Health. She distinguished three functions of the psychiatric social worker in such a service (which, being explicitly designed for aftercare pure and simple, was naturally patient-centred). These functions were: personal help to the patient, interpretation of his needs to the community, and "interpretation of the patient's problems and needs to the family, helping them to adjust to his often changed personality". This function is further elaborated in terms of "explaining the patient's difficulties and trying where necessary to modify the relatives' attitudes towards him" because "the psychiatrically disabled person is exceptionally dependent upon his environment and his family's ability to understand him, and his relationship with them greatly affects his prospects of eventual recovery". She goes on to discuss those unhelpful attitudes which, being based on deeply unconscious needs, are more resistive to change. She also mentions the possibility of having to deal with situations of acute conflict between the interests of a severely unstable patient and those of the spouse and young children, a theme which has been mentioned again by Jones and

Hammond,[3] but never fully discussed. Heimler also describes work focused on interpreting the patient's needs to the relatives,[4] but only Eden,[5] as far as I can ascertain, has written of short-term crisis casework with relatives, to relieve pressure of anxiety and guilt.

I would like to emphasise that I do not for a moment question the value and importance of the work described above. It must clearly remain a vital function of the worker in Community Care to seek out the "hard-to-reach" type of severely disturbed patient, whether in order to work with him directly, or to establish a bridge across which the patient can enter some kind of psychiatric treatment. This is a type of work which probably no-one else can do, and it certainly renders a great service to the relatives, who would otherwise be left with the burden indefinitely. It is also clearly important to interpret the patient's needs to the family and to modify their attitudes of over-anxiety, over-protection or uncomprehending irritation that so often defeat their own ends. I will not repeat the demonstration so excellently made by Goldberg[6] that there is often a deep psycho-pathological entanglement between patient and relatives which needs to be unravelled from both sides in the interests of both. I will merely state that I am in full agreement.

I have chosen to discuss a very limited aspect of the total problem of a family in which an overt psychotic breakdown has occurred. At this point the emotional disturbance in one member, which may have been creating serious problems for his relatives for years already, has been defined as insanity, or as a serious mental illness necessitating hospitalisation. One response to this is something very like a phobia of psychiatry, and a need to deny emotional problems in other family members. When a child is brought to a child guidance clinic reluctantly under pressure and years too late, when the parents steadfastly deny or minimise the problems which are so manifest and disquieting to others, when they would willingly accept remedial teaching but refuse to hear of psycho-therapy, all this defensiveness can very often be traced to intolerable anxiety arising from a history of mental illness in the family. Such illness, once recognised for what it is, is apt to arouse anxiety so acute that, unless something can be done to relieve it at an early stage, it can only be coped with by very primitive and maladaptive mechanisms, such as denial, which prevent the timely recognition of treatable problems and the acceptance of appropriate help.

So few of these cases come into treatment that those I shall describe are of another type, where acute anxiety could in fact be faced without denial. Mr. X broke down following five years in a Japanese prison camp. Returning home in 1946, he fathered twins in 1947, and shortly after this his temper became so violent that he was examined and certified as being of unsound mind. His family consisted of his wife, Tom (16), Rose (12), May (6), Jean (5) and the twins. He had always been a hot-tempered man, and the Ministry of Pensions claimed that he had been mentally ill before his call-up. The psychiatrist at the Observation Ward was reported to have elicited a history of tempers in boyhood, and to have said that these were the first sign of "mentality". Mrs. X lived in constant fear that her children were also "mental". Rose had a pretty hot temper, and both she and her mother feared that this was an early sign of mental trouble. (When Rose began to come and see me of her own free will, I think this probably confirmed her mother's fears!) Rose consulted the Clinic at the age of 22, on account of her daugher's tempers (Susan, 3½). At one point in our acquaintance she developed stomach pains and backache. Her doctor at first attributed these symptoms to "nerves", but examination revealed a duodenal ulcer, some kidney trouble and some defect of the spine. Rose was tremendously relieved, because she felt that had the pain been really "imaginary" this would have meant she was "going nuts" like her father.

You will have noticed that Rose's little girl, Susan, was referred for tempers. The parents were making very heavy weather of these, and in their anxiety were hitting her a good deal. Naturally, the anxiety was largely concerned with fears that tempers might lead to insanity. On the other hand, the attitude resembled that of the Duchess:

> Speak roughly to your little boy
> And beat him when he sneezes.
> He only does it to annoy
> Because he knows it teases.

This insistence that Susan was bad, and could help it, was a defence against fears that she could not help it, and was mad. The parents also feared that madness results from indulging one's temper. So they hit Susan as people used to flog lunatics, to drive out the evil spirits. . . .

When May reached adolescence she began to be promiscuous, and reacted to interference with all the resources of the family temper. This too was felt to be a variant of the family madness, especially when she was referred to a psychiatrist. Fortunately, the psychiatrist was felt to be very helpful, which partly accounted for Rose's subsequent surprising willingness to seek psychiatric help for Susan.

Rose and her family lived in very crowded conditions, and she eventually consulted me about her son Tommy, then aged 7, whose bed almost touched the parental bed, who was very observant, and who had at least once observed the sex act (and protested indignantly). Tommy's interest and curiosity had been greatly stimulated, and also his sexual feelings for his mother. Naturally, Rose was afraid that he was an incipient sex maniac.

In this case I did not meet any member of the family till Mr. X had been in hospital for ten years, but the anxieties created by his breakdown were still very active. I shall now describe a case where the wife suspected the husband's mental illness from the first, and was already in casework treatment when her suspicions were confirmed. Mr. Y had left his family on the birth of his third son. Mrs. Y, whose brother attended our Adult Department, consulted us later about the eldest child, John, whose violent tempers made her fear he had inherited his father's instability. It was decided after a diagnostic investigation that John should remain in boarding-school rather than stay at home to have treatment, but Mrs. Y kept in touch with us from time to time. Some months later, Mr. Y returned home, and then developed an illness which incapacitated him for his job, which involved some heavy manual work. Lacking qualifications for other work, in spite of good intelligence, he remained unemployed and became increasingly depressed, with vague thoughts of suicide or "going round the bend". Yet he insisted that he would not see a psychiatrist but that his wife should see one "because of her complexes and inhibitions".

Eventually, Mrs. Y arranged a joint interview with me to discuss some question about the children over which they disagreed. At this interview, Mr. Y announced that he had decided they should both have treatment. Mrs. Y agreed, and I continued to see her, and arranged for him to see another worker. Mrs. Y showed herself extremely vulnerable to her husband's complaints and accusations, and spent much time in her interviews marshalling the evidence that these were unjust, and that he was more ill than she. She admitted she sometimes wondered which of them was mad; one of them certainly must be. She was trying hard to adapt by regarding him as a patient and herself as his nurse.

For a time all three boys were at boarding-school, so that Mr. Y had his wife to himself, and they got on better. He became more depressed and less paranoid, showing a childish dependence which was not without its appeal for his wife. Mrs. Y became less preoccupied with who was ill, and explored a good many things about the value the relationship had for her, and her problems about dominance and submission. Then Mr. Y began to deteriorate, revealing himself as frankly schizophrenic. This was precipitated by a financial crisis, in which his wife decided to economise by bringing one boy home from boarding-school and to insist that Mr. Y must pay for his own keep from his Unemployment Benefit. He responded with frank delusions of grandeur, and his worker was able to persuade him to seek in-patient treatment, while I communicated to his wife our agreement that he was definitely ill. She continued to discuss his behaviour as if he were fully responsible; I contrasted this with her former efforts to persuade me that he was mad. She admitted very readily that this had been her defence against her fears that she herself was mad.

At this point Mr. Y entered hospital as a voluntary patient, and his wife expressed a whole series of anxieties:

Is mental illness hereditary?
Is it likely to lie dormant and break out in adolescence?
Are boys any less likely to break down than girls? (Mrs. Y had known a suicidal adolescent girl.)
What would become of the boys in a "hen-ridden" home without a father?
What could she tell the children about their father's illness? (She had known of children in like circumstances who had worried secretly for years lest they would go mad in due course.)

In such circumstances, one cannot deny the possibility of constitutional weakness, but I was able to give her some reassurance by contrasting the violently traumatic character of her husband's childhood with the material security she was able to give her sons and the care and thought she was devoting to protecting their mental health. She decided to tell them that her husband was ill — his nerves were bad. John wanted to know why he was ill. Cedric, the youngest, said he should have his nerves out — and his bad back was due to his giving John a piggy-back! Mrs. Y was about to qualify as a teacher, and was thinking of working with handicapped children, but needed my reassurance that she was not too ill for this. Anyone who knew she attended the Clinic would think she was as ill as her husband — or at least as her brother. Eventually she was able to see that, although she had problems, she was not incapacitated as they were.

Here I think I was able to give this mother some help in dealing with the anxieties concerning her husband's illness and breakdown. She has never been able to let the children express their feelings freely, especially any anger with their father (who left hospital on the basis of a partial remission, settled down with a girl he met in hospital, and eventually gave his wife a divorce). But I think her anxieties have been more manageable than they would have been otherwise, the children seem to be developing well, and she has now married again, a husband who is distinctly less unstable than the first.

In these two cases, the major anxiety might be summed up as: "Who next?", but in the second we begin to glimpse the other anxiety which plagues the relatives of the mentally ill, which we might express as "Whodunit?" (You remember Cedric saying it was the fault of John's piggy-back.) In my third case both these themes will emerge very clearly.

Dennis was 12 when first seen at the Clinic. His mother, aged 35, had had a depressive breakdown the previous year, had been twice admitted for in-patient treatment, and was now at home for a month's trial period. The father was 15 years older, so small that he felt deformed, worked a 9-hour day at a poorly paid job, and suffered from a gastric ulcer. Dennis was the only child.

Both parents were anxious about Dennis, and had taken steps to get help for him. They complained that he had never been clean or dry, stole, lied, smeared mirrors, rubbed his hands and dangled a plasticine man for the cat to claw. He was said to have "deteriorated in the last year or so". His mother, who had been abandoned at five and brought up in a Home, said she was "terrified of doing to Dennis what her mother had done to her". She "felt Dennis to be part of herself in a way she couldn't express". She had had similar symptoms to his when young. The father wanted us to take Dennis in for observation "to see how queerly he behaves". He told the psychiatrist that Dennis was a problem "because he worries his mother". He wondered if Dennis had inherited anything from her — nerves for instance. He kept on asking him not to worry her, but it did no good. He implied that Dennis had contributed to her illness by his insatiable demands. The mother too was afraid that Dennis would inherit her illness, though she had been reassured at the hospital. The parents often quarrelled about Dennis and his behaviour.

It seemed to us that Dennis was the least ill member of the family, and would be better off in a suitable boarding-school. We therefore invited the mother to see the caseworker again, with a view to helping her to accept this residential solution without too much anxiety and guilt. However, her husband turned up with her. He was off work with his ulcer and a damaged wrist, and was apparently making a full-time job of looking after his wife, hovering protectively around her on account of her "insecurity and uncertainty" — yesterday he had sat and watched her at work for two hours! He discouraged her attempts to explain her difficulties to the caseworker by constantly remarking: "It's her illness". When asked directly what he was feeling, he burst out: "You can see my wife alone, if that's what you mean". The worker recognised that life had not been easy for him either, and wondered if we could help him. He denied any need for help; Dennis must get better to look after his mother when his father was gone. He sometimes wondered if he ought to leave his wife — what did the worker think? "Home is the focus where it all starts — *I sometimes wonder if it's all my fault*".

Here on the one hand we can see very clearly the needs of the patient, and the way in which her husband's anxious over-protection undermines her. At one point, when he described his plans to take her straight back to work from the interview and buy her lunch later, she said: "You see, that's what he's like all the time. . . . Dad, I wish you wouldn't fuss me so — you make me worried." Further contact with this disturbed marriage made it seem probable that he had in fact a great deal to do with his wife's illness.

On the other hand, we can see in operation the basic anxieties which a mental breakdown in one member arouses in the family. There is the anxiety about heredity, and here we see the inefficacy of simple reassurance. Then the father accuses the son of having driven the mother mad — he goes on and on at him to do this or that, always with the implication that he has made his mother ill and is driving her mad again. This kind of nagging is as good a way as one could find of making the boy ill, by reinforcing the anxiety and guilt which he would in any case feel about his mother's illness, so hard to distinguish from simple unhappiness. Finally, the husband reveals his own compelling motivation — someone has driven his wife mad, and if it is not the boy it must be himself. No wonder this tormenting anxiety drives him repeatedly to seek relief by projecting his guilt on to his son.

These aspects of the case seem to me to be generic or situational. Anxiety about heredity and guilt about the breakdown seem to me to be as normal as mourning following bereavement; not of themselves pathogenic in robust constitutions, but liable to take a pathogenic turning if the soil or the circumstances are unfavourable. In my third case, the intensity of the father's guilt and the character of his defences approximated to the classic picture of "driving the other person mad". In addition to these "situational" reactions, the psycho-pathology of this family bore a sinister resemblance to the family backgrounds of certain schizophrenic young men, as described by Goldberg,[6] Morris[7] and others. As soon as the mother was allowed to talk alone with the caseworker, she spoke of her frigidity with her husband. We suspected at the time, and gained ample confirmation later, that this mother's over-indulgence of her son had a strong libidinal and seductive element in it. This helped to inflame the father's jealous hostility to the son, and no doubt accounted for the suffering of the plasticine hanged man.

This was evidently a very difficult case, in which it took a great deal of work to achieve a minimal result. My point is that these parents virtually found their own way to the child guidance clinic, because their defences were fortunately of a character which enabled them to seek help actively. But we come across far more families whose response is not to seek psychiatric help but to avoid it, and these make me feel that ideally there should be someone to investigate every breakdown involving a family, to see what help they need with the anxiety and guilt which may otherwise threaten their mental health.

If it has not been possible to pay much attention to this function hitherto, this is more than understandable, in view of the multitude of needs of all kinds, and the terrible shortage of workers. But at this moment, when the foundations of new mental health services are being laid, it is important to take stock of the need, and I think this need for preventive work with relatives should be firmly placed on the record. It may seem unrealistic to suppose that resources will ever be adequate in our lifetime to do more than "put Humpty Dumpty together again". Yet I would like to put forward the hypothesis that preventive work with relatives, if carried out promptly at the moment of crisis, would be a very economical investment of resources, and would not be likely to be very time-consuming, in spite of the depth of the anxieties involved. I base this opinion on Caplan's[8] theory of crisis as a time at which defences have crumbled and, just because deep anxieties are exposed to the light of day, there is an excellent opportunity to help the family sort out fantasy and reality, to reduce their anxiety to realistic and tolerable dimensions, and to deal with it without recourse to maladaptive defences. Not only would such work be more effective and economical than later attempts to remedy situations in which maladaptive defences have become habitual and indispensable; the contact would also serve to discover what other members of the family were at risk from whatever family pathology might have contributed to the patient's breakdown.

This is a most vital area for research, and until we know more about it the tendency for mental illness to run in families remains an unanalysed amalgam of environmental and constitutional factors. I would add the hope that we shall in time be able to entrust a good deal of after-care to other professional groups, such as mental welfare officers, mental nurses and health visitors and to devote more of our own time and skills to preventing the spread of mental ill-health in families where it has already established a bridgehead.

Acknowledgment

I am indebted to Miss Barbara Boyle for permission to quote the case of Dennis, on which she did the casework under my supervision. E.E.I.

References

1. Power, M. (1956) Community Care: A New Social Service, *British Journal of Psychiatric Social Work,* Vol. III, No. 3.
2. Goldberg, E.M. (1957) The Psychiatric Social Worker in the Community, *British Journal of Psychiatric Social Work,* Vol. IV, No. 2.
3. Jones, K.I. and Hammond, P. (1960) The Boundaries of Training, *British Journal of Psychiatric Social Work,* Vol. V. No. 4.
4. Heimler, E. (1955) Psychiatric Social Work with National Assistance Board Cases, *The Medical Officer.*
5. Eden, M. (1955) A Modern Observation Ward and the Psychiatric Social Worker, *British Journal of Psychiatric Social Work,* Vol. III, No. 1.
6. Goldberg, E.M. (1960) Parents and Psychotic Sons, *British Journal of Psychiatric Social Work,* Vol. V, No. 4.
7. Morris, P. (1958) Some Disturbances of Family Function Associated with Psychiatric Illness, *British Journal of Medical Psychiatry,* Vol XXX, Nos. 1/2.
8. Caplan, G. (1959) *Concepts of Mental Health and Consultation,* New York.

CHAPTER 13

Children at Risk*

Dr. Gerald Caplan has familiarised us, in several publications, with the crisis model of mental health and mental disorder (1959, 1961, 1962). This draws our attention to certain kinds of sharp discontinuity in development or experience which upset the equilibrium of the individual and expose him to the risk of adopting solutions that are dangerous for his future mental health. Not everyone will emerge from his crisis thus damaged. Some will have responded to the challenge by mobilising their forces in ways that increase strength and confidence, maturity, and ability to deal with stress. Those who emerge weakened, relying more heavily than before on rigid, brittle, and maladaptive defences, may well have been predictably more vulnerable at the outset, although Caplan shows reason to believe that the quality of social interaction during the crisis period can often have a decisive effect on the outcome. Young children are particularly vulnerable to separation from their mothers, as Dr. John Bowlby (1951, 1956) and others have demonstrated, whereas the mother's reliable presence often renders them surprisingly invulnerable to any stress situation that does not upset the mother herself too greatly. It also seems likely that disturbed relationships within the family, especially but not exclusively between the child and his mother, will enhance his vulnerability to most kinds of stress.

---

*First published in *Case Conference,* Vol. X, 1963/4.

Need for Preventive Services

It follows from this reasoning that a preventive mental health programme must be especially concerned to identify and support vulnerable individuals who are exposed to crisis situations. One such group, which as yet has received surprisingly little attention, comprises the children of parents who have recently been admitted to a mental hospital. Such children are likely to be particularly vulnerable on account of previous disturbed relationships within the family, especially if the onset of the illness has been insidious. They are now exposed to the sudden loss of a parent, in circumstances that are likely to tinge their natural grief and distress with a heavy colouring of anxiety and guilt. Some of these children may also be vulnerable by heredity. This hypothesis was at one time derived from belief in the tendency of mental illness to run in families, but it now seems likely that much of this tendency could be accounted for by disturbed relationships and the experience of recurrent crisis.

If this reasoning is correct, policy and practice in the treatment and care of the mentally ill should always take the interests of the children explicitly into account in order to harmonise or balance them with those of the patient. There is as yet little evidence that this is systematically done. A very few hospitals are experimentally admitting pre-school children with their mentally ill mothers (Douglas, 1956; Baker, Game, Morrison and Thorpe 1961; Glaser, 1962). This practice is usually advocated on the grounds of benefit to the mother, but it is believed to be of value to the children too, both as avoiding a separation and as affording an opportunity for the child to enjoy skilled support in dealing with the problems with which his mother's illness confronts him. Where no such arrangements exist, the children are automatically separated from the parent who goes into hospital. We should not underestimate the traumatic potential of separation from the father, which will vary according to the age of the child and the degree of attachment to him. Separation from the mother, however, often results in substitute care arrangements which involve separation from the father also, whereas if he is hospitalised the children are likely to remain with the mother. Such arrangements may be formal and official, in which case the child care service takes responsibility and is in a position to help the child deal with his inner crisis: or they may be unofficial, as when relatives open their homes to the child. In this case it is nobody's explicit job to make sure that the child is dealing adequately with the crisis, and the lack of public discussion suggests that social workers may be too busy dealing with other urgent problems to investigate whether the relatives are indeed able to give the child the help he needs.

How far can we assume that placement in a kindly family, related or otherwise, provides an adequate solution for the child's emotional need? Even in the simpler case where the mother goes to the hospital for physical illness, this is expecting a lot. Adults often find it difficult to tolerate a child's grief or his defences, or to let him express his feelings. If he is sad and listless, unable to respond affectionately, and particularly if he eats poorly and compares the food unfavourably with his mother's cooking, those who are trying so hard to make him happy often feel hurt and personally rejected. This is likely to be all the more so if the mother is insane and if her behaviour and care of the children have been the subject of dissatisfaction and friction for some time, or if there were other tensions between her and the relatives now caring for the children.

Other adults can readily sympathise with the child who grieves openly, but may be shocked or antagonised by one who wears a mask of indifference, is unnaturally cheerful, or who expresses hostility to the absent parent. These reactions may be taken at their face value, and the child perceived as a heartless little wretch, whereas a child who is using these defences is probably in need of professional understanding and help. Yet other children may express their emotional disturbance by rudeness and rebellion toward anyone who presumes to try to replace the absent parent, or may develop symptoms such as tics, enuresis or soiling. Many adults find it hard to recognise such behaviour as a signal of distress, and their sympathy may be alienated. There is another hazard when the absent parent is mentally ill; these manifestations are apt to be interpreted as the first signs of hereditary mental illness, in which case the child will be treated with anxious over-solicitude, or those in charge may try to protect themselves against this anxiety by nagging or scolding him in the hope that he will stop such behaviour and so prove that he is not ill after all.

When the Parent is Hospitalised

When a parent goes to hospital, the mere fact of separation, the pain of missing the absent person, is bound to be complicated more or less by the child's anxiety about the illness and the outcome, and by guilt for past unkindness, demandingness, or thoughtlessness. When these feelings are strong the child will need opportunity to talk them out; this some families or foster-parents can provide, but others may find it too hard to tolerate the expression of such feelings, and may smother it with reassurance or cheerful chatter in a way that relieves themselves more than the child. When the parent is mentally ill, everyone's anxieties are likely to be worse. Physical illness can often be labelled and explained, and the length of absence can often be predicted; this is helpful to all but the youngest children. Mental illness can usually not be named or explained, and questions are apt to evoke uneasy equivocation, which creates an atmosphere of shameful and embarrassing mystery. Older children may suspect madness, and will feel ashamed of this as they would not of a physical complaint. Guilt may well have been stimulated during the period of onset by repeated urging to be good, to keep quiet, for fear of giving mother a headache, or because daddy isn't well. They may have been more overtly accused of "getting on mother's nerves", or of "driving daddy round the bend". When mother or father eventually "goes round the bend" this will seem to be the fulfilment of a prophecy, the result of all those unheeded warnings.

There may have been scenes of violence, and the children may have not only been very frightened, but also quite confused about who was the victim and who was the aggressor. This is especially so if the child has been attached to a paranoid parent, who may for months or years have been accusing neighbours, relatives, or the other parent of conspiring to "put him (her) away". Now he has been "put away", so he was right all along; or perhaps the child feels he has been sent away as a punishment for difficult behaviour. Such children are apt to be both frightened and angry with those who "put away" the missing parent for obscure reasons which they are usually too embarrassed to explain. The children therefore "play up" in ways that set up a new round of anger and anxiety in relatives, since they seem to confirm all the natural fears about heredity.

For all these reasons, the children of parents who have recently entered a mental hospital need help which relatives, friends or foster-parents may be able to give, but on the other hand may not, on account of their own anxieties about grief and loss, and about mental illness in particular. Moreover, these children need help now. Within a few weeks they will have resolved the crisis one way or the other. If they adopt pathological defences and we wait until these have become so crippling or alarming that the children eventually get referred for treatment, it may well take years to undo what could have been prevented by a few timely interviews with the child or the adults about him. This is why an adequate preventive mental health programme would require that, in every case where the patient has children, someone should take responsibility, for seeing not only that they are being suitably cared for on the material level, but also that they are being allowed or helped to express their feelings freely, and not to be overcome by unrealistic anxiety and guilt — which are not susceptible to reassurance unless they have been fully expressed to someone who does not secretly or openly share them. Sometimes, as I mentioned in a former paper (1961), a parent or other member of the household may in fact be blaming the child as a way of dealing with his own intolerable guilt, and this may require more extensive casework help.

When the Children Stay at Home

Even where the separation crisis has been dealt with, further crises may arise from the patient's visits home. Moods may vary alarmingly, disappointments may lead to threats of breaking up the home and sending the children away. If the children are in care, there may be jealousy and rows with the foster parents. At all these points help may be needed. The parent's return home will necessitate further readjustments, especially when he or she is still far from well. Fortunately, simple supportive casework, not too time-consuming, can often prove remarkably effective.

Mrs. A, the mother of several children, returned home against advice after a long stay in a mental hospital, following a limited response to a new drug. Her eldest son, who had been living alone with the father meanwhile (the younger children being in care) committed a minor offence soon after his mother's return, and was put on probation. Mrs. A, who was still quite vague and confused, began to demand the return of the other children too, and there were grounds for concern about all these children if she got her way. However, with the support of the probation officer, the mother gradually improved, the younger children came home and settled down, and the eldest boy did not repeat his offence. As the probation officer eventually expressed it: "I think what helped him most was to know that I liked his mother and was not frightened by her in spite of her strangeness."

Not all children are so lucky, especially those with a parent who spends short periods in a mental hospital at frequent intervals. Health visitors are sometimes concerned about young children in this situation.

Mrs B's husband got her admitted to hospital whenever her appetite failed, but took her home again as soon as it recovered, even though she was still in terror of enemies whom she felt to be pursuing her with machine-guns from airplanes, and talked about this in a loud and agitated manner to the children and everyone else who would listen. These children were observed to be very strained and withdrawn whenever their mother was at home, and more happy and spontaneous when she was away. The health visitor arranged for the youngest (aged 20 months) to enter a day nursery, where for some time he was exceptionally difficult and withdrawn. He gradually improved, but was visibly disturbed at each recurrent separation and reunion with his mother. Eventually he became able to enjoy the opportunities for play in the nursery and to respond to the staff, though he was still a solitary child at the age of 4 years. The warm and stable environment provided by the nursery was probably an important factor in the child's gradual improvement.

Reaching Families under Stress

In a recent symposium, entitled Reluctantly to School, two authors stress the frequency of ambulant mental illness among the parents of school refusers, particularly the mothers (Walker, 1963; Burgess, 1963). Walker describes two examples, of which I shall summarise one.

An unmarried mother was epileptic, and was periodically admitted to hospital for severe depression. Her mother looked after the three children at these times, but died when the eldest boy was 10. From this time he felt increasingly responsible for his mother and siblings, especially for reminding his mother to take her medicine, and his school attendance suffered. At age 12 he was charged with non-attendance and, following a remand in custody, he was enabled to return to school with the help of the probation officer and the mental welfare officer, who was now presumably called in to relieve the boy of the home nursing which he had been doing unaided for two years.

This story illustrates how easily cases can slip through the aftercare net, even when the family is in no state to undertake responsibility for the patient and may be in urgent need of supportive and preventive services itself. It is unclear at the moment how far this is due to the undermanning of services, and how far to lack of liaison between mental hospitals and community services, whether specialised or not. The problem is too big to be solved by specialised services alone, even when the mental hospital really brings itself to trust and use the community service. Child care officers, probation officers and health visitors all have contact with these families, and the help they offer can be tremendously increased by communication and co-operation with those treating the parent. It is vital that there should be some machinery for ensuring that somebody is available and sensitive to the needs of every family exposed to such stress, or at least every family containing children, so that no family in need slips through the net unhelped. We do not know what proportion of these families can manage unaided — not simply to survive intact, but in such a way as to avoid developing a fresh round of mental disturbance. We do know that at present many are left to manage as best they can. We need a study of how families cope with this crisis similar to that reported by Caplan (1961) of families coping with the birth of a premature baby. The other necessity is that all professional people who have contact with such families should be recognised as potential helpers, and that those who do not already have adequate or appropriate training should recognise the need for consultation, and should be generously supported by those with more specialised knowledge, whether of mental illness, or of casework method.

References

Baker, A.A., Game, J.A., Morrison, M. and Thorpe, J.G. (1961) Admitting Schizophrenic Mothers with their Babies, *Lancet*, pp. 237-9.

Bowlby, J. (1951) *Maternal Care and Mental Health*, WHO.

174 Social Work and Human Problems

Bowlby, J. and Ainsworth, M. (1956) The Effects of Mother-Child Separation: A Follow-up Study, *British Journal of Medical Psychology.*

Burgess, E. (1963) Children Committed to Care for Non-attendance at School, *British Journal of Psychiatric Social Work,* Vol. VII, no. 2.

Caplan, G. (1959) *Concepts of Mental Health and Consultation,* U.S. Children's Bureau, Washington. (1961) *A Community Approach to Mental Health,* Tavistock, London. (1962) *Prevention of Mental Disorders in Children,* Tavistock, London.

Douglas, G. (1956) Psychotic Mothers, *Lancet,* pp. 124-5.

Glaser, T. (1962) A Unit for Mothers and Babies in a Psychiatric Hospital, *Journal of Child Psychology and Psychiatry,* Vol. III, no. 1.

Irvine, E.E. (1961) Psychosis in Parents: Mental Illness as a Problem for the Family, *British Journal of Psychiatric Social Work,* Vol. VI, no. 1.

Walker, A. (1963) Children who Refuse to go to School in a Reception Centre, *British Journal of Psychiatric Social Work,* Vol. VII, no. 2.

Part IV   Values and Knowledge
for Social Work

The Seebohm reorganisation of the social services posed enormous problems of integration for social workers of different background and training. BASW accordingly arranged a regional conference to explore what knowledge and values could be shared by caseworkers, residential workers and the untrained. In my contribution (Chapter 13) I dwelt particularly on the value of autonomy, because it seems to be often neglected in residential institutions and sometimes given too exclusive a priority by the new generation of fieldworkers, and is thus a frequent source of friction.

Chapter 14 was first presented before the amalgamation of the social services, to a conference on training for child care called by the Children's Department of the Home Office, which was then responsible for the child care service. I was more anxious then than I am now about the appearance of learning theory and behaviour modification in a few social work courses, and so were many of my colleagues. We felt there was a danger that learning theory might be used as an alternative to dynamic theories of human behaviour, and that social workers might be encouraged to manipulate their clients' behaviour without adequate consideration of its motivation and its possible defensive functions. However, several articles (Sluckin and Jehu, 1969; Sluckin, 1975) have demonstrated that some at least of the techniques of behaviour modification can be usefully combined with awareness of psycho-dynamic motivation and relationships. But there is still a need for vigilance against using these techniques as a short cut and focusing too exclusively on modifying behaviour without regard for the stresses and strains of the familial and social environment, which might lead us to relieve the client of his symptom and leave him undefended against those who are demanding too much of him, or quite the wrong thing.

At the end of that paper I briefly indicated my view that creative literature is an antidote to the dehumanising and distancing effect of too much social science regarding individuals as objects of scientific enquiry. The curriculum of basic courses of social work is so overloaded that one cannot impose much extra reading on students but certain novels, like *The Rainbow* or *The Mill on the Floss,* contain the experience of so many situations, relationships and personalities that even one of these greatly enriches the study of "human growth and behaviour". In my last years at York I would ask the students to read one or two of these novels and to discuss the family constellations, the development of the characters, the nature of the crises, which they contain. After retiring I was happy to find that Bill Bayley, the Training Officer for the Northern Probation Region, was also interested in the use of fiction, poetry, films and plays for deepening the insight of social workers, and together we have run short refresher courses for probation officers. My appointment at Smith College of Social Work enabled me to explore this method further, and to give the lecture which now forms Chapter 15.

References

Sluckin, A. and Jehu, D.A. (1969) A Behavioural Approach in the Treatment of Elective Mutism, *British Journal of Psychiatric Social work,* Vol. X, no. 2.

Sluckin, A. (1975) Encopresis: A Behavioural Approach Described, *Social Work Today,* Vol. V, no. 21.

CHAPTER 14

A Common Base for Social Work: Values and Knowledge*

I believe it was David Hume who demonstrated the complete independence of value from knowledge, and produced the axiom that what ought can never be derived from what is. I am not a philosopher, but (or perhaps so) my common sense has always revolted against this proposition, since in daily life our reasoning about what we ought to do is so often carried on in terms of the anticipated results of our actions: for instance, if we spare the rod, shall we really spoil the child or shall we help him to be kinder and more considerate? It seems to me that we have to distinguish between ultimate values, which are certainly independent of what is, and instrumental values: i.e. those things which we think we ought to do because we believe they will help to achieve goals based on our ultimate values. Now these instrumental values are properly open to modification by knowledge: it may be proved that some hallowed prescription is in certain circumstances impossible to carry out, or futile, or even that it defeats the ends it was intended to serve.

This may seem rather abstract, but I hope to show that it is highly relevant to the question of identifying a common stock of values and knowledge which can be shared by social workers of different training and specialised experience, and by those concerned with all varieties of day and residential care. Some of the hallowed "principles of casework" can be divisive in this context, and really seem to me to need reinterpretation in the light of further knowledge and thought. Let us take the principle of respecting the autonomy of the client, or

---

*First published in *A Common Base for Social Work*, B.A.S.W., 1972.

recognising his right to self-determination. This makes sense at first sight in relation to the healthy adult client — but what about children, or more or less senile old people? And then what about homicidal patients, what about prisoners, what about neglectful or cruel parents? Here we come up against the whole question of the conflict of interests between one individual and others; such parents, for instance, may be strongly opposed to any separation from their children, but their style of parenthood may be having a visibly disturbing or harmful effect on their offspring. In fact it becomes apparent when we think about such situations that none of us can claim absolute autonomy, or an absolute right to self-determination, because the behaviour of any member of a society affects the rights and the autonomy of all those in contact with him.

This brings us to the issue of social control: the accusation that while we proclaim our respect for autonomy and self-determination we are actually nothing but agents of social control. Some of us have reacted to these accusations, or "revelations", by passionately repudiating the social control function, and adopting the stance of being "on the side of the client" — almost, in certain cases, "my client right or wrong" — or is it "the client can do no wrong"? Is this what non-judgmentalism means? If so, it could only be practised by the individual caseworker, who could — and sometimes does — identify with his client against all comers; against his tyrannical parents, against his rebellious children, against his unreasonable spouse. Most of us realise that this is in fact a form of judgmentalism, unhelpful to the client and unfair to his family and other contacts; we try to avoid it, and we usually succeed in avoiding its cruder manifestations. However, it is difficult to avoid, and this requires constant vigilance. It was not uncommon before the Seebohm reorganisation for workers in the mental health service to focus pretty exclusively on the interests of a mentally ill parent, and for child care workers to focus equally strongly on those of the children. Some of us may now be becoming more aware of such bias, and doing our best to accept the much more painful situation of equal concern for various people whose interests cannot always be reconciled.

At this point I should express my view that social control is a necessary, and in fact an indispensable thing, without which no society could hang together at all, and few individuals would enjoy any rights with any degree of security. A good many people seem to disagree with this view, but to debate that would require another paper. I will simply assert that in my view social control is necessary for the protection of individuals against one another; that is the framework within which I say that social workers do have a social control function among others, and that this kind of control is the most humane we have. Consider the alternatives to social work help, for instance, for the neglectful or cruel parent.

A good many of the divisions in our ranks have been concerned with the social control function, owing to feelings that such control was not compatible with respect for autonomy or self-determination, and was therefore incompatible with casework. For many years P.S.W.s were inclined to hold up their hands in horror at the methods used by some M.W.O.s to get patients into hospital, while themselves avoiding a task which was felt to be unworthy of a caseworker (social control might be necessary, but it was felt to be dirty work). But by refusing the statutory duties and the risk of having to use pressure or compulsion, they also avoided the opportunity of dealing with the psychiatric emergency, with all the opportunities for using the crisis to uncover and resolve pathological processes in the family. Many P.S.W.s had come out of this ivory tower before the Seebohm reorganisation began, and found themselves the better for it; eventually it will not be possible for any worker in the local authority to avoid his share of compulsory admissions and project authoritarian badness onto specialists in compulsion. It will be easier for us all if we can accept authority, not as a Bad Thing, but as a Good Thing which can be abused but need not, and which cannot be dispensed with. Similarly, some of us avoided the probation service because of its rather obvious social control function, which seemed to blot out the "assisting and befriending"; and there have been serious discussions as to whether the element of control was compatible with respect for autonomy and self-determination. Oddly enough, people were less aware of their social control functions in the child care service, till Joel Handler (1968) rudely challenged this denial, by spelling out in no uncertain terms how extensively Children's Departments were involved in this process. I think it is time we stopped arguing and worrying about whether we do or should exercise social control; let us accept the fact that we do, and devote more thought to how and when we should do so. Acceptance of this would relieve us from the burden and handicap of self-deception, and would remove some of the fictitious barriers which have divided us till now.

There is of course a world of difference between having and exercising a social control function, and being nothing but an instrument of social control. The good social worker should never be a *mere* instrument of control, and this is what makes social work the most humane instrument of such control we have. Although we are properly concerned with other people besides the client (if we can identify a single client at all), this must always be balanced by an equal and genuine concern for him. If this is not so (and sometimes it is not) we are not, in that situation, operating as professional social workers. It is part of our professional discipline to keep our cool in situations where others often allow their blood to boil — for instance when dealing with the parents of battered babies. We must not allow our concern for the helpless, suffering child to blind us to the suffering and need of the offending parent, even though we may have to protect the child by an exercise of authority and control — i.e. by removing him to a safer environment against the expressed wishes of the parents. The child is our client, whom we must protect; the parents are equally our clients, whom we may have to protect against those who would like to punish them by imprisonment or otherwise. In working with them we shall indeed be hoping to improve their capacity for parental care, and this may even come about partly to please us; but they will not even want to please us unless we have been able to relieve their deprivation through a relationship in which we have provided something akin to an experience of parental care. This ability to remember and to sympathise with the client's suffering, to consider his motivation and his needs whatever he has done, is what we mean by acceptance — another of our ambiguous words.

I have chosen an extreme case which reminds us, among other things, that the ability to accept all comers is an ideal rather than a reality. Not all of us can genuinely accept the battering parent. Others of us may find other behaviour and its authors impossible to accept — for instance, robbery with violence to old people. Before April 1st,

1971, we could acknowledge these limitations in our choice or avoidance of special fields in social work; we chose old people's welfare rather than child care, or vice versa. But the setting up of generic services does not automatically make us more catholic in our sympathies, though contact with clients with new problems does a great deal towards this by revealing the familiar humanity behind the unfamiliar problems. (A student from a Middle-Eastern country, where unmarried mothers are usually killed by their relatives, was amazed and delighted to find in a placement that unmarried mothers were people to whom she could relate as well as to anyone else.) But many of us will find that we still cannot help drawing the line somewhere; and I think it important that the new services should recognise this and create a climate where people can be honest about such limitations, and not try to conceal and deny them. If they can be admitted and discussed, they often prove modifiable. On the other hand they may prove too deep-rooted to change, and it seems to me that there should be some flexibility in allowing people to avoid working with clients who for them personally are beyond the pale. Sincerity is one of the major values of social work, and should not be sacrificed to unrealistic ideals of being all-understanding and all-accepting. This can only result in pretended acceptance, and pretence is no use to anybody, least of all to the very damaged clients who are hardest to accept.

I set out to talk about autonomy (defined in the dictionary as "personal freedom; freedom of will"), and our respect for it; and I find myself talking about its limitations and our social control functions! However, autonomy or freedom is not negated by law and controls; it is limited in the interests of the autonomy of others, and is thus distributed more justly than if we had a free-for-all. However, it is still far from equally distributed, because of the inequalities of wealth, status, privilege, education and ability; some members of the community are subjected to restraint for the protection of others; other members are unable to claim a full measure of autonomy because they are too young, too old or too handicapped to live independently. I think "respect for the client's autonomy", is a phrase which doesn't hold water. It makes much more sense simply to respect the client (autonomous or not), and accept an obligation to help him maximise his legitimate autonomy. This can be done in many ways. Increasing a person's resources usually increases his autonomy (unless there are strings attached), whether we do this by providing appliances and conveniences for the physically handicapped, or by encouraging the poor to claim welfare rights of which they were too ignorant, or too apprehensive to apply. Campaigning for better general provision of income or appliances also increases the possibility of choice or freedom of movement of the beneficiaries; so can the encouragement of successful pressure-group activity.

But resources and autonomy are not identical, and should not be confused. Children and old people in Homes may be very well provided for, perhaps much better than they would be outside, but they may pay heavily for this in terms of the freedom to choose and decide. A weekly ration of sweets worth 20 pence represents virtually no autonomy, as compared with 10 pence to spend on sweets of ones own choice — or on something else. Old people also prefer to do their own shopping; they may become unable to carry the heavy bag, to make the journey safely alone or even to walk so far, but the answer (in terms of autonomy) is someone to go along and help, perhaps to drive, but not to do the shopping for them while they sit cosily at home.

Once old people are in Homes, it is particularly easy, in the goodness of our hearts, to do everything for them, forgetting the pleasure they derive from pottering down to the shops and choosing what to buy — from exercising this remnant of autonomy. Obviously, autonomy is progressively restricted by the increasing infirmities of old age; the principle of maximising autonomy enjoins on us not to reduce it unnecessarily, for reasons of administrative convenience, and in fact to take trouble to preserve it — e.g. by seeing that old people who have no relatives to take them shopping have someone else to escort them; a useful role for volunteers. This kind of concern for the client's autonomy is, I think, the Rubicon between residential (or custodial) care and residential social work.

Concern for the client's autonomy has two elements: (a) allowing him to decide as much as possible for himself, and (b) encouraging him to do as much for himself as possible. Every time we do for someone what he could do for himself, however well we mean, we infringe his autonomy, we undermine his independence and his self-respect, we help to transform his self-image into that of a helpless person.

This kind of thing is often a bone of contention between residential and field staff. Indeed, so many residential staff being untrained, or not having been sensitised to this issue in their training, it often happens that patients are institutionalised (i.e. deprived of their autonomy), and field staff then hold up their hands in horror and set about de-institutionalising them through groupwork, etc., to the horror and dismay of the residential workers. This problem should diminish as training for residential staff expands and pays more attention to these issues.

To maximise autonomy requires clarity about its limits: we often have to help the client to distinguish between the possible and the impossible, since effort expended on pursuing the impossible is wasted effort, which could have been used for achieving the possible. This is for me the true meaning of adaptation: doing the best one can for oneself and one's family within the limits of the possible. Socially, these boundaries are sometimes hard to determine; social workers are often accused of pressurising people to accept intolerable situations which could be improved, given enough thought and determination. No doubt this sometimes happens and it requires vigilance to avoid it. But in the short run at least there is a limit to the number of welfare benefits which can be claimed; and having maximised income, there is still the problem of managing it. There are other less mutable limitations on autonomy: physical handicap, for instance. The victim of an accident or a disabling disease often has great difficulty in adapting, at great cost to himself. He remains unemployed because he is waiting for the time, which will never come, when he can return to his former occupation; he refuses all recreation because he can no longer engage in the athletic activities which were his pride. It is a great service if we can help him to adapt by relinquishing unattainable goals, and finding new satisfaction in the possible: to choose, from those occupations or leisure activities which are available, those which will be most rewarding for him.

This brings us to the point that autonomy is limited by internal as well as external factors; and crying for the moon is only one of them.

The accumulated experience of the decades since the principles of casework were formulated has made us realise that many of our clients are incapable of self-determination, because they are not well enough organised psychologically to take their own decisions. I do not mean that they take decisions which we may think foolish or wrong; I mean that they never actually take decisions. To decide means to pause, however briefly, to exercise foresight and the hindsight on which that is based, to consider alternatives. This requires some degree of ability to learn from experience, to predict consequences and to control impulses in the light of this knowledge; those who have not achieved these abilities do not decide, but act directly on impulse, often with disastrous results for themselves and others. Again and again such people defeat their own ends, or bring about events which they did not want, or even which they feared. With these impulse-ridden people it does not make too much sense to talk of respecting their autonomy; the problem is to help them to *gain* some autonomy by learning to decide and plan, to exercise foresight and hindsight, and to control their impulses in the light of such knowledge so as to be able to achieve at least some of their desires more safely and securely. Usually this learning cannot occur unless anxiety and deprivation can be relieved. Here we should recognise that material and emotional deprivation often (though not always) go together. It is difficult to relieve emotional deprivation without doing something to relieve material deprivation, but to relieve the latter alone may do very little to relieve the former.

It is time to give some attention to knowledge. My personal bias leads me to mention first knowledge of human growth and behaviour. We need to know what kind of experience helps a child to grow up able to love and work and to take responsibility, to learn from experience and to control his impulses; how the family can help him to do all this, and why certain families are temporarily or permanently unable to do so. I would emphasise that we cannot understand either normal or distorted development without reference to feeling, both in parents and child; the good home, from the point of view of child development, may not be the home which is cleanest and tidiest and free from financial muddles, or even that which provides the best physical care. Lack of loving warmth may cancel out all these advantages. Our mental health functions require some knowledge of severe mental illness and also of neurosis. Much of our work with families requires especially knowledge of the so-called character disorders (one of the various labels which are used to distinguish the kind of immature or impulse-ridden people I described above). Many things about these people become easier to understand and accept when we recognise their deprivation, not only in the present but all through their lives; depriving or neglectful parents are usually the deprived children, for whom we are so concerned, grown up. This is a branch of knowledge which has improved a good deal since I was a student. Another is the understanding of what goes on in families, which is equally important, for instance, in relation to mental illness and to child care. It is only too easy for doctors, and for us, to accept as the patient the person of whom the family complains; whereas more attention to what goes on within the family, might make it clear that some other member is much more in need of treatment, and may actually be driving that one mad. Other problems too — delinquency, drink or gambling — may be impossible to understand properly by studying the individual alone, without reference to family relationships.

In the past, some of us have been mainly concerned with personal problems and problems of relationships, and have perhaps not paid enough attention to material problems and how to relieve them; others have specialised in material aid, whether financial or in terms of appliances for the handicapped, with relatively little attention to emotional problems. We shall all have to try to redress any former imbalance in our knowledge; unless and until the machinery of state welfare is very much simplified, there is a great deal more to know in this area than we used to realise. On the other hand, it sometimes happens that doctors or hospital social workers refer disabled patients to the social services department in the hope that they will get help in adapting to the disability, only to find that appliances are supplied but other help is lacking. This is another aspect of what I said about the importance of feeling; we all need to appreciate that illness, separation between family members, etc. lead to emotional as well as material problems, and that it is the function of the social services to give help with both kinds of problem.

Then there is the whole question of method. Should we be learning special techniques, and if so which? At one time I was fascinated with a particular kind of casework technique, but later I realised there were many caseworkers and many clients for whom this would not do (see Chapters 4 and 5). Florence Hollis and others have more recently distinguished a number of techniques which can be combined in various ways to meet the needs of various caseworkers and clients. This analysis of techniques was designed as a research tool, not a practice tool, and I think there is a serious risk in training of focusing too much attention on technique at the expense of the worker/client relationship, which is often much more important. Since social workers are now expected to learn to work with groups as well as individuals, we cannot afford to focus too much on the niceties of technique. I think the basic thing is understanding of people in all their variety of personality and need; this provides the best basis for a flexible adaptation on our part to such needs. One thing I would emphasise: the importance of clear formulation of each client's needs, what we aim to do and how we hope to do it. The new departments are uncovering a vast amount of unmet need, and we cannot afford (if we ever could) simply to drift along "seeing" people regularly, in the hope that we are providing some sort of non-specific support which may help them mature or cope more adequately with problems. There is even a danger in such work of doing worse than waste our time, of encouraging a chronic dependency. Far better to aim at specific objectives, however modest, and to review our progress every few months. If nothing has changed we should then review our method and see what else we could do to be more effective; if there has been change, there is also a need for new responses on our part to meet and encourage it. If the client is maturing the time may have come to be less protective, to expect and encourage more independence, even to close the case.

Looking back, I think we had a premature focus on methodology, which led to unhelpful rigidities and infinite waste of time and fury on battles of dubious relevance, which distracted us from the variety of need.

CHAPTER 15

The Study of Human Growth and Behaviour: Science or Humanity?*

Since professional education is a preparation for a profession, let us begin with the question: What is a profession? Definitions commonly emphasise the possession of a distinctive body of learning, the accepted responsibility to transmit this and to add to it, and a code of ethics and professional practice whose function is to protect the public against neglect or exploitation by practitioners whose role requires that their clients entrust them with considerable power and opportunity. In some professions, technique forms an important feature of practice and training; this applies for instance to surgery and psycho-analysis, but less so to the ministry of religion.

An important function of definition is to distinguish the subject from those with which it is most likely to be confused. I therefore want to emphasise what the professional is not: in particular, that he is not a scientist and that however impressive his technical equipment, he is far from being merely a technician.

Only a professional scientist is primarily a scientist. This may seem obvious, but is often forgotten. Doctors, social workers and other professionals may engage in scientific activity full-time or part-time, but this is a change of role and function. The primary task is then to collect facts, to test hypotheses and so on — perhaps to perform experiments. Since any therapeutic activity is then part of the experiment, it must, therefore, be standardised. (I leave aside the vexed question of whether psycho-analysis is primarily science or therapy.)

---

*First published in *Social Work,* Vol. XXVI, no. 4, 1969.

Qua doctor or *qua* social worker, the professional's task is to render a service — to serve the patient or the client, who is *not* his rabbit or guinea-pig. He may use the findings of a number of sciences, but he is not *merely* an applied scientist. Healing, helping, education are arts, in which it is appropriate to use not only all relevant knowledge but also all the imagination and intuition one has: disciplined, of course, by that attention to mistakes and failures as well as to successes which enables us to learn from experience, and thus to develop "clinical judgement" or its analogues. There is an old French saying — "It is necessary to know Geometry to build a Cathedral, which is an act of faith".

I shall not discuss here the ethical code which is proper to the profession of social work, though I shall naturally imply important elements of it, particularly that of respect for the individual. Nor shall I give differential attention to the three branches of social work method; I write from experience which is mainly in social casework, but I believe that my argument applies *mutatis mutandis* to social groupwork and community organisation (and to the "pastoral professions in general" (Halmos, 1965)). I also leave aside that important part of the curriculum which prepares the social worker for the administration of social services.

We sometimes describe social work process in the borrowed terms "diagnosis" and "treatment". But since these are somewhat loaded, let us say in the plainest of English, that the social worker has to understand the individual or the group with the problem or the need, and to help them to find appropriate means of arriving at a solution. The principle of respect for the individual implies that the person or the people with the need or the problem should be not only allowed, but encouraged to cooperate as actively and responsibly as they are able in the exploration of the problem and the search for a solution, and should make the final decision.

This double task of understanding and helping calls for knowledge and skill. Let us consider what kind of knowledge. Social work was greatly handicapped in the early years of its development by the lack of a workable psychology (i.e. a psychology which included an account of irrational and self-defeating behaviour). It therefore embraced, eagerly and rapidly in the New World, reluctantly and cautiously in the Old, the body of psychological theory of which Sigmund Freud laid the foundations. Psycho-analysis developed as a branch of medicine, and provided a flood of usable and useful insights at a time when academic psychology had nothing to offer to the arts of healing or helping.

Since that time, great strides have been made in other directions. Sociology and anthropology have made a notable contribution to the understanding of human behaviour. We have become aware that whatever goes on in the unconscious, the early experience of children differs widely from one culture to another, and even from one subculture to another. Family structure, the roles of father, mother and of children of different ages, the aims and methods of child-rearing, the various roles which the adult is expected to perform, the value system which permeates all these, all constitute a comprehensive pattern which moulds and evaluates personality and which defines normality and deviance. It is within the context of such patterns that individual experiences produce individual variation. Each pattern produces its characteristic problems or forms of general human problems, and provides its characteristic approved solutions (e.g. methods of controlling disobedient children, methods of dealing with ambivalence about mothers-in-law) and its characteristic forms of deviance. All this provides a further dimension to our understanding of the individual in relation to his social environment — as long as we remember that it is not the sole purpose of men to play social roles: as long as we do not forget about needs, goals and purposes. Also social workers need teachers of sociology who are prepared to consider its implications for use; who will criticise our value-systems constructively, rather than simply explain them away.

Similarly, the development of learning theory has produced a useful account of important factors in learning and social adaptation. To some extent this can be integrated with the knowledge derived from psycho-analysis, though much work remains to be done on this. Also, Jehu (1967) has shown that many of the procedures of casework can be translated into the language of learning theory, and their effectiveness accounted for in these terms. But by no means all learning theorists consider it worth while to relate their findings and theories with those of psycho-analysis. A body of socio-behavioural theory is being built up which not only commands academic respect more readily than psycho-analysis has been able to do, but which is also beginning to claim to be a sounder basis for social work.

How far does this kind of knowledge help us to understand people better? Socio-behavioural theory has achieved academic respectability largely by aligning itself with the physical sciences, by studying its phenomena entirely by means of external observation and experiment; by studying behaviour rather than experience. This yields a kind of knowledge and a kind of understanding similar in kind to our knowledge and understanding of machines or of animals. But we should note in passing that the socio-behaviouralist shows more interest in the laboratory animal than the animal in his natural habitat; although as Ardrey (1967) has shown, even the study of wild species in captivity leads to some highly distorted conclusions about their psychology and social structure.

We can learn a lot from the rat, and more from the monkey and the ape; but I have serious misgivings about theories of human psychology confidently built largely on the study of captive and domesticated animals in laboratories. Labs are the best places to study some problems; but we now know that behaviour in a laboratory, or even in a zoo, gives a very inadequate or even a grossly misleading picture of the psychological equipment of a species, especially of its social psychology. Freudian theory has been described by a not wholly unsympathetic critic (Farrell, 1963) as a premature empirical synthesis, but it is not nearly as premature as human psychology based on that of laboratory animals.

I should like at this point to recall the argument of the philosopher Bergson, that science, which confers control of the environment, also falsifies by abstraction. Science deals splendidly with all that can be weighed, measured or counted, but this involves excluding from the universe of discourse the intangible, the imponderable, all that cannot be reduced to statistics. Behavioural scientists, from Watson onwards, have sometimes implied that what they could not study does not exist, and very often that it does not matter. Occam's razor is sometimes used to reduce feeling to the status of an unnecessary hypothesis. But feeling is a phenomenon, a fact of experience, and any psychology which ignores it is a very incomplete psychology. Behavioural Man, like Economic Man and Sociological Man, is subhuman — a simplified model produced by studying people as if they were things. Many useful discoveries can be made by these methods; it is not only dynamic psychology which has revealed to us processes of which we were previously unconscious. But in order to help people with their personal problems and relationships we have to deal with the whole man; we have to consider the effect of what we say and do on his feelings, as well as their contribution to his problems. We cannot afford to throw away the peculiar knowledge each of us has of people just by being one of them. Behavioural psychology is unable to deal with experience except by translating it into terms of presumed behavioural or physiological correlates; feelings becomes muscle tension, rhythms of heartbeat and breathing, secretion of sweat or electrical discharges. All this adds to our store of accurate and interesting scientific results; but it adds little or nothing to our understanding of experience, and the words in which we used to describe it have become for this purpose less useful than they were. Moreover, behavioural theory leads to behaviour therapy. There is a slippery slope on which it is difficult to stop where we would wish. It is only reasonable that our work should be subject to testing as regards the effectiveness of our methods; we ourselves should wish to work in the most effective way. This calls for criteria, and behavioural criteria are the easiest to formulate and to validate. So effectiveness is measured in terms of behavioural change, rather than of experience and attitudes. So if the object is to change behaviour, it is tempting to argue that all we need to know is how to do it most effectively, and experience can be regarded as irrelevant. The practitioner's task becomes one of moulding behaviour by the various kinds of conditioning, selecting and discarding responses by reinforcing this and extinguishing that; is it not sufficient to learn the techniques of the animal trainer? To quote a perceptive answer from an examination on the probable effect of behavioural theory on the role of the social worker, the practitioner is likely to become "more of a technician and less of a helping person".

Is such an outcome desirable? As Halmos says (1965) "Ever since Pavlov, there has been a firm conviction among some clinical workers that the machine man's psyche requires only machines for maintenance and repair, and that all therapy of the psyche must therefore be pursued in the businesslike spirit of the garage mechanic." Only it is worse than that, because some "psychologists" refuse to talk about the psyche at all, and maintain that all discourse about this no-thing is meaningless. I would seriously suggest that there is more to be learned about the mind of man from literature than from this kind of psychology. Let me quote Hamlet:

> "'Tis not alone my inky cloak, good mother,
> Nor customary suits of solemn black,
> Nor windy suspiration of forc'd breath,
> No, nor the fruitful river in the eye,
> Nor the dejected 'haviour of the visage,
> Together with all forms, moods, shows of grief,
> That can denote me truly. These indeed seem,
> For they are actions that a man might play:
> But I have *that within which passeth show;*
> These but the trappings and the suits of woe."

There are many reasons why the social worker should be sensitive to "that within which passeth show", and I think the need is increasing rather than declining with the drift of modern society. Social work is traditionally concerned with welfare need. Although it is now clear that the "Welfare State" as yet falls far short of providing adequately for these, there is no reason why, in conditions of increasing affluence, this problem should not be solved in the next fifty years. But affluence itself is a product of modern technology and the social organisation which goes with it; other products are alienation and anomy, and to these many sociologists attribute much of what is called social pathology. These concepts can be defined in more or less objective terms. It is worth noting that Karl Marx himself was aware of the subjective as well as the objective aspect: "The more the worker spends himself, the more powerful becomes the alien world of objects which he creates over and against himself, the poorer he himself — his inner world — becomes, the less belongs to him as his own." Thus the technology of mass-production impoverishes the worker psychologically — and this technology is essentially similar under socialism and capitalism. It requires moreover social and geographical mobility, which not only breaks up the extended family, but interferes with the establishment of deep-rooted relationships outside the nuclear family, thus tightening its tensions and increasing its vulnerability.

Our "irreversibly technological future" (Erikson, 1968) therefore seems likely to increase the need for skilled emotional support both for families at risk of disintegration and for the "disordered dust of individuals" who are the fall-out from family fission. Moreover, the more the individual is psychologically impoverished and threatened by the bondage to machines (Lane, 1969), the more he is manipulated both as factor of production and as consumer, the more in fact he is treated as a thing, the more likely he is to need the help of professionals who will relate to him in his full humanity, who will be attuned to "that within which passeth show". Let us hope that the human race will find ways in time to avert the risk of "affluent slavery for all concerned" (Erikson, *ibid.*), to reverse the dehumanising effects of mass-production while retaining its economic advantages. But meanwhile, for the foreseeable future, an increasingly important part of the social worker's function will be to provide and to promote the capacity for existential encounter, whether in individual interview, or in family or unrelated groups.

In this task, academic knowledge can be an instrument or an incubus. No doubt the behavioural sciences will outgrow their present crudity, and their practitioners will overcome their objections to the integration of these various ways of studying man in his societies. But there is also a problem concerning the use of positivistic knowledge about people. Application of the physical sciences consists of the manipulation and control of the physical environment; but this would be an unfortunate analogy for the application of "social science". The more complete our scientific knowledge about people, the more effective our techniques, the greater the power, and the more insidious the temptation, to manipulate them (of course "for their own good"). How can we ensure that knowledge and power shall not corrupt our attitudes and decompose our values, even as we use them with intent to serve? I think it is vital that we explicitly reject the model of the social worker as "technician", and uphold that of "helping person". We must reject the implicit model of the client as one to or for whom things are done, and uphold that of a person who uses help in working on his problems. We need to clarify the concept of casework and groupwork processes as essentially forms of human cooperation. The teaching of philosophy is of vital importance. I have mentioned Bergson as an ally against positivism. I think we shall increasingly turn to existentialism for the affirmation of people as experiencing beings, who suffer both pain and damage when treated as things. Another antidote to the influence of science, of which man is the object, is art, of which he is the subject. Literature (the art I know best) provides a wealth of insights into the human condition, the experience and motivation of men in society. . . . No, let me use a living language, and speak of their loves and hates, their passions and their virtues, their temptations and their faults — just those insights which are needed to preserve our concept of the fully human, of man and his dignity. We can learn a good deal about mental illness from the textbook; there are things we can learn better from Shakespeare, Ibsen, Dostoevsky and Conrad.

References

Ardrey, R. (1967) *The Territorial Imperative.*
Erikson, E. (1968) *Identity: Youth and Crisis.*
Farrell, B.H. (1963) Psycho-analysis — The Theory, in *New Society,* June 20.
Halmos, P. (1965) *The Faith of the Counsellors.*
Jehu, D. (1967) *Learning Theory and Social Work.*
Lane, A.D. (1969) The Machine Minders, *New Society,* January 30.

CHAPTER 16

Knowledge and Language*

Social workers need to know a great deal about human personality, development, motivation, interaction and behaviour. Such knowledge is usually imparted under the rubric of "applied social studies" with various mixtures of psycho-analytic theory and "behavioural science" or "socio-behavioural theory". For many years I allowed myself to comply with social/academic pressure to teach in this way, with a fairly marked bias towards psycho-analytic theory rather than the newer forms of behavioural theory, disregarding as I did so an uneasy and partly suppressed awareness that at least as much of my personal knowledge and understanding of human nature was derived from the study of English and French literature. Retirement from academic harness is a great liberator from academic discipline, and in my experience it concentrates the mind wonderfully. Shortly before my retirement, the reading of a friend's essay on *The Mill on the Floss* brought to my attention the tremendous psychological and sociological insight which enabled George Eliot to create her rounded, living characters and the dense, rich and complex social world in which they exist, develop and work out their destinies. I began to set an occasional essay to my students (who were taking a Master's degree in social work) in which I invited them to bring their theoretical concepts to bear on this novel, and eventually on one or two others chosen for their rich content concerning human personality and relationships. It seemed to me that the exercise enriched what had been learned in other ways, and did much to ensure that what was cognitively mastered was also experienced in feeling, and related to personal experience. One student wrote, introducing an essay on

---

*Reprinted from *Literature and the Study of Human Experience,* Smith College, 1975.

"Separation and Individuation: Marriage in *The Rainbow*": "This essay is based not only on an understanding of *The Rainbow* ... but also on personal experience. Having been married for a year, I have struggled with the very issues about which I have written. This essay has enabled me to work through some of the dynamics involved, and also has deepened my appreciation of the value of literature as an experience of personal growth." This seems to me to describe exactly the kind of experience we hope that our students will have, which is not always achieved by more conventional methods. Perhaps it is not always achieved by this method either (not all those who have undergone our educational system achieve or preserve a receptiveness to literature) but it seems to me more likely to attain this kind of result than more conventional approaches unaided. Subsequently I found opportunities for using this approach exclusively on refresher courses for experienced social workers and eventually I had the opportunity to teach a course on these lines at Smith College.

I would certainly understand these novels less well had I no knowledge of Freudian psychology; I use them to complement, not to replace. But I will now quote some passages from Freud himself. "Creative writers are valuable allies and their evidence is to be prized highly, for they are apt to know a whole host of things between heaven and earth of which our philosophy has not yet let us dream" (note the allusion to Hamlet). "In their knowledge of the mind they are *far in advance of us everyday people* (my italics) for they draw upon sources which we have not yet opened up for science" (Freud, 1907).

Secondly, on the creative writer: "The description of the human mind is indeed the domain which is most his own; he has *from time immemorial* been the precursor of science, and so too of scientific psychology. . . . The creative writer cannot evade the psychologist nor can the psychologist the creative writer" (my italics), (Freud, 1907).

Here Freud appears to submit to the current positivistic ideology, which imposes the axiom that no knowledge is real knowledge which has not been achieved by scientific method, and formulated in quantitative terms and in unambiguous testable hypotheses; and which implies that everything worth knowing about human nature can be known by these methods and will eventually be so. I have argued elsewhere (Irvine, 1969) that these assumptions are of dubious validity when the subject matter is so fluid as human experience, and that the language of testable hypotheses already distorts and falsifies phenomena whose subtlety and fluidity can only be expressed in the language of the literary artist, so that what is eventually studied is not what originally was to be studied. I will simply add a quotation from the *Manual of Meteorology:* "Every theory of the course of events in Nature is necessarily based on some process of simplification of the phenomena, and is to some extent therefore a fairy tale." In practice Freud found that his positivistic model would have been a strait-jacket if closely adhered to: "It still strikes me myself as strange that the case histories I write should read like short stories and that, as one might say, they lack the serious stamp of science" (in fact, he can't write of people as if they were things). "I must console myself with the reflection that *the nature of the subject* (my italics) is evidently responsible for this, rather than any preference of my own" (Freud, 1895).

It takes great courage in these days to choose the tools that fit the nature of the subject rather than those which are academically respectable, especially if one'e ambition is to be taken seriously as a scientist. But fairy tale for fairy tale, let us consider the contribution of the humanities (recognising that human nature and the weather have much in common).

One more quotation (Barchilon and Kovel, 1966). "Had he" (Freud) "not studied his hysterical patients the way a writer describes his heroes, neither he nor anyone else would have discovered, in our day, the unconscious dimensions and rules of human behaviour." An opinion with which I concur.

From time immemorial, to adapt Freud's phrase, literature and art have been the traditional repository of accumulated knowledge and wisdom about human nature; and this had reached very considerable proportions before the psychologists and sociologists really got off the ground. Moreover, literature (including drama) studies the whole man (not those abstractions economic man, psychological man, sociological man) and observes him in his natural habitat (not the laboratory or the consulting-room) and in dynamic interaction with his family, his social circle and the wider society in which they exist. Furthermore, this whole man is observed *by* a whole man, not by that bit of a man contained in the role of social scientist; by an observer using greater empathy than the man in the street, unlike the social scientist, who uses less (he may have the capacity, but usually feels obliged to inhibit or disregard it so that it will not contaminate his objectivity). In this respect the psycho-analyst is on the borderline, and really in a double-bind: he cannot establish the kind of communication he needs to have with his patient without exercising great empathy, yet his reliance on empathy and intuition are often exploited by those who deny his claim to be any sort of scientist.

Yet another advantage of using literature in teaching about human nature is that it helps to counteract the distancing of human beings by scientific (or pseudo-scientific) approaches (note the terms "client", "client-system", "individual" or "subject"). The style of our case records (unlike Freud's) also contributes to the distancing effect. But paradoxically, our clients need to feel someone close to them; although this person must also be able to preserve some detachment so he then can pull them out of the ditch rather than jump in with them. Some of our distancing methods were developed at a time when the main problem was to avoid over-involvement with the client, but I think we leaned over backwards (sometimes, as imprecision eroded our language, we even proposed to avoid involvement, which seems to me distinctly anti-therapeutic). Now that we are securely rooted in the impersonalities of social science, we are at risk of becoming too detached and impersonal, too cool and distant; of transforming the object of our attention and our service into just an object (or thing to be intellectually understood). Literature deals with people as subjects, and brings us close to them — closer than close, often right inside — refreshing the sometimes jaded student of behavioural science with a revitalising draught of human experience.

Let us consider some instances of the creative writer as the precursor of science — or at least of psycho-analysis. In a novel published in 1860, George Eliot asserts that in their childhood her two central characters "were not wrong in believing that the thoughts and loves of these first years would always make part of their lives". In a subsequent episode, the child Maggie is bitterly hurt by her adored, but somewhat insensitive, brother. "Very trivial, perhaps, this anguish seems to weatherworn mortals who have to think of

Christmas bills, dead loves and broken friendships; but it was not less bitter to Maggie — perhaps it was even more bitter than what we are fond of calling antithetically the real troubles of mature life. "Ah, my child, you will have real troubles to fret about by-and-by" is the consolation we have almost all of us had administered to us in our childhood, and have repeated to other children since we have been grown-up. We have all sobbed so piteously ... when we have lost sight of our mother or nurse in some strange place; but we can no longer recall the poignancy of that moment and weep over it, as we do over the remembered sufferings of five or ten years ago. Every one of those keen moments has left its trace, and lives in us still, but such traces have blent themselves irrecoverably with the firmer texture of our youth and manhood; and so it comes that we can look on at the troubles of our children in the reality of their pain. Is there anyone who can recover the experience of his childhood, not merely with the memory of what he did and what happened to him, what he liked and disliked ... but with an intimate penetration, a revived consciousness of what he felt like them — when it was so long from one Midsummer to another? What he felt when his schoolfellows shut him out of their game because he would pitch the ball wrong out of mere wilfulness; or on a rainy day in the holidays, when he didn't know how to amuse himself and fell from idleness into mischief, from mischief into defiance, and from defiance into sulkiness; or when his mother absolutely refused to let him have a tailed coat that "half", although every other boy of his age had gone into tails already?"

Well someone can — George Eliot can — and here she tries to help us all to do so. Could anyone formulate better the kind of memory the social worker or the therapist needs to recover as a basis for that empathy which is so essential an ingredient of therapy? Memory and empathy are intimately fused in this passage since the author, careful to preserve her male disguise, has to transpose her own memories into those of a boy. But she has got it right, hasn't she? — expressing in a series of nutshells what male novelists such as James Joyce, Dostoevsky and Tolstoy have described at greater length from personal experience. Note the appreciation of the pain and importance of separation for a young child, which so many psychologists have denied, ignored or treated as unimportant, until John Bowlby forced them to admit it by accumulating a mountain of scientific evidence. Note the observation that time for the young is endlessly long — so relevant to separation, disappointment, hope deferred — the grief so easily interpreted as naughtiness. To quote, this time from Graham Greene: "Unhappiness in a child accumulates because he sees no end to the dark tunnel. The thirteen weeks of a term might just as well be thirteen years."

Let me introduce another precursor: Charlotte Brontë, in her novel *Villette*. Polly is a child of six, whose flighty mother had recently left her husband (and child) by mutual consent, and then very shortly died, leaving Polly with her father. The latter was "a man of very sensitive feelings", who "could hardly now ... be persuaded but that some over-severity on his part — some deficiency in patience and indulgence — had contributed to hasten her end. He had brooded over this idea till his spirits were seriously affected" (i.e. he was suffering from exaggerated and prolonged mourning, with marked guilt feelings). Having consulted his doctors, he was advised to travel, and sent Polly to his friends the Brettons, who were strangers to her.

Polly arrives very subdued, clearly unhappy, but very self-possessed, and soon asks to go to bed. Next morning, she surprises her nurse by dressing herself, for the first time. When asked why she did so, she replies: "I dressed myself to learn, against the time when you leave me". Polly has learned that people go away, and here we see accelerated independence as a defence against insecurity.

Polly gives no trouble, but she mopes: "No grown person could have performed that uncheering business better. No furrowed face of adult exile ... ever bore more legibly the signs of home-sickness than did her infant visage." This was published in 1852, about a hundred years before John Bowlby had to conduct massive researches and muster weighty arguments to convince his colleagues that the young child in such circumstances mourns and grieves with the same grief and mourning as bereaved or deserted adults.

I will now leave this theme of precursors to consider the language of science — even of psycho-analysis — in relation to that of literature.

Those who want to use words for constructing testable hypotheses cannot use the words of common speech unchanged. Either they invent neologisms, or they adopt the words of common speech and fit them for their new purpose of pure denotation by stripping them of their connotations, their over-tones and under-tones, pinning them down to a single unambiguous meaning. This is legitimate for certain purposes — as long as they and we do not suppose that the words thus doctored still represent what they originally represented before the operation. If the language of feeling — popular or literary — is ambiguous, this is because of the "nature of the subject" (as Freud says); because human feelings, moods and attitudes are fleeting, changeable, transient, always in motion, as the human body is never totally still until it is dead. When we say that a couple of human beings loved each other over many years, this certainly does not represent a static relationship. The love of the first years is not the same as that of the last; if we look close enough (like D.H. Lawrence) we shall find that the feelings of each partner for the other undergo at least subtle changes from day to day — sometimes quite dramatic changes several times in the course of a single day. A relationship is like the sky in the English climate — sometimes cloudless and blue, sometimes with slow, benign clouds drifting across it and casting their shadows below, sometimes with clouds in wild commotion or dramatic outbursts of thunder and lightning. And the love which is found to have survived the storm did not cease to exist during the storm, and then miraculously resurrect; it may have been totally concealed by the clouds, but it existed, and probably contributed to the bitterness or violence of the conflict. To sum up: an ambiguous language reflects a fluid reality, which can be evoked and thus to some extent communicated, but cannot be pinned down or immobilised.

I shall now compare a psycho-analyst (D.H. Winnicott) struggling to express pre-verbal experience, with a poet (W.H. Auden). I have chosen Winnicott, not as a bad communicator but as a particularly good one, who struggled manfully to find words in which to express the almost inexpressible and who occasionally achieved a truly poetic quality of communication. But here we shall see mainly the struggle, and the dissatisfaction with what he was able to do with the words at his disposal: "... the place where infants live — a queer place — where *nothing has yet been separated out as not-me,* so there is *not yet a* ME. Here identification is what the infant *starts with.* It is not that the infant identifies himself or herself with the mother, but rather that no mother, no object external to the self, is known; and even this statement is wrong, because there is not yet a self. It could be said that the self of the infant at this very early stage is only potential. In a *return* to this state an individual becomes merged with the mother's self. The infant self has not yet formed and so cannot be said to be merged, but memories and expectations can now start to accumulate and to form'' (Winnicott, 1965).

Compare this with a poem by W.H. Auden:

> This lunar beauty
> Has no history,
> Is complete and early;
> If beauty later
> Bear any feature
> It had a lover
> And is another.
> This like a dream
> Keeps other time,
> And daytime is
> The loss of this;
> For time is inches
> And the heart's changes
> Where ghost has haunted,
> Lost and wanted.
> But this was never
> A ghost's endeavour
> Nor, finished this,
> Was ghost at ease;
> And till it pass
> Love shall not near
> The sweetness here,
> Nor sorrow take
> His endless look.

The following little poem belongs to a fable by Samuel Beckett, in which Watt, who seems to stand for Man, lives for a time as servant in the house of Nott, who seems to stand for God, Watt only gets occasional glimpses of him, and never face to face.

> Watt will not
> Abate one jot,
> But of what?
>
> Of the going to,
> Of the being at,

Of the going from
Nott's habitat.

Of the long way
And the short stay
And the going back home
The way he had come.

Of the empty heart
And the empty hands
And the dim mind wayfaring
Through barren lands.

A flame with dark winds hedged about
Going out
Gone out.

Of the empty heart
And the empty hands
And the dark mind stumbling
Through barren lands.

I doubt if there is any finer expression of the essential sadness of separation and loss. Here they are deeply experienced, and I think we have a glimpse into the heart of mourning. But there is much in our culture to discourage mourning, and this social defence also has its expression in poetry. I will quote from a poem by an English poet, John Pudney, written for use in a wartime film of the R.A.F. called "Reach for the Stars". One of the many pilots who is shot down is found to have left for his wife a poem, of which these are two verses:

Do not despair
For Johnny Head-in-air;
He sleeps as sound
As Johnny-on-the-ground.

Better by far
For Johnny the bright star
To keep your head
And see his children fed.

In the context of a film which had generated strong feelings and great tensions about who would live and who would die, who would be widowed and who would be miraculously spared, this expression of understated heroic stoicism was extremely moving; in contrast with its explicit injunction, it moved many people to tears. But the explicit injunction is deeply engrained in our modern culture, and was reinforced at the time by the powerful social pressures of a nation fighting for life. Many widows tried to practise what was enjoined — and many still do, which usually means that they try to prevent their children from mourning also. Lindemann has told us of the cost of aborted mourning; here is a poem which expresses the first step on such a path.

> Life must go on
> And the dead be forgotten
> Life must go on
> Though good men die
>
> Ann, eat your breakfast
> Dan, take your medicine;
> Life must go on;
> I forget just why.
>   (Edna St. Vincent Millay)

I will add a comment by Tennyson on the facile consolations which are used in the attempt to induce people to forego their grief and mourning:

> Some say that other friends remain,
> That loss is common to the race;
> But common is the common-place
> And vacant chaff well-meant for grain.
>   *(In Memoriam)*

This verse expresses in its bitterness the resentment of the bereaved person whose friends defend themselves against sharing his mourning, and hints at the furious envy of the bereaved for the unbereaved.

The myth of Balder the Beautiful can help us to focus both on repression and on family secrets:

Balder was a Norse hero who was so beautiful and so universally beloved that some god gave him the blessing that no weapon made of the wood of any tree that grew could kill him. He was beloved — *almost* universally, but Loki, a deformed and ugly god, was envious, and Balder was only *almost* immune. Loki bethought him of the mistletoe — not a tree but a parasite: and with this parasitic wood and his own envy he fashioned a deadly arrow. The following poem by G.K. Chesterton is based on this myth:

There is always a thing forgotten
When all the world goes well;
A thing forgotten, as long ago,
When the gods forgot the mistletoe,
And softer than an arrow of snow
The arrow of anguish fell.

The thing on the blind side of the heart,
On the wrong side of the door.
The green thing groweth, menacing
Almighty lovers in the spring;
There is always a forgotten thing
And love is not secure.

Here we have a reminder of the dangers of idealisation, of secret envy and hostility — the things which mostly lurk on the blind side of the heart.

Let us take another poem about secret envy, by William Blake:

I was angry with my friend;
I told my wrath, my wrath did end.
I was angry with my foe;
I told it not, my wrath did grow.

And I watered it with tears
Night and morning with my fears;
And I sunned it with smiles
And with soft deceitful wiles.

And it grew both day and night
Till it bore an apple bright;
And my foe beheld it shine
And he knew that it was mine.

And into my garden stole
When the night had veiled the pole.
In the morning glad I see
My foe outstretched beneath the tree.

Here we have in a beautiful nutshell what could have been the fable of a whole novel. Let us note that there are two sources of poison which contribute to the fatal outcome: that of the original grievance, and the festering unexpressed resentment which make the fruit deadly; and that of the foe's envy and covetousness, which lead him to steal the deadly fruit.

I will close with a superb expression of conflict, guilt and anxiety, attributed to Queen Elizabeth I of England:

> I grieve, and dare not show my discontent;
>   I love, and yet am forced to seem to hate;
> I do, yet dare not say I ever meant;
>   I seem stark mute, yet inwardly do prate:
> I am, and not; I freeze, and yet am burned,
> Since from myself, my other self I turned.
>
> My care is like my shadow in the sun,
>   Follows me flying, flies when I pursue it;
> Stands and lies by me, does what I have done;
>   This too familiar care doth make me rue it;
> No means I find to rid him from my breast,
> Till by the end of things it be suppressed.
>
> Some gentler passions slide into my mind,
>   For I am soft, and made of melting snow;
> O be more cruel, Love, and so be kind;
>   Let me or float or sink, be high or low;
> Or let me live with some more sweet content,
> Or die, and so forget what love e'er meant.

References

Auden, W.H. (1960) *Poems, XXX.*
Barchilon, J. and Kovel, J.S. (1966) Huckleberry Finn: A Psychoanalytic Study, *Journal of American Psychoanalytic Association,* Vol. XIV.
Beckett, S. (1945) *Watt.*
Blake, W. A Poison Tree, in *Songs of Experience.*
Bowlby, J. (1951) *Maternal Care and Mental Health.*
Bowlby, J. (1969) *Attachment.*
Brontë, C. *Villette.*
Chesterton, G.K. *The Ballad of the White Horse.*
Eliot, G. *The Mill on the Floss.*
Freud, S. (1907) Delusions and Dreams in Jensen's "Gradiva", *Standard Edition,* Vol. IX.

Freud, S. (1895) *Studies on Hysteria,* S.E. Vol. II.
Greene, G. (1971) *A Sort of Life.*
Irvine, E.E. (1969) Education for Social Work. Science or Humanity? *Social Work* (U.K.), XXVI, 4.
Millay, Edna St. Vincent   Lament, in *Collected Poems.*
Tennyson, A. *In Memoriam.*
Winnicott, D.W. (1965) The Relationship of a Mother to her Baby in the Beginning, in *The Family and Individual Development.*

Part V   Miscellany: Adolescence, Prediction and Anxiety. The Contribution of a Great Psycho-analyst to Social Work

Chapters 16 and 17 were written for publications of the International Association for Child Psychiatry and Allied Professions, with which I have been associated for many years. At the time when I wrote Chapter 15 there was much concern about the shame and discouragement experienced by children who failed the examination at "eleven plus" (i.e. were allocated to a school for the less intellectually able), which tended to give them a negative self-image at a time when identity-formation is particularly vulnerable. For this and for egalitarian reasons the "grammar schools" in most parts of England have been merged with other secondary schools to form comprehensive secondary schools. This has done something to de-dramatise differential schooling, although in most comprehensive schools the pupils are allocated to different streams according to ability. It is perhaps too soon to say whether the pupils in the lowest streams have less sense of failure than if they were in a separate school, while the size of many comprehensive schools creates problems of its own. The resonance of educational success or failure in relation to the child's relationship with his parents has not received much attention; but I note that S. Hyatt Williams (1975) mentions among other reasons for dropping out educationally "an inhibition of the ambition to go one better than father or mother".

Chapter 17 raises an issue which I hope will receive much attention before long. The study of human behaviour is tremendously complex, so that one theory after another turns out to have been over-simplified. Yet each theory has its impact on parents, whether it is couched in terms of what they have or should have done, or worse still of the kind of people they are or should be. Since parents play a major role in the mental health of the child, and since their anxieties are apt to give rise to dysfunctional defences, it is of great importance that their morale be preserved and supported. Any disparaging references to their failings in public utterance tends to undermine their self-confidence and increase their anxiety, thus adding to the hazards of the children for whom they care. Happily there are now some indications that the tide is turning, and an increasing number of therapists are offering the parents of disturbed children a partner role, thus relieving their guilt and sense of failure and letting them play a vital role in the therapeutic process. I close with a tribute to the late Dr. Winnicott, who was so full of admiration for "the ordinary devoted mother", and so full of sympathy and respect for the many parents who have failed the child in some way for some reason, most of whom he found so eager to cooperate in restoring the child to health, however arduous the process.

CHAPTER 17

Psycho-social Aspects of Adolescence: Problems of Uncertain Role and Obscure Communication

Adolescence is a period of rapid physical development, culminating in the capacity for mature sexual experience. In some societies this physical maturation coincides with well-marked changes in social and financial status, often marked by *rites de passage* for one or both sexes. The Jewish Barmitzvah, for instance, reminds us of a society in which a boy could assume the responsibilities of a man at 13, whereas in advanced countries nowadays he remains in school for another 2-5 years. He changes status only within a religious frame of reference.

Recognition of adult status in advanced technological societies is usually delayed till the age of 18, when most of the rights and responsibilities of the adult have been conferred. However, a majority of young people have already left school at 15 or 16, and have become wage-earners. Many of them could be self-supporting, but in fact many families in Western countries ask them only for a minimal contribution to their own support, leaving them more to spend on pleasures and personal adornment than they may ever have again after marriage. This is itself a curious phenomenon in family life. It marks an accepted intermediate status when the youngster is not expected to make a full contribution to the family budget, and thus carries less than adult responsibility. The parents who thus encourage a partial economic dependence expect in turn to exercise control in certain matters; they expect their children to postpone sexual activity (particularly their daughters), to come home by a certain time in the evening, perhaps to save a proportion of the money they keep for themselves. These expectations are frequently unshared and become, as we shall see, the focus of a greal deal of friction.*

As Ruth Benedict has pointed out, different cultures emphasise different phases and aspects of life and development. Some make little of the transition from childhood to adulthood; Great Britain, a stratified but mobile society, is probably not unique in laying great stress on the determination of economic and social status, mainly by means of an educational steeple-chase; the hurdles are examinations, each of which imposes a limit to the vocational choices of the majority of competitors. It is these examinations which represent the real *rites de passage* of this society, dramatically focusing all the stresses on the moments of evaluation, selection and rejection through which individuals are said to "find their own level".

The first of these important and stressful events has occurred for the last 25 years at the age of 11, when the crucial selection is made for type and quality of secondary education.† This first step in the determination of his eventual social role and status naturally affects the processes of identity-formation. Like every stress, this is a test of the stability of the individual and of the family which defines and endures the crisis with him. Stable and reasonably intelligent parents will not usually be greatly surprised by the outcome, having formulated realistic hopes and plans. If disappointed, they will respond philosophically, without regarding the child as a shameful failure. They will propose reasonable aims and accept attainable results; although they may very reasonably be distressed if the child is allocated to a school of really poor quality, they will not blame him. However, many parents cannot accept with equanimity selection for any but the most academic and highly-valued type of school (Grammar School, cf. lycee, gymnasium). His status in the family and his self-respect may be permanently undermined; those parents who infect their children with insomnia as selection approaches are often those whose own siblings outclassed them educationally and vocationally.

---

*This passage, written in 1966, dramatically indicates the speed of social change in this area. It describes a situation of crumbling norms. In 1978 there seems to be no consensus at all and therefore many parents simply do not know what to expect.

† The so-called "eleven-plus" exam, now abandoned.

Children selected for the more academic schools have to prepare for a further ordeal in some years' time (General Certificate of Education, cf. Baccalaureat, Abitur). Standards are now higher than before and competition keener. These stresses, too, can be surmounted, given reasonable parental expectations and a secure position in the family. But if the child needs success to compete with a more favoured or gifted sibling, to gain parental approval or to bolster his precarious self-esteem, any loss of position in school may be deeply discouraging. In conditions of social mobility, the son's education may become entangled with his rivalry with his father. The working-class grammar school boy is expected to become more learned and respected than his father, thus fulfilling early fantasies of defeating, humiliating and supplanting a father who has seemed at times tyrannical and who is a powerful rival for the mother's affections. Guilt derived from such sources is often responsible for educational deterioration in Grammar School. The father's pride in his son's success may also be poisoned by similar fantasies; unless he is secure in his self-respect and his relationship with his wife, he may be acutely ambivalent, and may express his resentment by denying that reading books is real work, while also making excessive demands for industry and success.*

A mother who is disappointed in marriage may exacerbate these problems by emphasising the son's intellectual superiority to the father, thus involving them both in a thinly veiled acting-out of the Oedipal drama. This situation may result in delinquency or homosexuality as well as educational failure. Further down the educational scale, the boy with severe learning difficulties often has a father who is intellectually or educationally handicapped, whose ambivalence creates a double-bind situation. Consciously he wants his son to succeed but, as his wife complains, he undermines and belittles the boy in a way that clearly betrays his reluctance to be put in the shade. This rivalry does not usually reach the intensity which produces disabling conflict and learning inhibition in the boy without a combination of early deprivation and insecurity in the father and an overt or covert preference for the boy on the part of the mother. On

---

*This failure of the father to participate by identification in the son's success appears to be culture-linked; while common in England, it is rare in Scottish or Jewish families. It would be interesting to know of its incidence in other cultures.

the other hand, over-ambitious parents often defeat their own ends by over-pressure, creating a conflict between the child's wish to succeed and be a credit to them and his resentful wish to fail and disgrace them. There is a rather narrow path between this risky over-involvement in the child's education, and a degree of detachment which can be interpreted by the adolescent as indifference. In the latter case, increased parental concern with school-work often contributes to a striking improvement.

Identity, Rebellion and Discipline

Adolescence is the time when all the chickens come home to roost. "The Oedipal child had to repress his sexual and hostile impulses in favour of affectionate attachments to his parents" (Jacobson, 1961), and to renounce a good deal of his earlier infantile dependency in favour of his drive for independence. In the long identity crisis of adolescence (Erikson, 1950) all these underground impulses and drives become reactivated in an individual who now has the ability to impregnate or to conceive, to inflict grievous bodily harm or even to kill. It takes time and effort to withdraw the sexual libido from mother or father and to redirect it towards potential mates, as well as mastering the anger with both parents for their exclusive sexual relationship, especially since it is important not to know what is going on. Hence the regressive flight into renewed infantile dependence, the intensified repression of sexuality, which often leads to anxieties about sexual normality or the compulsive and often joyless sexual activity. Hence also the outbursts of physical violence, and the aggression underlying the attack on the parents' values and standards. But there are other reasons for this revolt. Since the adolescent must not know what he wants, he cannot know who he is; hence the well-known sense of unreality and the detection all round him of the false and the phoney. "The adolescent is engaged in trying to find the self to be true to" (Winnicott, 1964), and the identifications which he has built up are often repudiated, felt to be "not-him", dangerous representatives of the parents who want to mould him into a false, externally imposed, identity. These fears are perhaps stronger in modern Western conditions, with small nuclear families and relatively subtle and insidious parental pressures than in times and places where families are larger, parent-child relations less intimate and discipline harsher. Withdrawal from parents or revolt against them, with sexual or delinquent acting out, certainly occur quite often in families where parent-child relations have a fraternal quality, as well as in those where standards are unusually high and discipline unusually strict. In a less dramatic way, the uneasy alienation from the parents is often expressed by extreme reserve, combined with the search for an adult confidant outside the home.

Writing of the urgent problems of management with which this behaviour confronts parents, Winnicott (1964) mentions: "The need to avoid false solutions: the need to feel real or to tolerate not feeling at all. The need to defy — in a setting where their dependence is met and can be relied on to be met."

Defiance requires a firm authority to defy, but this is becoming hard for parents to provide. Adolescence forces on parents a radical change in their accustomed role. Parents of infants and children usually have a reasonably good idea of their task in supplying the needs of their offspring for love, care, protection, training and control. The pre-pubertal child may or may not be easy to manage, but throughout the latency period he is relatively understandable and predictable (apart from a minority who are recognisably emotionally disturbed) and his parents' role is reasonably clear. But it is not only the disturbed minority who cause concern in adolescence; many children who had previously been regarded as normal, or even exceptionally good, now become both difficult and unpredictable. At one moment they rebel violently against their parents' authority, challenging all their standards and opinions; at the next this exaggerated self-confidence ebbs away and leaves them dejected, hopeless and utterly dependent. Children may now present problems of aggression for the first time, and sexuality, which is often unrecognised in its secret childish manifestations, now emerges unmistakably, often some years before the parents can remember having such interests themselves, and in much more vigorous forms.

Such youngsters need on the one hand great tolerance and understanding, on the other firmness and consistency. This balance each parental couple now has to find for itself, since absolute standards of right and wrong have ceased to prevail in large sections of society. Modern parents have been trained to depend for their standard of child care on the advice of a host of "experts", ranging from the genuinely professional to the popular journalistic. Such advice has never been unanimous and has varied greatly over short periods of time; but these discrepancies are as nothing compared with the babel of conflicting opinions concerning the adolescent and his needs. Every shade of permissiveness and strictness finds its authoritative advocates, and the bewildered parent often becomes as inconsistent as the adolescent himself. Extreme permissiveness is often the line of least resistance, sanctioned by similar permissiveness in the available reference groups; it is hoped that the youngsters will appreciate their privileges and will not let their parents down by going too far. But many young people seem determined to do just that — to go just as far as is necessary to force their parents to resume protective control. They subject their parents to a kind of trial by ordeal — ordeal by battle and argument and defiance — whose object seems to be to find out how real the parents are, how genuine their values, their courage and their concern for their children. It is an ordeal by confusion and mystification, with deception based on self-deception and with outright lying. The adolescents passionately demand unfettered freedom to play with every kind of danger, and accuse recalcitrant parents of everything from senility and imbecility to corruption and tyranny; yet they are far from pleased if they get what they seem to want — as they often do.

This confused and misleading communication, often accompanied with great sound and fury, is extremely demoralising to parents, many of whom crack in some way under the strain. Inner uncertainties are ruthlessly exposed, and any latent disharmonies between them exacerbated. Harmonious parents will support each other against these attacks on their authority, their personal values and parental performance, but a precarious partnership is likely to be split by mutual projection of blame for the situation. Parents whose own identity crisis was hastily and superficially resolved find all the unsolved questions reopened, and may suffer a new crisis in which they become extremely unsure of themselves and their motives. The modern parent knows that personal jealousies and rivalries can be disguised as overstrict discipline, and often fears to exert realistic discipline through distrust of his own motives. These may well be mixed, since even the happily married are liable to suffer some envy of their children's emergent sexuality at a time when their own is beginning to wane. Many also identify with the adolescent's demand for freedom, having never really forgiven their own parents for restrictions imposed at that stage of their development. Johnson and Szurek (1954) have described the highly pathological ways in which parents can consciously or unconsciously manipulate their children into acting-out the parents' own forbidden impulses. We are concerned not with the more dramatic extreme, but with the milder degrees of this process which can occur within the normal range of parent-child relations.

Yet if parents are over-permissive, the adolescent becomes visibly more depressed, anxious, irritable and insecure, acting-out more and more wildly, making it clearer and clearer that he can *not* look after himself. Those who get into real trouble often express deep resentment towards the parents, who would not (they say) have allowed it if they really cared, *whatever he told them.* At this point the parents sometimes slam on the brakes too hard or too angrily; but those who recover (with or without professional help) their ability to assert genuine protective authority are often surprised to find how relieved and grateful the youngsters prove to be. (All this applies to girls too, despite the use of masculine pronouns.)

Oedipus Redivivus

We have mentioned the adolescent's difficulty in detaching his reawakened and maturing sexuality from its original object in father or mother. Wise and mature parents can do much to facilitate this task by offering warm, supportive parental love and encouraging responsible independence and hetero-sexual friendships within reasonable limits. Many parents, however, are handicapped in this task because something in themselves secretly responds to the changing quality of the child's love, so that sexual tensions develop all round the parent/child triangle. Parents whose sexuality is waning may find it hard to tolerate the waxing powers and attractions of their children. At the same time, father may find in daughter a reincarnation of the girl he married, and mother rediscover in son her Springtime lover. If the marital relationship has developed into a source of mature and ample satisfactions, such feelings are fleeting and easily controlled, but if it is worn and staled by custom the parents may collude with the child's regressive tendencies. The mother may encourage a kind of courtship in her son, thus stimulating her husband's jealousy while she also reproaches him with neglecting or discouraging the son. Seductive behaviour by mother, and the mutual antagonism of father and son involve the boy in painful conflict and anxiety; he also becomes angry with his mother for creating this position and discouraging his search for a mate of his own age. Such conflicts, when severe and long-standing, can lead to serious breakdown or anti-social behaviour.

Girls are prone to similar problems, *mutatis mutandis.* The most dangerous situation for either boy or girl is that where serious marital problems are latent or open. If, for instance, the father has been accustomed to console himself for his wife's short-comings by an extra affectionate relationship with his daughter, this may lead to serious trouble in adolescence. He may compete openly with her boyfriends, letting the relationship develop into a tantalising aim-inhibited courtship. Or he may dimly perceive the temptation to do this, and overcompensate it by becoming much cooler in his manner, while interfering in his daughter's social life by excessive strictness, hostility and suspicion of her boyfriends and by unfounded accusations of misconduct. Both these situations are common in the background of young unmarried mothers.

These problems take other, and acuter, forms in the one-parent family. The loss of either parent is of course a serious bereavement. The loss of the same-sex parent deprives the child of a living parental model for identification, and often imposes a burden of guilt about the untimely death of the Oedipal rival. It also intensifies the danger of a seductive attitude on the part of the surviving parent and the vulnerability of the adolescent to this. Even in the absence of excessive erotic tension, the oldest or only son of a widow is often burdened with a heavy sense of responsibility for his bereaved and struggling mother, which makes it hard to progress to courtship with girls, while a daughter who has not had the support of a father's appreciation in developing her feminine self-esteem is apt to seek reassurance in promiscuous relationships. The unmarried mother, and the bereaved parent of either sex, are apt to try ineffectively to be both father and mother, thus failing in both roles and bitterly resenting the impossible task. Such parents can give little support to the child in mourning the lost parent, so that the child is apt to be thrown back on pathological defences.

It is hard to generalise about sibling relationships, as these are so various. In adolescence, siblings may draw together in alliance against the parents, or their rivalries may be sharpened. Where communication between generations is poor, an older sibling may serve as confidant and substitute parent, or even as a channel of communication. A boy who tolerates or expects sexual freedom in his girlfriend may betray his moral conflict by his disapproval of any deviance by his sister from the strictest moral code. Similarly the rebellious adolescent girl may betray her need for control by disapproval of the parents' leniency with a sibling, or express her hostility towards them indirectly through exaggerated accounts of her siblings' antagonism and accusations against them.

Hazards for the Parental Marriage

We have seen what profound conflicts may be aroused in parents by the awakening sexuality of their children as well as by the adolescent rebellion in general, and how latent dissatisfactions in the marriage may be precipitated. The damage done may well be hard to repair. Another problem is that dissatisfied couples often get along by projecting or displacing onto dependent children those traits which each dislikes in himself of his partner. As the children grow up and detach themselves, these devices are likely to break down. Husband and wife may for the first time have to look at the basis of their marriage as they face the prospect of life alone with each other. Thus marriages which had seemed on the surface reasonably stable may begin to show cracks and may in extreme cases break up. Even harmonious couples have to make a considerable readjustment as their children grow up and cease to be a major focus of family life, having moved to the periphery. The parents thus become more dependent on each other for their emotional satisfaction. The problem tends to be more acute for the mother, and may represent a real crisis for her if her husband cannot make the necessary adjustment.

In modern Western societies there is an increasing tendency for the mother to solve the problem of the empty nest by employment outside the home, often beginning some time before the children leave school. Women who lack the inclination, the capacity or the opportunity to redirect their interests and energies in this way often cling desperately and destructively to the youngest child or to an unmarried daughter; failing this they may lapse into illness or depression.

Conclusion

Just as it is easier to describe mental illness than mental health, it is easier to describe the manifold ways in which parents can fail their children in adolescence than those in which they can help them to resolve their identity crisis. Even when it has been safely weathered, most parents can only say they rode out the storm or muddled through. This is a very great subject; we can only say that those who try to help parents when things go seriously wrong have certain general principles in mind. There is no doubt that what parents do is important; we have emphasised, for instance, the need for a degree of control adapted to the adolescent's actual capacity for sensible self-direction. This firmness in control needs to be combined with a warm and sensitive responsiveness to the adolescent mood; the ability to be interested in their views and ideas, to receive any confidences they may offer, and the ability to let them alone in their moods of withdrawal. The successful achievement of satisfactory identifications depends to a great extent on what kind of people the parents are; on their personal maturity, their capacity for good relationships, and on the firmness of the parental identities and ego-boundaries. One of the reasons why adolescents become insecure and angry when their parents show weakness towards them is that they want models who are strong as well as kind, models who really believe in themselves and their values. But they have little respect for parents who are merely conformist. Most disturbing to identity formation are those parents who treat their children as extensions of themselves, either demanding that they replicate their own careers or pursue their own unachieved ambitions, or projecting onto them the shadow side of their own natures.

References

Erikson, F. (1950) *Childhood and Society.*

Jacobson, E. (1961) Adolescent Moods and the Remodelling of Psychic Structures in Adolescence, *The Psychoanalytic Study of the Child,* XVI, 164-183.

Johnson, A.M. and Szurek, S.A. (1954) Etiology of Antisocial Behaviour in Delinquents and Psychopaths, *Journal of the American Medical Association,* March 6th.

Winnicott, D. (1964) *The Family and Individual Development,* Tavistock Publications, London.

CHAPTER 18

The Risks of the Register: or the Management of Expectation*

It is clear that the child, from the moment of conception, is exposed to many risks which threaten his development — we all live more or less dangerously. We can also agree that in many conditions of handicap or disturbance a number of factors conspire to produce the problem; aetiology is usually multi-factorial. Many of these risks can be predicted, and some can be avoided or counteracted by appropriate and timely action. It is therefore unquestionable that research into risk is valuable and should be pursued and that strategies for counteracting or minimising risk should be explored.

However, serious questions arise concerning the diffusion of the knowledge we gain through such research, and the effects of such diffusion. How far should we try to control these effects, how far can this be done? The social sciences, like some branches of natural science, affect what they observe, in this case largely through the dissemination and popularisation of their findings, or even their hypotheses. Kinsey's report is published and widely read, whether in the original or transmuted and distorted by the media. Sexual behaviour is unlikely to be unaffected by such information. The work of Freud underwent a similar process. It has been used by some to justify the sexual gratification, and some think the sexual over-stimulation, of children; by others to justify the partial separation of parents and child in the kibbutz. Early traumatic theories of the origins of neurosis and vulgar misunderstanding of the term

*First published in *The Child in his Family: Children at Psychiatric Risk,* Vol. III, Ed. Anthony & Koupernik, 1974.

"repression" were used to justify what most clinicians now consider a harmful degree of over-indulgence, intended to avoid "repressing" the child.

To come to our present topic, the recognition of risk entails anxiety; anxiety for the professionals concerned, anxiety for the parents, the relatives, the social network. We know that anxiety has its uses; it also has its abuses. Anxiety may provide the motive for appropriate action or for more or less inappropriate defensive manoeuvres, according to its intensity and according to the ego strength and coping repertoire of those concerned and the environmental support available.

We are not unfamiliar with this at the family level. We know how the anxiety and guilt provoked in parents by handicaps in young children often constitute a serious risk to the child's development potential by giving rise to defences of denial, over-indulgence, over-protection, rejection, or simply to despair. We know how these responses may engender risks for other members of the family — neglect of healthy siblings, mutual projection of blame between parents, with consequent threat to the marriage, and so on.

It is relevant here to recall Leiderman's investigation (Leiderman, 1974)[6] into the unintended interference with the establishment of the mother-child relationship arising from the traditional precautions against infection in the case of premature babies. This work appears to show the further side-effect of a risk to the parental union. It also suggests the possibility of reducing the double risk of impaired mother-child relationship (and maternal self-confidence) and of a broken home. Similarly, it is common medical practice to postpone contact between mothers (or parents) and babies suffering any obvious physical handicap or deformity, with the good intention of protecting the mother against shock till she is stronger, but with the unintended consequence in many cases of arousing her suspicions (sometimes to the point of horrifying fantasies) and anxieties, which can reach traumatic intensity. Here, too, the kindly precaution creates a risk both for the mother-child relationship and quite possibly (following Leiderman) for the marriage. It is relevant here that Graham and Rutter[5] found a significant correlation between psychiatric disorder in epileptic children and "nervous breakdown" in the mothers, although not with broken homes. On the other hand, as regards children with cerebral palsy and similar brain disorders, psychiatric disturbance in the child was not significantly associated with maternal breakdown, but was correlated with broken homes.

It is hard for a large-scale statistical study to disentangle the various strands of the chicken-egg cycle. Had the mother shown signs of emotional disturbance before the birth of the handicapped child, or should we suppose that she was a vulnerable individual who broke down under this specific stress? How far is the harmony or strength of the marriage related to the vulnerability of either parent? Do vulnerable fathers tend to leave home? Are vulnerable mothers more likely to break down? How often is an apparently satisfactory marriage destroyed either by a psychiatric illness in the mother with which the father cannot cope, or by the vulnerability of both parents to the anxiety and guilt aroused by the birth of a handicapped child, and the mutual projection of guilt, with all the subsequent recriminations? Or again, how many fathers are driven away from home by their wives' excessive preoccupation with a handicapped child?

Williams[12] states: "Most authors of studies on handicapped children conclude that parental attitudes to a child and its handicap are of more significance in its personality development than the handicap itself." In particular, he refers to the work of Pond[9] and Drillien[4], who found (in the words of his summary) "that disturbed behaviour in children is common where there have been severe complications of pregnancy and/or delivery. When children suffer environmental stress in infancy and early childhood, they are more likely to become disturbed if they suffered complications of pregnancy and birth, and even more predisposed if they were immature. However, *the quality of maternal handling and the early environment of the child is of more significance in personality development and in the causation of behaviour disorders than complications of pregnancy, length of gestation or birthweight"* (my italics).

Williams continues: In examining the contribution of environmental factors to the aetiology of behaviour disorder, one is struck by the fact that psychiatrists are still predominantly concerned with the gross aspects of child-mother relationships. Such global terms as rejection, over-protection, guilt, withdrawal and denial are used to account for behaviour disorder in a child. There is no doubt that these maternal attitudes correlate well with disturbed behaviour. But in more cases these maternal attitudes are *secondary phenomena.* This is not to deny that there is a proportion of mothers who are seriously disturbed psychiatrically and who affect their children adversely. But there is a fair proportion of mothers (and fathers for that matter), who have disturbed handicapped children, who have frequently demonstrated their capacity for good parenthood by the normality of their other children. *The majority of parents of maladjusted handicapped children are ordinary good, devoted parents"* (my italics).

If parental attitudes and behaviour are such an important factor in the development or prevention of psychiatric disturbance in handicapped children, it behoves us in our deliberations to give very serious attention — not to say pride of place — to the morale of parents and to the effect on this of our own communications. It may be legitimate, for scientific purposes, to regard parents simply as adverse environmental factors for their child, even though this seems to fall under the indictment of "treating people as things". Even scientifically, this has its dangers. For obvious reasons, psychiatrists and their colleagues have more opportunity to observe malfunctioning individuals and families than those who master their problems without specialist help. Thus there is a natural tendency to know much more about and to feel much more interest in the pathological than in the normal. Our knowledge of how parents bring up a mentally healthy child, even when there is a serious handicap to contend with, is extremely rudimentary; by and large, we know very much more about "how not to do it". However, this does not matter so much when we talk among ourselves; no doubt we shall achieve a better balance in the long run. But every time we talk in public, or publish and mention emotionally disturbed parents as noxious factors in the child's environment without recognition of their existence as suffering people (and I mean people — like us — not "persons") and without recognising the existence of many parents who do more than any professional can to help their children to contend with their handicaps without psychiatric damage, we are in fact increasing the risk of maladjustment among parents, undermining their precious self-confidence, reinforcing those social beliefs and stereotypes which favour parental demoralisation and incompetence, and thus increasing the risk for an incalculable number of children.

There was a phase when many child psychiatrists heavily scape-goated parents. This has now been corrected to a great extent, but the attitudes of many doctors, social workers, public health nurses, and journalists are still affected by this literature and the stereotypes derived from it, while the work of Ronald Laing and his associates has recently poured fresh fuel on the flames. Some enthusiasts among sociologists and others are already proclaiming the death of the family, and there is a real danger that before we get around to serious study of how many families contribute to the normal development of their children, enthusiastic "reformers" will mount a campaign encouraging society to abandon the family in favour of untried substitutes.

Little has been done to redress the balance against the effects of the scape-goating literature. Few "experts" explicitly recognise, with Williams, that many parents of disturbed handicapped children are at least non-factors in the child's disturbance, while some provide a quality of devoted and intelligent home nursing which few professionals could emulate, all round the clock and all round the calendar. The late D.W. Winnicott and Dr. John Bowlby have been almost alone in their loving and scrupulous study of "the ordinary devoted mother" and how she lays the foundations of mental health for her children. Winnicott[13] also advised social workers to take as a model "therapy of the kind that is always being carried on by the parents in correction of relative failures in environmental provision. What do such parents do? They exaggerate some parental function and keep it up for a length of time, in fact until the child has used it up and is ready to be released from special care." This passage could equally well be applied to children suffering from a variety of handicaps rather than from previous failure of "environmental provision".

But apart from Winnicott, who has described the contribution of "the ordinary devoted mother" to the care and education of a vulnerable or damaged child? Virtually the only literature I have found on this has been written by those few parents who are capable not only of providing such care but also of writing about it.

The most notable of these books is *The Siege* by Clara Claiborne Park,[8] who comes across as a gifted, sensitive, and remarkably stable woman, mother of three normal children, struggling very effectively to come to terms with the condition of an autistic child, to understand it as far as possible, and to find ways of expanding the child's interests and abilities — methods which called for incredible patience and delicacy of touch, lest the child take fright and withdraw instead of advancing. Beginning without professional help as a lone inventor, Mrs. Park eventually found first-rate professional advice and support, but this was after a long struggle, and she has an eloquent chapter ("The Amateurs") on the potential contribution of parents and the reluctance of many professionals to recognise or encourage this, let alone to guide it. Recognising the dangers of parental over-anxiety, over-sensitivity, over-activity, or despair, she goes on to say: "But since we parents, in clinical literature, have found few eulogists, it is up to us to put our handicaps into perspective. Since we are conscious of them, we can go a long way towards overcoming even the severest. And we, and others, should realise that they may be counter-balanced by special advantages that even the most gifted psychiatrist cannot match."

One of the few professional writers to make this point is Margaret Adams[1] of the Eunice Kennedy Shriver Center, who writes: "Parents, because they are fully acquainted by hard experience, have a very strong emotional investment in the situation that if not taken into account, may sabotage the more carefully laid, objectively sensible plans." Mrs. Park's point is more than this, since the parental expertise and devotion are resources which we can ill afford to waste. As she says: "Perhaps the most important of all the parents' advantages" is "that they know the child's language ... gesture by gesture, sound by sound, word (at last) by word. . . . They hear the anxiety in the high squeal the outsider cannot distinguish from laughter; they understand that assent is conveyed by running across the room or jumping up and down."

Despite their outstanding ability and stability, the Parks had difficulty in finding professional advisers who were willing to trust them and to accept them as partners (at this point major partners) in the educational/therapeutic exercise. Mrs. Park writes: "Far from denigrating the knowledge of psycho-therapists, I only ask that they let parents share it. I learned from my child slowly and painfully, she and I together. But I would have learned faster, and with fewer gaps, if I had been in contact from the beginning with skilled and sympathetic professionals.'' She describes a first experience of very thorough professional study of the child, combined with a cold, impersonal attitude to the parents, a passive listening to what they had to say, with minimal feedback, a total lack of interest in the records they had kept, an uninformative report, and a total lack of guidance or encouragement.

Later she reports, with great gratitude and detailed appreciation, an experience of real partnership with the staff of another clinic. The social worker commented (''the words dropped into my mind like balm'') on the unusual persistence and energy shown by the parents. '''I think', she said, 'that we will be able to learn from you'. I could scarcely believe I had heard it. They did not think that in my lonely and presumptuous work I had injured my child. They thought I had helped her. Their present recommendation was not that Elly should begin analytic therapy but that I continue to work with her as before, with one difference. I would now have professional guidance from an analyst on the staff of the clinic.'' For some weeks there were regular, frequent sessions, mainly concerned with the mother's emotions; then the focus shifted to the child, and less frequent office interviews were supplemented with an occasional home visit when the mother could observe the therapist's approach to the child and find new ideas for her own approaches, as she also did later when the child was able to enter a good nursery school.

I have written about this book at some length because of its intrinsic value, and because of its scarcity value. It makes my point about the morale of the parents, about their need for encouragement and appreciation, and about how easily and how often this morale is not only neglected but unintentionally undermined. The Parks were certainly outstandingly able, but Williams has emphasised the good performance of many parents of more average ability and the secondary nature of much of the parental emotional disturbance observed and reported.

Insofar as the disturbance is secondary to the child's handicap, it is worth considering the possibilities of preventing parental disturbance and thus reducing the risk to the child. Caplan's crisis theory is clearly relevant here, and has provided the framework for several attempts at early intervention.[2,6] The project described by Nurse[7] arose partly from the observation that the families of retarded children were subjected to multiple and not necessarily coherent visiting by social workers, public health nurses, and officials mainly concerned with regular school attendance; such families are particularly likely to be transferred from one worker or service to another at times of stress or crisis. "This fragmentation of service and lack of continuity is being inflicted on particularly vulnerable people, and a common experience of social workers in this field is to be confronted with families in which disturbed patterns of adjustment and relationship have become firmly rooted over many years."

Two social workers and a senior public health nurse therefore decided to assemble a group of parents within at least two years of learning that their children were retarded, with the aim of helping them to adjust to their predicament. They hoped that by providing "some superficial support to the parents early in the life of the child" the group could obviate the need for long-term regular visiting by social workers later. However, once the lid came off Pandora's box, superficial support was soon forgotten, and the six months' planned duration also proved to be quite inadequate. (It is worth observing here that the crisis, in Caplan's sense, had already been missed, since the children in question were aged two or more at the start of the group.)

The members were deeply and passionately concerned with grief at the handicap, anger at the child's exacting demands, guilt and problems of "Who's to blame?", desperate wishes that the child could have been aborted, with guilt about these, and conflict about wishes to get rid of the child by sending it to an institution (at a time of great public concern about scandalous conditions in a hospital for the retarded). Since "every handicapped child is a risk for the parents" (Solnit, 1974),[11] and since every parent who succumbs to this risk increases the risk of maladjustment for the child, it behoves us to consider what we can do to minimize this risk — in fact to give this question a high priority. Much of the risk is inherent in the situation;

disappointment, grief, resentment, anxiety and guilt are normal expectable reactions to severe handicap in a child, and are liable to give rise to dysfunctional defences. All parents have to struggle with these responses with various degrees of success and failure. The outcome of this struggle, for parents and child, is partly determined by what the parents bring to the situation from their store of previous good and bad experiences, in terms of confidence in their ability to love, to create, to repair; partly by the degree of support they enjoy among their friends and relations; partly by the attitude and skill of their professional advisers; and partly by the general climate of opinion which affects the attitudes alike of parents, friends and relations and professional advisers.

If we agree that it should be a major objective to preserve parental morale, we have to approach the problem at various levels. On the one hand, all those parents who are not totally incapacitated by severe mental illness should be treated as partners in the preventive enterprise. Their potential or actual strengths should be recognised and encouraged, just as we hope they will in turn encourage those of their children. Many of them will need some help with their own feelings, as described by Mrs. Park and also by Brody,[3] and this is likely to be most effective if given at the point when the diagnosis or the information of risk is communicated. But the help they need is likely to be educational as well as therapeutic. The child's potential for development and for mastery of any handicap needs to be fully and carefully explained (though not exaggerated), together with the most appropriate ways in which the parents can help the child. This may need to be explained one step at a time, and perhaps with the simpler or more anxious parents many times, or a long-term strategy may be grasped in one or two sessions by the more intelligent. Most parents will need opportunities to report progress at intervals to some encouraging "expert", and will also need advice as to the timing of new methods, as well as help in noting and valuing the very small increments of success which occur in many cases. Two considerations are important:

1. If the parents' potential for helping the child to develop his competence and master his handicap is mobilised, they will have more to give the child than any therapist can give — although

expert intervention may occasionally be needed to supplement parental care or to remove some obstacle which prevents the child from accepting it.

2. It is vital for the parents' own stability to be given a method for helping the child to overcome his handicap and encouraged to use it and to enjoy some success. This provides a truly functional outlet for their drive toward reparation, together with reassurance that they are indeed capable of achieving it. Failing such help, many parents attempt reparation in ways of their own devising, which are often dysfunctional, such as over-protection and infantilisation; or else they are liable to fall back on more primitive defences against guilt, such as denial or rejection.

On the societal level, we have to give very serious consideration to the effect of our deliberations and our publications on the parents of those children whom we identify as vulnerable. We know that these communications will be filtered to them through the popular press, and through the professional press and its impact on their professional advisers; we know that distortion in inevitable, but at least we can avoid inviting it by the imbalance of our emphasis. We should also make some serious attempt to counteract the harm which has been done by previous publications which have unintentionally, but nonetheless powerfully, undermined many potentially helpful parents and added to the burdens they already carried in caring for a handicapped or disturbed child. Anything we say about the unwilling and unwitting contribution of some parents to the maladjustment of their children should be carefully balanced by recognition of the role of the parents in relation to all those children who are able to adapt to their handicaps without succumbing to the risks to which they are exposed. When therapeutic or preventive interventions in which parents were involved (Provence, 1974)[10] are reported, the work with the parents and the contribution which they were able to make should be at least as fully reported as other elements in the interventive programme.

We must never forget that scientific meetings, publications, and publicity affect the situations we describe in unintended ways, as well as those we intend. Let us remember how often the arrogance of the "experts" has led society, and parents in particular, in directions we have later bitterly regretted. Since we inevitably leave "footsteps on the sands of time", let us be careful which way they will lead those who follow.

References

1. Adams, M. (1972) Social Aspects of Medical Care for the Mentally Retarded, *New England Journal of Medicine.*
2. Booth, B.L. (1966) Residential Courses for Families with a Handicapped Child, *Case Conference,* 13,2.
3. Brody, S. (1961) Preventive Intervention in Current Problems of Early Childhood, in *Prevention of Mental Disorders in Children,* G. Caplan (Ed.), New York: Basic Books.
4. Drillien, C.M. (1964) *The Growth and Development of the Prematurely Born Child,* Livingstone, Edinburgh.
5. Graham, P. and Rutter, M. (1968) Organic Brain Dysfunction and Child Psychiatric Disorder, *British Medical Journal,* 3, 695.
6. Leiderman, P.H. (1974) Mothers at Risk: A Potential Consequence of the Hospital Care of the Premature Infant, in Anthony & Koupernik, *The Child in his Family: Children at Psychiatric Risk.*
7. Nurse, J. (1972) Retarded Infants and Their Parents. A Group for Fathers and Mothers, *British Journal of Social Work,* 2,2.
8. Park, C.C. (1967) *The Siege,* Pelican Books, London.
9. Pond, D.A. (1961) Psychiatric Aspects of Epileptic and Brain-damaged Children, *British Medical Journal,* 5264, 1377-82.
10. Provence, S. (1974) Some Relationships between Activity and Vulnerability in the Early Years, in Anthony & Koupernik, *The Child in His Family: Children at Psychiatric Risk.*
11. Solnit, A. (1974) A Summing up of the Dakar Conference, in Anthony & Koupernik, *The Child in His Family: Children at Psychiatric Risk.*
12. Williams, C.E. (1968) Behaviour Disorders in Handicapped Children, *Developmental Medicine and Child Neurology,* 10,6.
13. Winnicott, D.W. (1958) The Mentally Ill in your Caseload, in *Collected Papers,* Tavistock, London: Basic Books, New York.

CHAPTER 19

The Role of Donald Winnicott: Healing, Teaching, Nurture*

Donald Winnicott came to psycho-analysis through paediatrics. Thus he had more occasion than most analysts to observe the delicate interaction between "the ordinary devoted mother and her child", and to this task he brought a unique quality of observation, involving a profound use of disciplined imagination; like Blake, he saw "not with but through the eye". Only relatively late in life did he cease to practise partly in the paediatric setting, and he retained a keener awareness of the dynamics of the mother/baby system that can often be achieved by the analyst who works with patients alone. Even in the consulting-room, he combined regular analysis of children and adults with another kind of child psychiatry (described in *Therapeutic Consultations* and elsewhere) in which he used a deep-going diagnostic appraisal of the child and his problem as a basis for increasing parental insight and exploring with the parents how, in the light of this fresh understanding, they could make good what was missing and restore what was damaged.

In his collected papers, Winnicott frequently acknowledges his debt to Melanie Klein, especially in relation to the concept of internal objects and the theory of the depressive position. Yet he was too original to be a follower, and his contribution to the corpus of psycho-analytic thought is very distinctive. His major contribution concerns the first half-year of life (which can only be "known" by inference and imagination) and the corresponding phase of the mother's life; even here, the difference is mainly one of emphasis, yet it is important as well as subtle. In a book written jointly with Melanie Klein (1937),

British Journal of Social Work, 3, 3, Printed in Great Britain.

Joan Riviere writes, "a baby does not recognise anyone's existence but his own (his mother's breast is to him merely a part of himself — just a sensation at first) and he expects all his wants to be fulfilled". This contains the essence of much that Winnicott has written, but Mrs. Riviere passes on immediately to the child's discovery of "the not-me" through frustration (the experience which Winnicott later called disillusion) and the phenomena of introjection and projection which then develop as the child tries to order and control the complications of his developing conceptual world and the chaos of the associated feelings. Later in the same book, Melanie Klein gives an account of motherhood which closely resembles Winnicott's, but is expressed almost entirely in terms of earlier individual experience, the fulfilment of early childhood longings and the resolution of problems arising from early relationships with parents. Winnicott's concept of "primary maternal preoccupation" has a more biological flavour, of which there is only a hint in Mrs. Klein's account: "the child's helplessness and its great need for its mother's care call for more love than can be given to any other person, and thus all the mother's loving and constructive tendencies now have scope".

Winnicott was fascinated with the period preceding the child's discovery of "the me and the not-me", which he conceived as a period of illusion, in which the baby assumes (and is allowed or encouraged to assume) that he omnipotently creates the objects of his desire. Although it is clear that illusion must often be threatened from a very early age by inevitable frustrations, his view was that if all goes well illusion remains relatively intact till what he called "the weaning age". Recognising that "the actual time of weaning varies according to the cultural pattern", he specifies, "for me the weaning age is that at which the infant becomes able to play at droppings things . . . somewhere about five months". The relevance of the child's game to weaning is not immediately obvious; it seems that what the author really had in mind is the perception of objects as separate from the self, and a beginning ability to use symbols.

Here I would like to protest against the widespread tendency of psycho-analysts to obscure an important area of theory by expressing it in imagery derived from breast-feeding, in a culture where most infants are bottle-fed from the start, and where weaning as a maternal technique now emphasises the gradual introduction of more solid food rather than the withdrawal of the bottle, which the child is often allowed to renounce in his own good time. Just as Winnicott reveals above that he used the term "weaning" to represent a turning-point in the child's internal cognitive and affective development, so he spells out elsewhere the symbolic use of the term "breast". "When it is said that the first object is the breast, the word 'breast' is used, I believe, to stand for the technique of mothering as well as for the actual flesh. It is not impossible for a mother to be a good-enough mother ... with a bottle for the actual feeding." It is of great value for the reader to be provided with this kind of gloss, but why do analysts continue to increase the difficulty of communicating their difficult subject by such unnecessary obscurities of language?

To return to "primary maternal preoccupation": this was Winnicott's term for an innate biologically-determined wisdom and capacity for devotion, expressed in a high degree of active and pleasurable adaptation to the infant's needs. This enables the mother's response to the infant's cues to be sufficiently prompt and accurate to sustain the illusion that he has created the external object whom he eventually comes to discern (dimly, by fits and starts, and gradually more clearly and continuously) out of the needs which she satisfies, and out of "an innate capacity to love". In other words, he creates a perceptual object out of many experiences of need satisfied (and sometimes unsatisfied) and at the same time he makes this care-taking woman into his mother by the development of his attachment to her.

This is a major achievement in disillusion, the process by which illusion makes way for reality, and the mother brings him to this point largely as a result of a dwindling of her maternal preoccupation, which leads to an increasing imperfection of adaptation. This psycho-biological change usually keeps step with the infant's growing capacity to tolerate delay and frustration, his development of security, the confidence that sooner or later need will be met (Erikson's "basic trust") — unless social pressures, or the theories of "experts", induce her to force the pace, or some problem in her own development induces a pathological and pathogenic prolongation of maternal preoccupation.

Perhaps Winnicott's greatest divergence from the Kleinian picture lies in his account of the genesis of hate. Following the passage quoted above, Joan Riviere refers to the earliest frustration "at the breast", and describes the baby as "exploding with hate and aggressive craving". Winnicott, on the other hand, suggests (1947) that "the personality must be integrated before an infant can be said to hate. However early integration may be achieved — perhaps integration occurs earliest at the height of excitement or rage — there is a theoretical earlier stage in which whatever the infant does that hurts is not done in hate. I have used the term 'ruthless love' in describing this stage. . . . As the infant becomes able to feel to be a whole person, so does the word hate develop meaning as a description of a certain group of his feelings."

Here I think Winnicott is saying that during the stage of illusion the infant may rage, but he cannot hate, because there is not yet an object to hate. Hate, like projection and introjection, appears, according to him, at the stage of "weaning". It is also interesting that I can find in his work no mention of the "death instinct", nor any reference to an inevitable experience of the "paranoid-schizoid" position. It seems as if he joins hands with Melanie Klein at the onset of the depressive position, and that this is the point at which he sees the internal objects, as well as the external object, developing.

We have mentioned the danger of trying to force the pace, and this is a constant theme in Winnicott's work. Maturation is a process in time, which can easily fail, or be replaced by pseudo-maturation, if the pace is forced. This may seem obvious enough; but learning theory has provided a basis for various attempts to accelerate development, of which "teach your baby to read" was only one outstanding example. Time is needed for the development of a "completed experience", a total happening, which can be relinquished without conflict because it is complete. Winnicott describes a baby playing with a spoon (with the author's co-operation) till he loses interest: "he has 'had time to go right through an experience. This is good for the baby' " (1975, p. 35). But this is already a successor to the initial good feeding experience, in which the mother allows time for the child to hesitate, to turn to the breast, to suck, to get over-excited, to withdraw, to return to the breast; by waiting and giving each at the right time, she adapts to the child in a way that supports the illusion which Winnicott considers so vital in the early months, after which he considers the experience can safely be more occasional. He understands that many mothers will not have time to provide it often; but this is sad, because "the baby is the poorer" (and the mother too). The same emphasis on the right time underlies the approach to toilet-training: "Perhaps there is a whimpering sound which the sensitive mother knows that if she comes quickly she may be able to attend personally to a motion which otherwise just becomes a wasted mess. This is the very beginning of cooperation and social sense, and is worth all the trouble it involves" (1957, p. 61). This sort of thing is what makes the difference between toilet-training as a basis for attitudes of autonomy, submission or rebellion.

Any understanding of the needs of children can be a source of anxiety to those mothers who are for some reason ill-equipped for some aspect of the role. Thus Bowlby has been criticised for chaining the conscientious mother to her pre-school child by guilt and anxiety. Winnicott confirmed the vital importance for the young child of almost uninterrupted contact with his mother, adding that he had found most mothers to be capable of a very high quality of devoted maternal response, although this could be disturbed by the pressure of material cares (or the theories of "experts"). His broadcasts to mothers are full of reassurance and encouragement, rather than warnings of the risks of failure. Although he believed that "the ordinary mother" would enjoy the kind of mothering experience described almost as much as the baby, he recognised that she might easily be too busy or harassed to do things that way very often. Necessity must be respected, but his heart bled for the waste. He suggests that many bedwetters "are going back in the night to their infancy, trying to ... find and correct something that was missing ... the mother's sensitive attention to signals of excitement or distress that would have enabled her to make personal and good what otherwise had to be wasted, because there was no one there to participate in what happened" (1957, p. 62).

This is very moving writing, with a marked poetical quality; it comes from a broadcast to mothers, and if it had not spoken to their feelings it too would have been just another waste product. These statements are not couched in a language which permits easy experimental verification; yet Winnicott insisted that his conclusions were based on a truly scientific process of testing and refining in the appropriate situations: therapeutic settings, where mother-infant interactions could be observed and influenced and observed again; residential settings, where staff could apply his theories in their attempts to understand and help distubed children, report the results in great detail, and again, if necessary, modify their management on the basis of fresh insight. The language of the published work varies to some extent according to the habits and expectations of the audience, professional or otherwise, but Winnicott never succumbed to the dehumanising professional language in which concepts are reified in the service of a pseudo-objectivity. His broadcasts to mothers are not translated from some more abstract theoretical formulation; they arise directly and visibly from deep personal experience, in which feeling and rigorous thought are intimately fused; and this applies no less to the professional papers. Winnicott was a great practitioner of the rare and undervalued art of holding feeling and thought in balance, and giving them combined expression. His aim was "verstehen" of the human being in all his depth and complexity, with particular emphasis on the elusive and the imponderable which, as Bergson argued, are overlooked or distorted by positivistic approaches, resulting in a false mechanistic view of mankind. Winnicott's insights did not always lend themselves to clarity of expression, being concerned with phenomena so subtle and elusive; one observes in him the struggle of the creative writer to communicate and make intelligible experience which has not previously been expressed in words — very literally "a raid on the inarticulate". Hence the varied and resourceful attempts to say the same thing in different words, to find new words in which to make it clearer, or to bring out some new facet; hence the use of imagery, particularly images of space to be filled; hence the triumphant moments when prose becomes poetry, "a simple concentration of difficult meaning". Le style, c'est l'homme.

There are times when Winnicott's "ordinary devoted mother", absorbed in her primary maternal preoccupation, sounds suspiciously like an idealised mother-image. He did not, however, believe a mother to be free from ambivalence, and in fact he put this very strongly in his paper on "Hate in the Countertransference" (1947). "The mother hates her infant from the word go." Here follows a long list of reasons why hate may be present. "A mother has to be able to tolerate hating her baby without doing anything about it. She cannot express it to him. . . . The most remarkable thing about a mother is her ability to be hurt so much by her baby and to hate so much without paying the child out, and her ability to wait for rewards that may or may not come at a later date." So social workers need not feel guilty about their own ambivalence as mothers, or shocked at that of their clients. Nor, in view of the title and content of this paper, need they expect to be free of ambivalence towards their clients.

There is, of course, great danger for the baby if the hate preponderates or gets out of control. A more common risk, about which Winnicott was very concerned, was the incapacity of many women "who are good mothers in every other way and who are capable of a rich and fruitful life" to develop a primary maternal preoccupation. "The result is that such women, having produced a child, but having missed the boat at the earliest stage, are faced with the task of making up for what has been missed. They have a long period" (assuming that they are motivated to put things right) "in which they must closely adapt to their growing child's needs, and it is not certain that they can succeed in mending the early distortion." Failing this, the child may well come into professional care, and if he is very lucky he may find himself in the hands of somebody who is both motivated and skilful enough to undertake the repairs successfully.

This leads us to Winnicott's role as a teacher of other professions than his own. Martin James (1968) has recorded that by the time of the last World War most psycho-analysts had abandoned the earlier attempt to communicate with the educated and professional lay public, having been discouraged by a wave of uncritical enthusiasms and misapplication of analytic theory among lay followers, extremists and cranks. However, Winnicott's concern for the protection of spontaneous maternal response made it impossible for him to stand aloof, and led to his famous series of war-time broadcasts to mothers. The war also led to his extremely fruitful professional partnership with Clare Britton (who eventually became his wife), and with many untrained but carefully selected residential workers, in the residential management of evacuated children who had proved too deprived and disturbed to be contained within the voluntary billeting system. This experience revealed the therapeutic potential of good "residential management", which brought him to disagree strongly with the view of some colleagues that only psycho-analysis can repair the consequences of any variety of early emotional damage. Analysis, in his view, was for those who had enjoyed at least some primary experience of good mothering, a treasure lost through interruption or overlaid by subsequent distortions of relationship. Where such primary experience had not existed, the only hope was to provide, however belatedly, opportunity for the kind of relationship where it could develop. On the other hand, he was by no means one of those optimists who suppose that the sad effects of severe environmental failure are to be easily corrected by the provision of a better environment. "A deprived child is ill", he wrote, "and it is never so simple a matter that environmental readjustment will bring about a change-over in the child from ill to healthy. At best, the child who can benefit from a simple environmental provision begins to get better, and as the change takes place from ill to less ill the child becomes increasingly able to get angry about the past deprivation. Hate of the world is there somewhere, and health has not arrived unless the hate has been felt" (1965, p. 134). Here in a nutshell is one of the basic problems of long-term substitute care.

But neither was Winnicott an easy pessimist, and he generously supported the efforts of Barbara Dockar-Drysdale and others to expand the possibilities of making good at a later date the damage inflicted by early deprivation, even when so severe as to have been previously found irreversible. These workers used his detailed analysis of health-producing experiences in the earliest years to build up a very sophisticated quality of residential care, which accepts and works through hate and destruction, rather than reacting repressively against them; they have increasingly focused on the needs of the child who is still unintegrated during his schooldays, and on ways of promoting integration, even as late as adolescence. This must involve provision of the quality of primary experience which was lacking at the appropriate time, although in group care this can only be done in a "localised" way, at certain times or in certain situations. Clearly the problem of the gaps between these experiences of quasi-maternal adaptation must be an acute one, and here Winnicott's concept of transitional object is probably familiar to readers — the special toy or scrap of material out of which the child creates a special symbol scrap of material which out of which the child creates a special symbol for his mother. The term "transitional phenomena" covers a wide range of rituals, often co-operatively created by mother and child; the bed-time story, the special way of tucking in, the last kiss in a special place, which, like transitional objects, "enables the child to stand frustrations and deprivations". Such transitional phenomena are an essential ingredient in the quality of child care described, but Winnicott warns us that they cannot be used as a gimmick. "There must be someone for the object to stand for, which means that the condition of these children cannot be cured simply by giving them a new object. A child may, however, grow to such confidence in the person who is caring for him that objects that are deeply symbolical of that person will appear."

I wrote this paper before deciding on the title. The eventual need to formulate one concentrates the mind wonderfully on the crucial question: why is it so clearly appropriate to commemorate Donald Winnicott in a social work journal? In many ways I hope the answer is implicit in what I have written; there has been much occasion to mention his two-way involvement with the fields of social work and residential care to which Clare Winnicott has done so much to bring together in mutual identification. As we have seen, many analysts have tried, perhaps prematurely, to tease out the implications of their knowledge and clinical experience for normal child development, and to make them available to parents and the relevant professions. Such a task is beset by special difficulties in communication; many became discouraged, and Winnicott was one of the few who persevered. It is partly because he devoted so much time to communicating with these professions, in terms of a real exchange of views and experience, that he gained such deep understanding and empathy for them (analogous to his empathic understanding of parents). He became an outstanding communicator, but much more than that; in a very real, though symbolic, sense he nurtured the nurturing professions, feeding them with a continual flow of wisdom, insight, experience, support. It is an honour to have been asked to add a fragment to his memorial.

References

Klein, M. and Riviere, J. (1937) *Love, Hate and Reparation.*
James, M. (1968) Psychoanalysis and Childhood 1967, in Sutherland (Ed.), *The Psychoanalytic Approach.*
The following is a list of Donald Winnicott's books which are currently in print.
The Child and the Family, Tavistock Publications, 1957.
The Child and the Outside World, Tavistock Publications, 1957.
The Child, his Family and the Outside World, Penguin Books Ltd., 1969.
Collected Papers, Tavistock Publications, 1958.
Family and Individual Development, Tavistock Publications, 1965.
The Maturational Process and Facilitating Environment, Hogarth Press, 1965.
Playing and Reality, Tavistock Publications, 1971.
Therapeutic Consultations in Child Psychiatry, Hogarth Press, 1971.

Conclusion

It has been a curious experience to review my writings of twenty-five years, to realise the illusions I entertained in my middle years. I began to write in 1950. Behind me lay the Thirties, a great slump and its aftermath, the desperate poverty proclaimed by the Hunger Marches, the threat of international Fascism. The profession and the movement with which I had identified had barely struck root in Britain, had barely achieved visibility. Then during the Second World War, things had begun to move. Children of all ages were evacuated from the cities and billeted with householders in the safer countryside. This spot-lit, as perhaps nothing else could have done, the material conditions of the urban slums from which many of these children had come, the extent of emotional disturbance among them, and the insufficiency of kindness and common sense in dealing with them. Psychiatric social workers were suddenly in great demand to help the host communities with these unexpected problems, to help the innumerable residential and day nurseries to provide for the developmental needs of their charges, to provide social care for the discharged psychiatric casualties of the armed forces.

The immediate post-War period was one of great progress and great hope. The Welfare State was established, and seemed for a time to be solving the problem of poverty, so that interest in people's other problems, their tangled relationships, their inner conflicts and self-defeating tendencies, became stronger. It was at last accepted that the model of casework inherited unchanged from the Charity Organization Society was inadequate, and that all caseworkers needed to understand these matters in terms of dynamic psychology. Some of these changes are more fully described in Chapter 1.

I did not foresee that my "renaissance" would prove to be only a thesis, which would be strongly, even violently, confronted with a

243

powerful antithesis before the end of my working life. It did not occur to me to question the social worker's right to intervene until the publication of Barbara Wootton's *Social Science and Social Pathology* (1960). My personal experience was sheltered by the conditions of child guidance, where the client is under no obligation to use the service, and a potential client who proves unwilling is encouraged to withdraw. Our right to intervene depended entirely on our ability to convince the parents of each child that the service we offered was relevant to their problem and likely to help, so that all our consumers were willing clients. There were times when we had reason to regret this limitation. I remember a psychotic woman whose husband admitted in confidence that she was severely maltreating her adopted child, and who refused to cooperate with us or to allow the child to be placed in a boarding-school. This left us powerless to protect the child. The father was too much afraid of his wife to call in the N.S.P.C.C., and all we could do was to alert those agencies which had routine contact with the child and which might find evidence to justify such a referral.

At the Tavistock Clinic I had supervised workers from probation and child care departments and had taken for granted the authority component of their roles. I had seen it as a factor which might create some initial difficulty in establishing rapport, and which called for special skills in demonstrating to the unwilling client that the worker was not only trustworthy and benevolent, but that a relationship with him had something to offer. I believed then, as I do now, that the probation officer's dual role as a benign authority, concerned for the client as well as for society, is of vital importance, since it provides an opportunity to dissipate the client's hostile stereotype of authority, which benignity alone would not do. Some students were uneasy about the apparent contradiction between the principle of "client self-determination" and the professional authority which probation officers are obliged to exercise; our discussion on this point covered the ground which I explored in Chapter 14.

The Tavistock students were all qualified and experienced social workers, who had either trained before the impact of psycho-analytic theory or who wished to deepen their knowledge of it. In contrast, the M.Phil. course at the University of York provided basic professional training for graduate students, some of whom had no experience of social work, and very few, more than two years.

Some of these students were seriously exercised about the right to intervene, particularly during the early part of their fieldwork, while still uncertain of their ability to help. This is of course appropriate, and far better than over-confidence. It wears off with experience of success, and the student usually comes to realise that to withdraw at the first rebuff often deprives the client of needed help, which he may prove able to accept if the worker has the skill to explore the client's ambivalence and realises that to accept hostile feelings without withdrawing may provide the client with a new and encouraging experience.

However, there is also now an ideological problem. Social work teachers are accused by some sociologists of indoctrinating their students with "the ideology of casework". (It might equally well be said that a certain number of students show every sign of having been indoctrinated by this school of sociologists before they embark on professional training.) Neither staff nor students can ignore the argument that casework is merely an insidious method of social control, a latterday opium of the people; that it does more harm than good by retarding the radical reorganisation of society, which is said to be the only true way to eliminate poverty and inequality. Deviancy theory points out that society creates the delinquent by making the laws he breaks; change the law and the homosexual is no longer a delinquent, provided he accepts certain limitations. This is true, and it is also true that our laws need reform in many respects and that reforms come slowly but, as this example shows, it comes. It is initiated, of course, by the activity of pressure groups and it may be that social workers have not till recently been as politically active as they might. But I sense an undermining of confidence in the whole democratic process, a preference for direct action and provocation, which seem to me to endanger the whole gradual process of social engineering and entail the risk of producing a lawless free-for-all, followed by a more authoritarian system than we have now. It seems to me we have a great deal to lose.

There is, of course, a very real problem about labelling and stigma, the problem of the deviant career. It is true that imprisonment of delinquents and the hospitalisation of the mentally ill inflict a stigma which militates against successful rehabilitation; yet delinquency and mental illness cannot be ignored. The problem is to find methods of rehabilitation which will inflict as little stigma as possible. The community care of the mentally ill and the gradual opening of the mental hospital to the community have considerably reduced the stigma of mental illness, and will almost certainly continue to do so. The treatment of delinquency has lagged far behind that of mental illness, although more adequate after-care now gives better hope of reintegration into society; while the greatest hope of reducing stigma lies in the New Careers movement and that towards devising alternatives to prison. However, I am not convinced that the majority of human beings are capable of stigmatising nobody at all.

I think it is true that social work in general militates against revolutionary solutions of problems and favours the more gradual process of social reform; from my standpoint this is a useful function. In spite of the poverty which still exists and our unsolved housing and employment problems, things have improved in my lifetime very much more than the younger generation will believe; for the sick, the aged, and particularly for the unemployed. It is natural for the young to be keenly concerned with the injustices of our society and impatient with the slow pace of social reform. I was a student during the great slump of the Thirties, when there seemed to be regress rather than progress, followed by some social reform at a snail's pace only. My friends and I were horrified by the poverty revealed by the Hunger Marches and felt desperately impatient of the failure either to prevent or relieve it. There followed the interlude of the Second World War, and then the post-war reforms. I well remember the moment in 1951 when I suddenly felt glad surprise that so much had been achieved in the last ten years. Now as then the young, with their narrow span of personal history, are tempted to despair at the ups and downs, the slow and unsteady pace of social reform, but our society stands to lose a great deal if revolutionary solutions come to be preferred. Experience in many countries has shown such solutions to require pretty harsh social control to maintain themselves. There is no sign as yet in any such regime of the State withering away as the original revolutionaries hoped.

I have tried to show, in Chapters 5 and 14, that it is a false dichotomy to present care and control as mutually exclusive alternatives, however difficult and painful it may be for the social worker to find and apply the appropriate combination in practice. A similar unreal dichotomy underlies the current debate as to whether social workers should help their clients with material *or* emotional problems. People whose felt needs are exclusively material and who are able to accept and use appropriate material help need the services of a welfare worker, not those of a professional social worker (see the Younghusband Report, 1959). But there are many people who for various emotional reasons are unable to use the services available or to make the most of their opportunities; there are many others whose problems concerning marital or parent-child relationships are compounded by material problems. These people need a service which combines help with both kinds of problem, and it is the distinctive character of casework that it is able to deal with both at once. In the classical model of casework the worker explores the client's material problems with him, helps him to think out workable solutions, encourages him to make and carry out plans, and tries to understand and help him to understand what sometimes prevents him from doing so, and what are the reasons for any self-defeating behaviour which he shows. It is sometimes argued or implied that caseworkers should immediately supply the client's wants or needs. Caseworkers prefer to encourage the client to do for himself whatever he can, rather than to do such things for him; the first course ministers to his self-respect and self-confidence, the second tends to undermine them.

However, Mayer and Timms (1971) have revealed a serious defect in the practice of this model. It seems that caseworkers too often fail to take the client with them as co-explorer of his situation by neglecting to share their growing understanding with him step by step. While the caseworker asks questions and explores, the client becomes mystified and often does not wait for the moment when the worker will eventually impart his understanding to him. It is possible that the psychiatric model has contributed to this failure of empathy and technique, particularly if the caseworker insists on compiling a full psychiatric history before addressing the client's problem. It seems clear that social workers and those who train them should pay more attention to establishing a genuine understanding and cooperation between worker and client. The notion of contract is a step in this direction, but this often tends to get whittled down into an agreement about frequency, length and possibly number of interviews, omitting the essential element of consensus concerning the goals of all this activity. At present it seems that casework based on learning theory deals most adequately with this problem (Hudson, 1975, 1976). I should add that, despite what I said above, the principle of client self-help should not be rigidly applied without regard to the chances of success. There are many cases where the dice are so loaded against the client that it is appropriate for the social worker to act as his advocate or even to take action on his behalf. Once again, behavioural casework and task-centred casework offer a valuable example of clarifying explicitly with the client who will do what.

On the other hand, many people seek help concerning conflict between marital partners or between parents and children. Such people may or may not need material help, but in any case this alone will not solve their problems, without some attempt to understand relationships past and present. The parents of handicapped children also often present considerable needs for material help, but a recent study has shown that this alone does little to reduce the stress under which they labour (Bradshaw and Lawton, 1978).

It is true that in the hey-day of Freudian casework some of us devoted a disproportionate amount of attention to the unconscious roots of behaviour and too little to the stresses with which the individual had to contend. I have tried to redress the imbalance between psycho-social and societal factors in Chapter 11, but I believe that the pendulum has swung much too far towards considering societal factors only. To quote a recent paper by Joan Cooper: "Social problems and private sorrows are not rooted exclusively in the economic, social or political structure. Neither are they rooted exclusively in biology, character or personality." Only a multi-factorial model which includes psycho-social as well as socio-economic factors can do justice to the rich complexity of human problems and human needs.

I prefer to think in terms of factors influencing human behaviour rather than of determinants, a concept which leaves no room for individual responsibility. The probation officer, for instance, has to take into account the personal and social deprivation and stresses to which the client has responded by turning to delinquent activities, so that they may be made good or alleviated as far as possible; but he must not encourage the client to use them as *excuses* or to see himself as a passive victim, since rehabilitation depends to some extent on reinforcing or developing his sense of personal responsibility.

The social worker has a complex role, being responsible to the client, to his employers and to society. In recent years a vocal group of younger social workers have tried to escape from this complexity by proclaiming that he is responsible only to the client. This does not seem to me a tenable position; it seems to indicate a suspect but not uncommon tendency to identify with the rebel, the under-dog, the delinquent. Few students find it hard to understand the feelings of the adolescent who is at odds with his parents; some over-identify with him and see his parents no more objectively than he does, not appreciating that some parental control is justified, even in the adolescent's own interests, and that many of his complaints may be based on misinterpretation of their motives. Even where the parents are indeed harsh or depriving, it is important for the social worker to learn to understand and accept them, which can often be done by evoking the deprived or ill-treated children from whom they developed. Unresolved problems about authority also often underlie the identification with the anti-social client as victim which I mentioned above. But one cannot make for the client, any more than for oneself, a world in which it is never necessary to subordinate one's own desires to those of others, to obey rules and accept some degree of authority. Damaged as he may have been by the slings and arrows of his family and society, his welfare depends on coming to terms with authority and on finding how to obtain as much satisfaction as possible by legitimate means. While it is important that we understand and accept his feelings about authority and authorities, we cannot encourage him to hope for a world without constraints and compulsions; we may encourage him to claim all his legitimate rights, and I think we have to help him see that these rights are accorded to him by society, as well as the restrictions which he resents.

Casework is also criticised for enjoining on the worker a controlled professional relationship, which is felt to be artificial or unauthentic; Chapters 2 and 3 are illustrations of the self-conscious use of relationship which is rejected. It is true that the model described may be inappropriate for many clients, as I recognised in Chapter 4, and that a number of social workers have demonstrated that a less formal kind of relationship, more resembling friendship, is more acceptable and helpful to many clients; but it is still important that the relationship be used purposefully to achieve a goal which should be agreed between social worker and client (the contract). Heimler (1958) has described meeting some of his clients in the pub or the park, but in spite of these informal settings he used the occasions therapeutically, sharing with the client his effort to understand him by using all the clues of his non-verbal communication as well as his spoken words.

The development of a more informal and flexible style in casework, the reduction of professional distance between worker and client, are, I think, a great step forward, providing the dynamics of the situation are understood and care is taken not to arouse false hopes of intimacy and permanence. If the social worker becomes the first close friend the client has ever had, or if he plays a parental role with a deeply deprived client, his holidays will seem like desertions to the client, while his leaving and losing contact will feel like total abandonment. To raise such hopes and disappoint them is not only cruel; the client may act out his anger in ways which harm himself and his family, or the disillusion may drive him further into isolation and withdrawal. To handle such intense situations safely requires an extremely good understanding of transference and great skill in handling it, possibly too much to expect of all social workers. However, various agencies are now developing approaches which enable workers to dispense with the usual professional distance without inviting an intense and exclusive personal attachment. Family Service Units encourage their clients to rely on the Unit as a whole, often combining casework with groupwork, so that the client has some relationship with more than one worker as well as with other clients.

One of the IMPACT units in the probation service, which specifically studied the differential use of various methods according to the needs of different clients, also allowed the clients to use the unit as a base, and combined casework with groupwork for some of them;

it also offered clients the services of a pair of caseworkers, thus minimising the risk of leaving a client suddenly with no familiar worker (although this is not the main reason for using this device). Family casework is also developing rapidly, and one of the many advantages of this method is that it, too, avoids the investment in the worker of unrealistic hopes, and encourages family members to understand and satisfy each others' needs better.

Both the Family Service Units and the IMPACT unit referred to above provide a generous amount of supervision and group discussion for their workers. It seems to me particularly important that this should be so in any agency whose workers are relying more on intuition and spontaneity rather than on a more formal technique, which makes it much more difficult to distinguish behaviour which is a valid response to the client's needs from that which meets one's own — possibly at his expense.

This profusion of ideas, methods and approaches seems to indicate that casework is still a vigorous plant, which is thriving and renewing itself under the cold blasts of criticism. At present it seems to be flourishing best in private agencies and child guidance clinics. The social services departments, twice reorganised in five years, are finding it hard to provide a structure in which casework can thrive, and there is a danger that it may be deformed and discredited by too much dilution with welfare tasks and heavy caseloads. However, some social services departments are now creating conditions which enable social caseworkers to practise their skills in the service of their clients, as well as devising imaginative forms of intermediate treatment. We must hope that other departments will follow their example, but if casework should be widely rejected by social service departments they will find themselves unable to offer significant help with marital or parent/child problems, and there will be a growing demand for private agencies to supply such help. It is tantalizing to be only a spectator of further developments, but they will be well worth watching.

References

Bradshaw, J. and Lawton, D. (1978) Tracing the Causes of Stress in Families with Handicapped Children, *British Journal of Social Work,* Vol. VIII, no. 2.

Heimler, E. (1958) New Roads in Psychiatric Community Care, *The Medical Officer,* C, 295.

Hudson, B. (1965) The Inadequate Personality, *Social Work Today,* Vol. VI, no. 16.

Hudson, B. (1976) The Haunted Bedroom: A case study in behaviour modification, *Social Work Today,* Vol. VIII, no. 10.

Mayer, H.J. and Timms, N. (1970) *The Client Speaks,* London, Routledge & Kegan Paul.

Wootton, B. (1960) *Social Science and Social Pathology,* London, Allen & Unwin.

Younghusband, E. (1959) *Report of the Working Party on Social Workers in the Local Authority Health & Welfare Services,* London, H.M.S.O.

Author Index

Subject Index

256   *Subject Index*

258   Subject Index

Knowledge vii, xi, 4, 22ff., 57, 63, 66,
74, 76, 82, 146, 177, 184ff., 188, 193,
195ff., 222, 228, 241

Labelling 42, 63, 99, 144, 245
Language 45, 195, 198, 200ff., 227, 235,
238
Learning theory 175, 189, 236, 248
Listening 44, 112, 115, 120, 126, 131ff.
Loss 60, 168ff., 203
Love 104, 184, 198ff., 215, 217, 230,
234ff.

Mackenzie, M. 57, 71
Maladjustment 10, 14, 22, 43, 225, 229,
231
Manipulation 25, 37, 43, 153, 175, 193,
217
Maternity & Child Welfare Service 57,
71, 83
Maturation 122ff., 136ff., 167, 186, 236
Mental
after-care 157, 165, 173
breakdown 158, 160, 162, 164ff., 218,
223ff.
health 50, 57, 70, 80, 162, 165, 167,
185, 209, 226
Mental health
consultation 57, 70, 80
education 57, 70ff., 80ff., 178
services 29, 50, 93, 156ff., 165, 173
Mental hospitals 93, 156, 168ff., 246
Mental illness, ill-health 10, 53, 146,
160ff., 168ff., 182, 185, 194, 230,
236
prevention of 57ff., 71, 74, 156, 165,
168, 171, 173, 222, 229, 231
Money 97, 102, 112, 116, 123, 126, 211
Mothering 124, 235, 236, 240
Mothers 59, 61, 64, 73ff., 84ff., 95ff.,
107ff., 136ff., 150ff., 156, 167ff.,
189, 199ff., 210, 213ff., 223, 233ff.
Motivation 4, 21, 40, 43, 99, 108, 136,
154, 163, 175, 180, 194ff., 216ff.,
223, 239, 249
Mourning 164, 200, 203ff., 219

Needs 28ff., 39, 41ff., 65, 69, 97ff.,
107ff., 124, 147, 154, 157, 163, 169,
180, 186, 188ff., 215ff., 234ff., 237,
239ff., 243, 245, 247ff., 250
Neglect 52ff., 141, 145, 153ff., 185ff.,
218, 223, 228
Norms 62, 65, 108, 145
Nurturing 114ff., 140, 241

Organisations 61ff, 72, 77, 80ff.
Over-compensation 218, 233
Over-indulgence 164, 223
Over-protection 70, 158, 163, 223ff., 231

Parents vii, 10, 27, 50ff., 59ff., 104ff.,
145, 152ff., 178ff., 184, 209ff.,
222ff., 234, 241, 244, 249
psychotic 93, 159ff., 168ff.
Permissiveness 43, 77, 216ff.
Personality 4ff., 22, 31, 40ff., 65, 71ff.,
136, 157, 176, 185, 189, 195, 224,
236, 248
Positivism 193ff., 196ff., 238
Poverty 111, 118, 123, 146ff., 243,
245ff.
Prejudice 18, 116, 129, 154
Primary maternal preoccupation 148,
234ff.
Probation 9, 39, 51, 151, 172, 179, 244,
250
officers 6, 8ff., 28, 49ff., 173, 176,
244, 249
Problems
emotional 61, 67, 70, 158, 185, 191
in relationships 12ff., 32ff., 54, 70,
185, 213, 234
marital 6, 111, 120, 123, 129, 218ff.,
248, 251
parent-child 14, 31ff., 248, 251
Projection 14, 16, 27, 30, 34, 36, 46,
61ff., 65ff., 77, 115, 123, 162, 216,
219, 221, 223ff., 234, 236
Protection 179ff., 187, 215ff., 223, 239,
244
Psychiatric social workers ix, 1, 4ff.,
12ff., 21ff., 28, 63, 70ff., 80, 179,
243

260   *Subject Index*